SMOOTH MOVES

SMOOTH

Juking,
Jamming,
Hooking &
Slamming

MOVES

Basketball's
Plays,
Players,
Action &
Style

Derek Gentile

Published by
Black Dog & Leventhal Publishers, Inc.
151 West 19th Street
New York, NY 10011

Distributed by
Workman Publishing Company
708 Broadway
New York, NY 10003

Manufactured in China

Cover and interior design by Liz Trovato

Cover photographs
AP/Wide World Photographs

All photographs provided by
AP/Wide World Photographs

ISBN: 1-57912-284-1

h g f e d c b a

Library of Congress Cataloging-in-Publication
Data available on file.

Contents

Introduction 8

PART 1 THE SHOTS

Chapter 1
The Jump Shot:
The Origin of the Elevated Offense 14

Chapter 2
The Hook Shot:
The Art of Shooting Gracefully 20

Chapter 3
The Slam Dunk:
Making a Statement With the Ball 26

Chapter 4
The Alley-Oop:
Beating the Defense by Throwing
the Ball Over it 34

Chapter 5
The Drive:
Taking the Ball to the Hoop With Flair 40

Chapter 6
The Foul Shot:
It's the Little Things that Count 46

Chapter 7
The Lay Up:
The Easiest Shot of All, Sometimes 52

Chapter 8
The Set Shot:
So Out, It's In 56

Chapter 9
The Bank Shot:
Using the Glass .60

PART 2 THE BALLHANDLING MOVES

Chapter 10
The Artful Pass:
Getting the Rock to the Person Who
Will Do the Most Good With It 66

Chapter 11
The No-Look Pass:
The Fancy Way to Move the Ball 72

Chapter 12
The Behind-the-Back-Dribble:
Tricky But Effective 78

Chapter 13
The Crossover Dribble:
A "Shake-and-Bake" Move 82

Chapter 14
The Pick and Roll:
The Two-Man Game 86

RT 3 THE DEFENSIVE MOVES

Chapter 15
The Steal:
Taking the Ball Away from
Your Opponent 92

Chapter 16
The Reject:
Get That Stuff Out of Here! 98

Chapter 17
The Defenders' Moves:
The Guys They Call "the Gloves" 104

RT 4 THE OFFENSIVE MOVES

Chapter 18
The Pivot:
Doing the Job in the Paint 112

Chapter 19
The Scorers:
Putting Up the Numbers 120

Chapter 20
The Garbage Men's Moves:
The Guys Who Do All the
Dirty Work .126

Chapter 21
The Rebound:
The Guys Who Get the
Ball For You 132

Chapter 22
The Little Big Men's Moves:
Players Who Play With Heart 138

Chapter 23
The Big Little Men's Moves:
How to be a Big Guard in a Big League . .144

Chapter 24
The Big Big Men's Moves:
The Biggest Players of All 150

Chapter 25
The Little Little Men's Moves:
Getting By In a Big Man's World 156

Chapter 26
The In-Betweener's Moves:
The Truly Unclassifiable Players 162

Chapter 27
The Playground Moves:
How Stylin' Began 168

Chapter 28
The One-On-One Moves:
The Gunslingers of the 20th Century 176

Chapter 29
The Fast Break:
Getting it Done in a Hurry 182

PART 5 THE REST OF THE MOVES

Chapter 30
The Trash-Talking Moves:
When Not to Keep Your Mouth Shut 190

Chapter 31
The Innovative Moves:
The All-Stars and Other Innovations 194

Chapter 32
The Coaching Moves:
Where Bench Jockeys Came From 198

Chapter 33
The Stylin' Moves:
It's All About Looking Good 204

The Last Second Moves 208

Ten Things We Couldn't Leave Out 212

Index 217

Introduction

Unlike many sports, whose origins are lost to antiquity or legend, the man who invented basketball is well-known. It was a Canadian, James J. Naismith, an 1887 graduate of McGill University.

The story of the creation of the game is equally well-known. And it is an interesting tale. Naismith was one of the best athletes in the history of McGill. He played soccer, rugby, track and lacrosse, and was a professional lacrosse player with a team called the Montreal Shamrocks.

Naismith was a fitness fanatic, and in 1890, he traveled to the School for Christian Workers (presently Springfield College) to take a course in physical training. His eventual plan was to become a physical director at one of the Young Men's Christian Association clubs springing up around the country.

Upon completion of the course, Naismith, 30, was invited to remain at the school to become an instructor there. This was the first of a series of serendipitous events that would lead to the creation of basketball. Had Naismith taken a job elsewhere, the game might never have been invented.

As the winter loomed, the school had a problem. One of the classes, made up of men training to be administrative secretaries for the YMCA, was becoming a nuisance. The 18 men were tired of the indoor athletic and gymnastic exercises that were being offered as recreation. In addition, the school ruled out indoor football and rugby as being too dangerous.

These were also older men, who were not afraid to convey their dissatisfaction to the school. So the board of directors asked Naismith, a personable man whom everyone liked, to see what he could do—and to do it within two weeks.

Naismith approached his task systematically. Smaller balls required equipment to catch and throw them, which would be too complicated for indoor sport. Naismith opted for a soccer-ball sized sphere instead.

Running with the ball in order to move it towards a goal would lead, Naismith realized, to players tackling or otherwise physically obstructing each other. So the ball was to be thrown or tapped.

Scoring was also a question. Goals close to the ground would seem, Naismith thought, to invite players massing close to the scoring area. So perhaps the goal would have to be elevated.

But how high? Well, that was actually a fluke. The balcony around the gym was 10 feet high. So that, Naismith decided, was to be the height of the goal.

The configuration of the goal was another fluke. After some thought, Naismith decided that the ball must thrown into the goal, as opposed to at the goal, as in darts. He asked the school janitor for a pair of boxes, about 18 inches square. But there were no boxes at hand, he was told. Instead, the janitor gave Naismith two peach baskets. Naismith thought that was a great idea. He tacked the baskets up at opposite ends of the gym, 10 feet off the floor.

The next day, he divided the 18 secretaries into two teams of nine men and showed them how to play the new game. It was an unqualified success. The secretaries ran around and had a grand old time, with a minimum of pushing and shoving. The final

score was 1-0, and the players all agreed to give it another go at the next class.

A few years later, when the game really began to catch on, one of Naismith's students suggested it be officially dubbed "Naismith-ball" after it's creator. Naismith hooted. The game, he said, is called basketball. That's the way it would stay.

Smooth Moves is a history of that game as seen from a slightly different angle. Most basketball histories take the game through its various permutations from the perspective of the men who played it and the teams on which they played. Basketball is a game that may have had one point of origin, but it also has many different styles, even now. Baseball is played the same way everywhere. Ditto soccer and hockey. But basketball can be played at a fast pace or a slow pace; with emphasis on long-rang shooting, or in-close shooting; with small, quick players or tall, slow players.

This book is an attempt to follow how these styles or moves evolved, and which players were key in the development of those moves.

There are, at times, differing versions of how a specific move evolved. The book attempts to sort through the stories and tall tales and present as balanced a picture as possible. We may not succeed in every case, but one thing we promise: you'll love reading about the moves.

This book was written in an interesting time; I started it was a few weeks after September 11, 2001. As a result, some of my written inquiries to the pioneers of the game went, understandably in that time of Anthrax-filled envelopes, unanswered. But to those men who either agreed to correspond or speak with me, my deepest gratitude.

These include Hall-of-Famers Al Cervi, George Yardley, Paul Arizin, Bob Kurland, coach John Kundla, coach (and player!) John Wooden, Arnie Risen, Frank Ramsey and Bill Sharman. In addition Al Attles of the Golden State Warriors and Kim Hughes of the Denver Nuggets were kind enough to speak with me on select subjects.

I regret to say that as I was attempting to contact Hall-of-Famer Angelo "Hank" Luisetti, he passed away. My condolences and apologies to Mr. Luisetti's family. If I intruded, it was not my intent.

Thanks to the NBA Retired Players Association, and to Robin Deutsch of the Basketball Hall of Fame. Mr. Deutsch was particularly helpful in tracking down members of the Hall of Fame.

My thanks to the indefatigable Harvey Pollock for allowing me the use of some of the stats from his amazing yearbook. One of the reasons the stats were included at all is frankly, a naked plug for Pollock's book, a labor of love that any true hoops fan will relish and available from the Philadelphia 76ers for $10. Accept no substitutes.

A tip of the hat must also go to former Kentucky great Ralph Beard, who was also a star in the NBA's early years. Beard, banned from the NBA for associating with gamblers (a specious charge at best), was gracious and generous with his time in an extended interview that proves that people from Kentucky are among the nicest in the world.

My research assistant, Brian Sullivan, was equally gracious and patient when I made requests that we both knew would be difficult to do in a short period of time. It should be noted that Sullivan, sports editor for *The Berkshire Eagle* in Pittsfield, Massachusetts remains in my eyes the expert on the modern NBA. His insights were priceless.

I had the support of many friends along the way. These include, first and foremost, my parents, Joseph and Margaret Gentile; my four sisters, Mary Beth, Melanie, Hilary and Karla and their families and kids. Also, Erik Bruun, a fellow author and the best listener I know; Donna Mattoon, the epitome of a supportive friend; Lisi de Bourbon, a big shot in New York City who still finds time to remind me to save my money, and my former collegue and pal, Tim Cebula. And once again, like the 7th Cavalry, great thanks to Susan Strong for saving several chunks of this book from computer oblivion and never being annoyed when I asked for help.

Basketball is a team game, and so thanks, too, to all my old teammates from all those teams, especially Tim Morey, Pete Morey, Jeff Kurpaska, John (nothin' we can't handle) Cronin, Greg Schwartz, Chris Sampson, Mike Urquhart, Tom Mitchell, Kit Foster, Dick Farnham, Stevie and Billy Hakes, Tom Kondel, Tiger Pause, T.K McBride, Al and Dave Meier, Bruce Viani and, of course, the old guys, Mike and Tom and Dave Kinne and John Beacco.

Thanks to my two editors, Will "the Thrill" Kiester and Becky "Steady" Koh, who didn't let me screw this up. Also, again, great thanks to my publisher, J.P. Leventhal, who, incredibly, pays me to do this again and again.

Part 1

The Shots

1 The Jump Shot
The Origin of Elevated Offense

ORIGIN: **The early 1940s**

THE FIRST: **Kenny Sailors, University of Wyoming**
Shot the first one-handed jumper.

THE ALL-TIMERS:
Joe Fulks (1946–54)
Bill Sharman (1950–61)
George Yardley (1953–60)
Jerry West (1960–74)
Hal Greer (1958–73)
George Gervin (1972–86)
Reggie Miller (1987–present)
All but Miller are in the Hall of Fame.

Above: The Knicks Allan Houston shows perfect jump shot form.

THE TECHNIQUE:
As you jump straight up into the air, bring the ball into shooting position above your head. Try to set your fingers on the seams of the ball, which will enable you to better control it.

Keep your shoulders square. Push the ball with your shooting hand until your arm extends completely and your elbow locks. Follow through by snapping the wrist in a downward motion. By keeping your elbow in line with your body, the ball has to go straight up and out.

Remember, try to make sure your shoulders are squared, even if your body is not. That will guide the ball.

The first jump shooter, Kenny Sailors.

In the mid-1940s, the idea of a man jumping in the air to attempt a shot on a basketball court was as ridiculous a notion as playing without pants.

The NBA was a grounded league then: players were ordered never to leave their feet on defense. They were taught to dribble the basketball close to the floor, to set picks by getting into a wide, low-to-the-ground stance. They were exhorted by coaches to dive for loose balls. Being airborne was a sin, unless one was driving close to the hoop.

Jumpin' Joe Fulks of the Philadelphia Warriors changed that forever.

The Pioneer

At 6' 5", Fulks wasn't particularly tall, but he was fast. The press called him "Jumpin' Joe" Fulks, not because he could jump, but because he *did* jump. Fulks was one of the

Above: Joe Fulks preparing to shoot.

Right: The Lakers Jerry West: unstoppable.

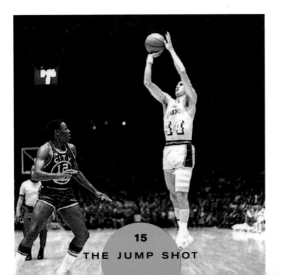

JUNE 14, 1998, NBA PLAYOFFS, GAME 6

As the final 15 seconds of the sixth game of the NBA championship ticked down, the Chicago Bulls, trailing 86–85, needed a basket. Everybody in the Salt Palace in Salt Lake City knew that Bulls guard Michael Jordan would get the ball. He did. The rest of the Bulls cleared out, and Jazz guard Byron Russell, an athletic, energetic defender, suddenly became a very lonely man. Jordan took a strong first step to the hoop from about 17' out and Russell, respecting Jordan's ability to drive, backed up and actually stumbled. But instead of driving, Jordan leaped into the air, the basketball rolling easily off his fingertips and arcing toward the basket. Russell, like Brooklyn Dodgers pitcher Ralph Branca 47 years earlier, could only watch helplessly as his team's championship hopes were obliterated. Bulls 87, Jazz 86. Game, championship, dynasty.

pioneers of the jump shot. In Fulks's case, his jumper was shot with two hands, launched at the apex of his leap. Actually, sportswriters of the time called Fulks's funny-looking shot an "ear shot" rather than a jump shot, because Fulks brought the ball all the way back behind his head and seemed to launch it from behind his ear.

Fulks, who played pro ball from 1946 through 1954, was not the originator of the move. The best guess anyone has is that Kenny Sailors, a 5' 10" guard from the University of Wyoming, was seen jumping into the air in the early 1940s to get his shot off over bigger opponents. Sailors parlayed that move into a brief professional career. Another college player, 6' 4" forward Lauren "Laddie" Gale, who played for the University of Oregon and in the National Basketball League (NBL) from 1940 through 1943, was also using a one-hander in those days. Gale was named to the Hall of Fame in 1977 as a college player.

In addition, there have been individual players who toiled at the turn of the 20th century who eschewed the standard set shot and tried other means of launching a basketball that involved leaving terra firma.

But Fulks made the jump shot sing.

In fact, during Fulks's first few years in the Basketball Association of America (the forerunner of the NBA), nobody knew what to do with the guy. Why? Because the popular coaching strategy at the time was that a good player never left his feet on defense or offense. Players who did, the theory went, were then at the mercy of their opponents. No one had any idea how to guard Fulks because going airborne to try to stop him was almost as alien a concept as jumping to shoot. As one sportswriter noted in somewhat wide-eyed prose, "Fulks has a vertical jump of well over 18 inches, which means he begins his shot 8 feet off the floor."

Eight feet? Whoa.

For the record, Fulks was a much better jumper than that. Observers estimated he had about a 26" vertical jump, which is good, but not amazing. Michael Jordan, for example, had at one point a vertical leap of 42". But in 1947, Fulks was a handful.

"Fulks was a hell of a shooter," recalled Ralph Beard, a two-time All-NBA performer with the Indianapolis Olympians who played against Fulks many times in the late 1940s. "That man could flat-out put the ball in the basket. He would just get on a roll, and you couldn't stop him."

He was a streak shooter. And going along with that, like all great shooters, Jumpin' Joe had no conscience. When he was hot, he kept shooting. When he was not, well, he kept shooting until he got hot again.

"Once, in a game against us," recalled former Rochester Royals center Arnie Risen,

Great Shooting Performances

Fulks Runs Wild
On February 10, 1949, Joe Fulks hit 27 field goals and 9 of 14 free throws to score 63 points and smash the league's scoring record of 48 points set a little over a week before by George Mikan. Philadelphia defeated the Indianapolis Jets, 108–87.

Fulks, according to contemporary reports, hit his 27 field goals on a variety of shots: spinning one-handers, running shots with either hand and long set shots. At different times in the game, Jets coach Burl Friddle tried five different players on Fulks: Price Brookfield was 6' 4", while John Mandic, Leo Mogus, Carlisle Towery and rookie Jack Eskridge were all 6' 5". Fulks shot over all of them as though they weren't even there.

To his credit, Friddle, who would be replaced the next year, went over to Fulks after he was taken out with 58 seconds to play and shook his hand.

Fulks's scoring spree was a record that stood until Elgin Baylor broke the mark in 1959 with 64 points.

West Sets a Record
On January 17, 1962, Lakers guard Jerry West wasn't feeling good. He had a touch of the flu, and while he did not consider *not* playing, he did admit to Lakers coach Fred Schaus that he might not go as many minutes as he usually did.

Portland's Clifford Robinson shoots a jump shot over Boston's Rick Fox.

West played only 39 of 48 minutes, a little under his average. He hit 22 of 36 shots, as well as 19 free throws, to score 63 points, then an NBA record for a guard.

Scott Wedman Kills the Lakers
On May 27, 1985, Celtics forward Scott Wedman (1974–87) took 11 shots from the floor, including 4 from beyond the three-point line. He made them all, which is still a finals record. Wedman was a reserve forward for the Celtics renowned for his shooting. But this was an exceptional performance, even for him. While the Celtics won that contest, 148–114 (the so-called Boston Massacre), the Lakers came back to win the series, four games to two.

Reggie Miller's Amazing 18 Seconds
By May 7, 1995, the rivalry between the New York Knicks and the Indiana Pacers had heated up to boiler room temperatures. The year before, New York had edged the Pacers in a tough seven-game series in the playoffs that featured its share of woofing and posturing on both sides. By Game 1 of the 1995 series, the Knicks had a 105–99 lead with 18.7 sec-

Left: Reggie Miller was a thorn in the Knicks side in their attempt to win the NBA Championship.

The NBA is a jump-shooters' league. The Knicks' Allan Houston, the Celtics' Paul Pierce, the Kings' Peja Stojakovic and the Supersonics' Brent Barry have the best form. For big men, Dirk Nowitzki of the Mavericks is sort of the Bob McAdoo of the 21st century: A big mobile guy who can shoot from the perimeter. And Nowitzki has better range than McAdoo.

Honorable mention goes to the Bulls' Jalen Rose. The art of shooting from behind a pick is nearly lost, but the Bulls run this nice little two-man screen that Rose curls around and pops. The Bucks like to do the same thing for Ray Allen.

PLAYERS TO WATCH

onds left and fans were starting to head for the exits.

"Realistically?" mused then-Pacers coach Larry Brown after the game. "I didn't think we had a chance."

But Pacer Mark Jackson (1987–present) hit Miller with the inbounds pass at the three-point line, and Reggie whirled and drained a three-pointer, 105–102. Now Knicks fans were nervous, but still composed.

But Knick Anthony Mason (1989–present) then threw a hideous inbounds pass that Miller picked off (after, Knick fans still contend, illegally knocking over New York guard Greg Anthony [1991–present]). Reggie scrambled back behind the three-point arc again and fired up a somewhat awkward three-pointer.

Swish. 105–105. Unreal. And there were still 13.3 seconds left!

Knicks guard John Starks (1988–present) was fouled, and with the entire Madison Square Garden fan contingent holding its collective breath, he obligingly missed both free throws. The Pacers got the ball, and this time the Knicks took no chances that another Miller bomb might detonate. They fouled him intentionally.

No matter. With the entire crowd screaming its displeasure, Miller canned both free throws, capping an eight-points-in-nine-seconds spree that is still hard to believe. Indiana now led, 107–105, and the now-catatonic Knickerbockers could not generate a successful shot.

And as he walked off the court, Reggie taunted the crowd one last time, clutching his throat in the "choke sign." The Pacers won the series in seven games.

now a Hall of Famer, "I believe he took 40 shots… in the first half. And I think he made two. But that didn't stop him from shooting in the second half."

But Fulks's jumper was kind of like a flying set shot: he still launched it, for the most part, with two hands. That was fine for him, but other midair pioneers perfected a technique that was more accurate.

Luisetti's Game

The athletic and amazing Angelo "Hank" Luisetti, of Stanford, had patented a one-hand "push" shot while an undergrad out West in the mid-1930s. Angelo didn't really jump, though. He sort of hopped just enough to maybe slide a piece of paper under his shoes. It wasn't a jumper, but it was a closer cousin than the set shot.

Luisetti and his team came East in 1936 and lit up a number of heavy-duty eastern collegiate powers, notably Long Island University, on a holiday tour. Long Island coach Clair Bee was unimpressed by Luisetti, declaring that no player of his would ever shoot a one-handed shot. It was, insisted Bee, an aberration: too hard to control and impossible to properly aim. Luisetti became a Hall of Famer in 1959.

Bee, a coaching genius for sure, was wrong here. Within a few years, the one-hander caught on faster than poodle skirts, and players realized that jumping and then shooting the ball gave them an edge. Sailors, as we have mentioned, was using it at Wisconsin. A pale-faced schoolboy guard by the name of Meyer "Whitey" Skoog was shooting a jumper up in Minnesota in the mid-1940s and becoming a legend. Skoog would later star for the Minneapolis Lakers from 1951 through 1957.

By the late 1940s, Ray Lumpp (1948–53) and Carl Braun (1947–62), of the New York Knickerbockers, were throwing in shots via a jumper, and legions of players, including George "the Bird" Yardley, a star for the Fort Wayne Pistons and Syracuse Nationals from 1953 through 1960, would soon follow.

But defenses didn't lag too far behind. If a player was going to jump on offense then, his defenders realized pretty soon that they needed to follow suit. And they did. Defensive specialists like the Lakers' Slater Martin (1949–60) and the Pistons' Mel Hutchins (1951–58) soon learned the value of jumping and sticking a hand in their opponents' faces to distract them. Still, there were a couple of ways to beat that. One was the old chestnut, the head fake, which has been in vogue almost since Dr. James Naismith set up peach baskets in Springfield, Massachusetts. The other way was to run like hell, and get open. By the mid-1950s, the Boston Celtics had this down to a science. The Celtics would get the ball off the boards, and their All-Star guard

CHAMPION SHOOTERS

Super Stats

Only two jump shooters have ever won the NBA field goal percentage crown, which perennially goes to players who rarely stray far from the basket. In the 1951–52 season, 6' 4" Philadelphia Warriors forward Paul Arizin (1950–62) hit 44.8 percent of his shots to lead the league. Arizin also won the scoring championship with a 25.4 scoring average. And in 1957 to 1958, Cincinnati Royals forward Jack Twyman (1955–66) won the crown with a .452 mark.

Bob Cousy (1950–63, 1969–70) would fly down the court. Cousy always had a couple options, but his principal one was fellow All-Star guard Bill Sharman (1950–61).

Sharman, a rugged 6' 2" guard, was the Felix Unger of basketball: neat as a pin, and meticulous to a fault. In superb condition at all times, Sharman ran and ran and ran and got open and got open and got open. Cousy would feed him, and usually he would drill a 15- to 20-footer. He was the first, or one of the first, of the spot jump shooters.

Above: Michael Cooper exhibiting full extension and follow through along the sidelines.

The Stop-and-Pop

As the 1950s melted into the 1960s, players also discovered another way of shaking a defender: the stop-and-pop. The move was simple: a player burst down the court, usually with the ball, stopped dead and launched his shot anywhere from 15' to 30' out.

A few players turned this into an art form. Los Angeles Lakers guard Jerry West (1960–74) was the principal practitioner of the stop-and-pop. West was simply so quick and accurate that he could dribble, stop and drain jump shot after jump shot while even the best of defensive players watched helplessly.

West was like a metronome; he was as relentlessly accurate in the waning seconds of a game as he was moments after the opening tap. Such killer consistency made him deadly as games wound down, and he was aptly named "Mr. Clutch," a name he hated.

Left: Oscar Robertson pulling up for two.

Fans these days don't see the stop-and-pop anymore. At all, in fact. That is explained by three words: the three-point basket.

The three-point line, which was legislated into the NBA for the 1979–80 season, pushed jump shooters back, and turned them into, for the most part, spot shooters. The Lakers' Michael Cooper (1978–90), the well-traveled Dana Barros (1989–present), Jeff Hornacek (1986–2002), of the Utah Jazz, and the Pacers' Reggie Miller (1987–present) all work (or worked) their defenders off picks or around double-teams, found their favorite spot and launched a three-point shot.

A few players, such as former Sixers guard Andrew Toney (1980–88) and, currently, Allan Houston (1993–present), of the Knickerbockers, can still stop at lip of

CAREER FIELD GOAL PERCENTAGE	
Scott Wedman: .481	
Reggie Miller: .480	
Jerry West: .474	
Sam Jones: .456	
Hal Greer: .452	
Jack Twyman: .450	
Bill Sharman: .426	
Kenny Sailors: .329	
Joe Fulks: .302	

Right: Jordan's balanced jump shot is a trademark of his remarkable talent.

Below: David Thompson extends beyond the reach of three Detroit defenders.

Fulks's Dominance

Jumpin' Joe Fulks was the NBA's first star and his influence was considerable. He averaged 23.2 points per game in the BAA/NBA's first year. Less than a decade ago, many teams did not average that many points.

To get an idea of Joe's dominance, consider this: the number two scorer in the league, Bob Feerick, averaged 16.8 points per game. Only four other players in league history have won scoring titles by larger margins than Fulks that first year: George Mikan (1950–51), Wilt Chamberlain (1961–62, 1962–63), Kareem Abdul-Jabbar (1971–72) and Michael Jordan (1986–87).

the line and throw up a three, but the stop-and-pop as we know it is gone, while its fraternal twin, the medium-range jumper, is now mainly the purview of midsize centers such as the Seattle SuperSonics' Vitaly Potapenko (1996–present), who use the 15-footer to pull bigger centers away from the basket.

2

The Hook Shot

The Art of Shooting Gracefully

ORIGIN: The early 20th century

THE FIRST: Ed Wachter, New York Trojans

THE ALL-TIMERS:
George Mikan (1946–56)
Harry Gallatin (1948–58)
Bob Houbregs (1953–58)
Neil Johnston (1951–59)
Kareem Abdul-Jabbar (1969–89)
Hall of Famers, all, including Wachter.

THE TECHNIQUE:
Instead of facing the basket, turn your body slightly to the side. If you're a right-handed player, raise your right leg as you shoot. If shooting left-handed, reverse the leg. Try to jump straight up and keep your body straight. Extend your opposite elbow for balance and to keep your opponent away from the ball.

Bring the ball up, out and over your head in a sweeping motion. Push off your left foot, extend your arm over your head and flip the ball toward the basket. Aim for either the backboard or the basket. Follow through by snapping your wrist in a downward motion. Angling your body instead of going straight up will result in a missed or off-balance shot.

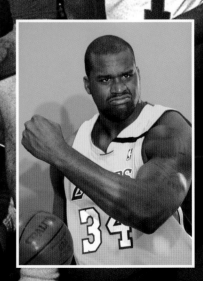

Alcindor/Abdul-Jabbar (33): The master of the hook shot.

Inset: Shaq: an intimidating force.

As basketball unfolded in the 20th century, it became clear that close-in shots were preferable to long-range attempts. The problem was that sometimes a defender was taller than the offensive player or his arms were longer, so the straight push shot, or layup, could easily be blocked. Players had to devise a way of getting their shot off in close quarters without it being deflected.

It's difficult to determine exactly who came up with the hook shot as we know it today. What is probable is that the shot developed from a straight one-handed layup to an over-the-head push shot where a player would shoot a push shot but protect the ball by angling his body toward the defender to what Earvin Johnson used to call a "baby hook" or "half hook," which was a more looping shot launched following a shallow jump. The straight hook shot evolved sometime in the 1920s from those moves.

Ed Wachter, who played professionally from 1896 to 1918, along with other players, was launching Cro-Magnon hook shots soon after basketball was invented.

Wachter was a 6' 2" center (accounts of that early era list him, variously, at 6' 2" to 6' 6") who was hard as nails. He had a blacksmith's arms and huge hands. He played for a host of teams in his 22-year career, including 12 league title teams and five "World Champions." (World Champions being, for the most part, a matter of interpretation, since no other country in the world actually played basketball at the time.)

Wachter was the leading scorer in virtually every league in which he played and was an innovator and thinker. He and his brother, Lew, were said to have invented the bounce pass, and Wachter's teams were among the first to use the fast break.

The Cowboy

The first player to be known almost exclusively for his hook shot was a 6' 4" center from the University of Kentucky named LeRoy "Cowboy" Edwards (NBL, 1935–43).

The Cowboy was a cocky one. His hook shot—a full, looping shot he could deliver from either side of the basket or coming across the middle—was a thing of beauty, and Edwards knew it. He was known in those days as a "gunner," for once the ball went into him in the low post, it almost never went back out again.

Edwards led the Oshkosh All-Stars to the championship of the National Basketball League for three consecutive years (1935, '36, '37), leading the league in scoring every one of those years. In 1936, Edwards scored 30 points in a game. That total was more than the total average of most of the teams in the NBL, and at the time was regarded as an amazing feat.

By the 1940s, the hook shot was established as the principal shot from the pivot. Just about every good big man could throw it up, and many players could do so with either hand.

And by this time, the foremost practitioner of the hook shot was a 6' 11" center, formerly of DePaul University, named George Mikan (1946–56). Mikan first played in the NBL with the Chicago Gears and later the Minneapolis Lakers. In 1949, the Lakers jumped to the BAA, soon to become the NBA, and Mikan and his hook shot was the spearhead for one of the great pro dynasties of the early years of professional basketball.

Big George

Mikan, or "Big George," as he was often known, used the hook shot almost exclusively. If he had to, he could shoot a soft set shot, and he was an excellent foul shooter, but his

The Los Angeles Lakers and Boston Celtics were locked into what would be the rubber series of their decade-long rivalry. Los Angeles had won the first two games, while the Celtics had come back to win Game 3 in Boston Garden. With seconds left, the Celtics were on the verge of tying the series, leading 106–105. But Lakers guard Earvin "Magic" Johnson had one more trick up his proverbial sleeve. Rolling into the lane with time ticking down, he turned his body away from the Celtics' two twin towers, Robert Parish and Kevin McHale, and lofted a soft hook shot over both. Parish is 7', McHale is 6' 11", but Johnson's perfect execution of the hook allowed the shot to slide beyond their fingertips and settle into the net. The Lakers had taken a commanding three games to one lead in a series they would eventually win in six games.

Magic's patented baby-hook.

George Mikan's early hook shot.

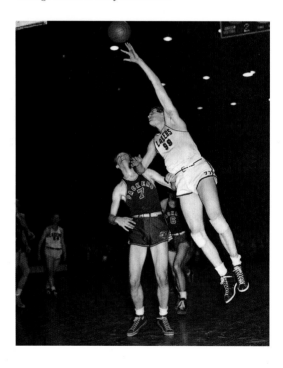

The right-handed Mikan could hook with either hand.

bread, butter and, in fact, most of his main meal was the hooker. The Lakers playbook was a slim one: it consisted, generally, of a pass into Mikan on either side of the basket. From either spot, he would whirl and shoot the hook.

Mikan was nearly unstoppable down low. At this point in NBA history, the lane was

HOOK SHOT DOMINANCE

Hook shot artists dominated the scoring leaders in the early days of the NBA. Laker center George Mikan won three consecutive scoring crowns from 1949 to 1951. Neil Johnston (1951–59), of the Philadelphia Warriors, won three scoring championships from 1953 to 1955 and won three field goal percentage crowns in the 1950s as well. And in the 1970s, Kareem Abdul-Jabbar won three consecutive scoring championships from 1970 to 1972.

only 6' wide, which meant that "the Leaning Tower of Minneapolis," as Mikan was also called, could position himself almost under the hoop, take a pass and roll in a hook shot from very close.

"He was very big and strong, and the Lakers looked for him almost every time down the court," recalled Hall of Famer Arnie Risen (1945–58), a 6' 9" center who played against Mikan when Risen toiled in the pivot for the Rochester Royals, the Lakers' archrivals in the early days of the league. "He was very tough to guard."

Too, opponents swore that Lakers management actually bent the front of the rims on the Lakers' home court slightly upward to better corral Mikan's offerings.

Mikan dominated the NBA's early years. In an attempt to curb his excessive scoring, the league widened the lane from 6' to 12' prior to the 1951 to 1952 season, which pushed Big George out a little, but didn't seem to stop him from scoring points in bunches.

Still, for the most part, the hook shot was a short-range weapon. In the late 1940s,

Tony Lavelli (1949–50), a 6' 3" guard from Yale, began shooting hook shots from farther out, sometimes as far as the foul line, or the top of the key.

That brought on the next big wave.

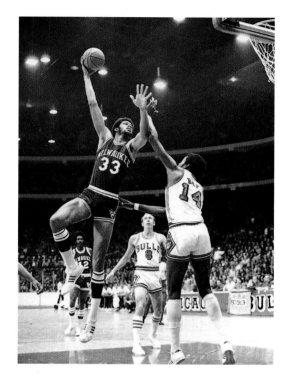

Lew Alcindor extends over Clifford Ray of the Bulls in 1971.

Through the 1950s and into the 1960s, the long-range hook was a weapon in many players' arsenals. Bob Houbregs, a 6' 8" forward-center who was a star at the University of Washington and who played five years (1953–58) in the NBA, fired up hook shots from all over the court. Houbregs took, and converted, hook shots from 25' out and beyond. Think of a guy launching hook shots from the three-point area and you get an idea of what Houbregs could do.

If Mikan was the best hook shooter from underneath the basket, Houbregs was the best from long range. But virtually every NBA player in that era could shoot a hook shot of some kind.

Another big man of that era, Neil Johnston, was the first player to shoot hook shots almost exclusively and win a scoring title. Johnston, a 6' 8" center-forward from Ohio State, could shoot hook shots with either hand. Johnston, who played from 1951 to 1959, led the league in scoring three consecutive years, from 1953 to 1955, averaging 24.4, 22.7 and 22.1 points per game, respectively.

But more important, Johnston was also a perennial league leader in field goal percentage, meaning not only did he score a lot, but that his hooker was pretty accurate as well. Johnston led the league in field goal percentage in the 1952–53, 1955–56 and 1956–57 seasons.

Kareem's Game

But nobody has shot the hooker as well, before or since, as Ferdinand Lewis Alcindor Jr., later known as Kareem Abdul-Jabbar.

The 7' 2" Abdul-Jabbar became a low-post scoring machine—the most consistent, reliable two points in the NBA from his rookie year until well into the 1980s. His hook shot, and his alone, became known as "the skyhook."

Abdul-Jabbar at a later time in his career still maintained his deadly accuracy with the hook.

The Greatest Hook Shots of All Time

Kareem's Clutch Hook
The greatest hook shot of all time in the NBA was also one of the great clutch shots of all time as well. In the 1974 playoffs, the Milwaukee Bucks and Boston Celtics were locked in a tremendous playoff battle. Game 6 was in Boston, and the Celtics were pretty sure they would wrap the series up at home, having taken a 96–87 win over the Bucks in Game 5 in Milwaukee.

But the Bucks hung tough and kept the game close throughout. With minutes running down in overtime, the Bucks trailed, 101–100. But Milwaukee knew enough to get the ball to its bread-and-butter man, Kareem Abdul-Jabbar. With only seconds left in the contest, Abdul-Jabbar flipped a hook shot over 7' Henry Finkle (1966–75) of the Celtics for the game winner.

Abdul-Jabbar Breaks a Record
On April 5, 1984, midway through the fourth quarter of a 129–115 win over the Utah Jazz, Abdul-Jabbar took a pass from Laker guard Earvin Johnson, wheeled to his right and flipped in a hook shot over Utah's 7' 4" center, Mark Eaton (1982–93). With that shot, Abdul-Jabbar had eclipsed former rival Wilt Chamberlain's career scoring mark of 31,439, a number few thought would ever be broken. The irony was, Abdul-Jabbar would score more than 7,000 points more in his career, which would last another five years.

A Good One to Quit On
It was the middle of the fourth quarter, and the Boston Celtics were enjoying a ten-point lead over the Los Angeles Lakers in the sixth game of the 1963 NBA Finals. Boston guard Bob Cousy dribbled down the right side of the court and launched a long, right-handed hook shot at the basket.

"The Cooz" was one of many guards who could shoot hook shots in those days, but a 20' hook from the corner was a little audacious, even for "the Houdini of the Hardwood," as Cousy was called then. But the ball swished through the net. It was Cousy's final basket as a Boston Celtic, and the Green would go on to win their fifth consecutive world championship that day.

Abdul-Jabbar (1969–89) was a product of the New York playgrounds. He learned to shoot the hook shot in the fourth grade, and refined it during his high school career at Power Memorial Academy. By the time he had matriculated at UCLA, the Alcindor hook was the most devastating weapon in college basketball.

Kareem Abdul-Jabbar over Bill Walton in the 1977 NBA Playoffs.

PLAYERS TO WATCH

Not too many. In the playoffs, Shaquille O'Neal uses a little baby hook he learned from Magic Johnson. The Spurs' Tim Duncan also has a soft jump hook he uses when he gets in the lane. Now that Arvidas Sabonis is back with the Blazers, he is the last pure, Bob Houbregs-type in the league. When the mood strikes (about every five games or so), Sabonis will wheel into the lane and toss a nice sweeping hook shot up. As for opposite hand hook shots, the last one seen was by Larry Bird in 1987.

Jamal Mashburn's baby-hook keeps the ball away from the outstretched hand of Kevin Garnett.

Abdul-Jabbar, still known as Lew Alcindor in those days, led UCLA to national championships from 1967 to 1969. He was drafted by the Milwaukee Bucks and, in his second year as a professional, led the Bucks in 1971 to a 66–16 record and the only championship in the history of the franchise.

Alcindor officially changed his name to Abdul-Jabbar in 1971. Prior to the 1975–76 season, he was traded to the Los Angeles Lakers. He teamed with Lakers guard Earvin Johnson to win five more championships from 1979 to 1988. Abdul-Jabbar retired in 1989, the all-time leader in the NBA in points (38,387), field goals made (15,837), field goals attempted (28,307) and minutes played (57,446).

Abdul-Jabbar's hook shot was a study in grace. He usually launched the shot after jumping, so that he was actually shooting down at the basket. He usually shot the ball from either side of the basket, but sometimes would shoot from the foul line, just to give his opponents a different look.

Abdul-Jabbar positioned his body between his defender (or, often, defenders) and the arm that released the shot. It was virtually impossible to block. The number of opponents (Wilt Chamberlain, George Johnson, Mark Eaton, Manute Bol) who even blocked it once in a while can be counted on one hand. And every time it happened, rare as it was, Kareem's coaches, probably correctly, complained that such a block was goaltending.

And he was not afraid to share his expertise. Earvin Johnson won Game 4 of the 1987 NBA Finals using a "baby hook" that Abdul-Jabbar had taught him.

"You expect to lose a game on a hook shot when you play the Lakers," said Celtics forward Larry Bird after the contest. "You don't

expect a hook shot from Magic Johnson."

In the 1980s and 1990s, there were other excellent hook shooters, including Bob Lanier (1970–84) of the Detroit Pistons and the Milwaukee Bucks, and the Celtics' Robert Parish (1976–97).

Since Abdul-Jabbar's retirement, though, the hook shot has become something of a lost art. Certainly, Abdul-Jabbar's eventual successor in the Laker pivot, Shaquille O'Neal (1992–present), has developed the "baby hook," but it is more in the style of Johnson's move than the unstoppable Kareem "skyhook."

San Antonio Spur center-forward Tim Duncan (1997–present) has developed a very nice hook shot, along with Sacramento forward Chris Webber (1993–present) and Minnesota big man Kevin Garnett (1995–present), but for the most part, post-up centers in the NBA of the 21st century shoot jump shots or drive to the basket. That isn't necessarily a bad thing, but few centers or forwards or guards can make one of the more graceful-looking and effective moves in basketball anymore.

CAREER HIGHS
GEORGE MIKAN, MINNEAPOLIS LAKERS
January 20, 1952: 61 points
CLIFF HAGAN, ST. LOUIS HAWKS
February 11, 1962: 55 points
KAREEM ABDUL-JABBAR, MILWAUKEE BUCKS
December 10, 1971: 55 points
NEIL JOHNSTON, PHILADELPHIA WARRIORS
February 15, 1954: 50 points
LEROY "COWBOY" EDWARDS,
UNIVERSITY OF KENTUCKY
January, 1935: 30 points

Right: Bill Walton's deadly lefty hook from inside the paint.

THE BEST HOOK SHOOTER OF ALL

Super Stats

As accurate a scorer as Neil Johnston was, Kareem Abdul-Jabbar was even more so. For 13 consecutive years, from 1970 to 1983, Abdul-Jabbar was in the top five in field goal accuracy, and his career mark was 56 percent. (His career three-point field goal average, in contrast, was a little less stellar: 6 percent on 1–18 shooting.)

3

The Slam Dunk

Making a Statement with the Ball

ORIGIN: As soon as baskets were put up in 1891

THE FIRST: The Harlem Globetrotters

THE ALL-TIMERS:
Jim Pollard (1947-55)
Wilt Chamberlain (1959-73)
Connie Hawkins (1967-76)
Julius Erving (1971-87)
Earl Manigault (NA)
Dominique Wilkins (1982-99)
Michael Jordan (1985-93 1994-98, 2000-present)
Vince Carter (1998-present)
Pollard, Chamberlain, Hawkins and Erving are in the Hall of Fame. Jordan is pending.

Dr. Julius Erving: the original dunking king.

Inset: Vince Carter slamming for a deuce.

THE TECHNIQUE:
Grab the ball firmly in one or both hands. Bend your knees and jump. When you get to the apex of your leap, throw the ball down through the hoop. Don't hang on the rim or you'll get a technical foul.

Also, know your limitations. Get as close to the basket as you can. The object (unless you are participating in a slam dunk contest) is still to score the two points.

The dunk shot is a natural offshoot of the layup, which was practiced almost from the day basketball was invented. But for most of the latter half of the 20th century and into the 21st, the dunk has assumed much more prominence in the shot-making pantheon. It is to the layup what Eminem is to James Taylor.

Popular legend has the dunk beginning in the late 1950s or early 1960s, as bigger and stronger players made their way into the NBA. That's wrong. Players were dunking long before that. For example, as early as the 1920s, the Harlem Globetrotters would often end one of their dizzying ballhandling exhibitions with a flashy pass that ended in a dunk.

But for a variety of reasons, many professional players almost never did so in a game.

"I could dunk, a lot of players could dunk," said George Mikan in an interview once. "But we didn't, because we didn't want to show the other player up."

That was only part of it. The other part was that as basketball evolved through the 1940's, bigger and bigger players were being recruited. This led, initially anyway, to a criticism that basketball was becoming a "freak show." In connection with that freakish tag, the dunk shot was regarded in that era as an easy shot that required no real skill. Thus, most big men never used a dunk shot, preferring to lay the ball into the basket.

So the players of that early era, up to the 1950s, largely eschewed the dunk shot.

At least most of them. In Minneapolis, 6' 4" forward Jim Pollard (1947–55) loved to jump in the air and throw down crazy dunk shots. In practice anyway. In addition to having a vertical jump of more than 40" (that's an estimate; nobody did things like measure players' vertical jumps in the 1940s),

OCTOBER 2, 1973, NEW YORK KNICKS (NBA) VS. NEW YORK NETS (ABA)

In 1971, rumor had it that the NBA and ABA were going to merge. So, anticipating that they would be playing each other sooner or later anyway, the two leagues began playing interleague contests. The merger didn't happen for a couple of years, but the interleague games were big revenue producers, and the two leagues continued them.

A majority of these games were on either neutral sites or on the ABA's home court. The NBA, frankly, was still wary of bringing in ABA teams to their buildings and promoting the other league.

One of the first games in 1971 was between the defending ABA champion Utah Stars and the defending NBA champion Milwaukee Bucks in Salt Lake City. It was billed as "the First World Series of Basketball." Milwaukee won a fairly close game, 122–116, with Kareem Abdul-Jabbar scoring 36 points and Oscar Robertson 24.

The game set the tone. The NBA teams generally downplayed the games in public, but teams in both leagues really tried to beat the hell out of each other.

On October 2, 1973, perhaps the most significant "exhibition" between an NBA and ABA team took place when the defending NBA champion New York Knickerbockers hosted the up-and-coming New York Nets in Madison Square Garden. It was Net forward Julius Erving's first professional game in the Garden, and the first time an ABA team played there. The Nets would win the ABA title that year, and had, in addition to Erving, center Bill Paultz, forward Larry Kenon and guards Brian Taylor and Bill Melchionni. The Knicks had Dave DeBusschere, Bill Bradley, Willis Reed, Jerry Lucas, Walt Frazier and Dean Meminger.

The Doctor delivering another patented house call.

The Nets pounded the Knicks, 97–87, and at one point, led by 13 points midway through the fourth quarter. Erving scored 27 points. Several Knicks downplayed the game, but Frazier played all 48 minutes, Bradley 41 and Meminger, filling in for the injured Earl Monroe, 38.

Midway through the third period, Erving took off from the left side of the court, jumped around forward Phil Jackson and slammed the ball home. The 17,225 patrons at the Garden gasped at the athleticism and power of Erving's dunk.

"The Nets," wrote *New York Times* reporter Sam Goldaper, who covered the game, "looked more like an NBA team. They were well-schooled in defense, broke fast and put pressure on the Knicks."

But beyond that, the Nets—and Erving—had demonstrated that no matter what people were saying, the red-white-and-blue league was no longer a joke league.

"Jumpin' Jim," as he was known, could palm a basketball.

In Your Face

George "the Bird" Yardley, a 6' 6" forward who played with the Fort Wayne and later Detroit Pistons and the Syracuse Nationals from 1953 to 1960, was one of the great leapers in the early years of the NBA. He, too, wasn't big on dunking, but he threw one down at least once in an official game during his career, in unusual circumstances.

Yardley was the top scorer in the league in 1957 to 1958, and was on track to score 2,000 points in one regular season, then a record. In the Pistons' last regular-season game, Yardley needed 27 points to crack the 2,000 mark. In the first quarter, his teammates obligingly fed him and he had 14 at the end of the period.

But Syracuse coach Paul Seymour had no interest in letting Yardley set the record. He ordered his players to double-team Yardley, a maneuver sometimes used on centers at the time, but never on a forward or guard. Yardley picked up a basket here and

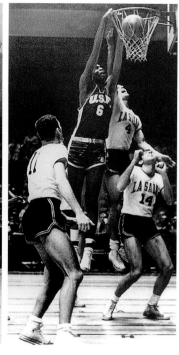

Bill Russell defying the entire LaSalle team with his two-handed dunk.

Dr. J showing off the two-handed jam.

there, but as the game wound down, he was still a point short.

"There was much effort on the part of Paul Seymour to prevent me from scoring 2,000 points," said Yardley recently. "I was more concerned with breaking George Mikan's record [which he did earlier in the year] of 1,932 points, because I thought that was a much more important record." (Mikan set that record in the 1950–51 season.)

Still, 2,000 points was a milestone. And now, Seymour was making it a little personal. So Yardley just hung around at half-court, for the Pistons' final few possessions. With only a minute or so left, he sprinted ahead of the field, took a pass and threw down a defiant dunk shot. It was probably the first "take that" dunk in league history.

"When I went from 1,999 points to 2,000, Seymour was fit to be tied," said Yardley. "Interestingly, I later played for the Syracuse Nationals and Paul was my coach,

and we eventually became very close friends."

Here Comes Wilt

The first player to dunk regularly in the NBA was Celtics center Bill Russell (1956–69). According to Bob Cousy, Russell's dunks consisted of quick jumps up to the rim and low-key flushes. Rarely did Russell, even at the end of his career, actually slam the ball into the basket.

That was the purview of Wilt Chamberlain. The 7' 1" Chamberlain, who played for the Philadelphia–San Francisco Warriors, Philadelphia 76ers and Los Angeles Lakers in a pro career that lasted from 1959 to 1973, often drew appreciative "oohs" and "aaahs" when he slammed a ball through the hoop, even in enemy arenas.

David Zinkoff, the colorful public-address man for the 76ers, would pronounce, "Another Dipper Dunk!" after Wilt slammed

Dominique Wilkins could always be counted on for a highlight-reel dunk as he does here against Larry Bird's Celtics.

one in. One of Chamberlain's nicknames was "the Big Dipper."

Chamberlain clearly was not worried whether he showed up an opponent, and obviously didn't fret about being called a freak. He was big and strong and remarkably agile. No one could stop his dunks when he had a mind to go to the hoop. Even Russell's principal strategy was to allow Wilt the dunk, then streak down the court ahead of Chamberlain, take a return pass and dunk the ball himself.

As the 1960s passed into the 1970s, the

dunk began evolving as a means of self-expression. In playgrounds across the country, ballplayers were dunking with style.

Where the dunk really came into its own professionally was in the NBA's rival league, the ABA. And ironically, the man who popularized the dunk as an art form as well as a way to score never had a chance to practice his craft in college.

When Julius Erving (1971–87) began his varsity career at the University of Massachusetts (1969–70), the dunk shot had been outlawed the previous year. Thus, fans at UMass missed what fans of the Virginia Squires were treated to: an airborne Erving, throwing down acrobatic slam after slam during games. From Day One in the ABA, Erving was unbelievably good, averaging 27.4 points per game (sixth in the league) and 15.7 rebounds, third in the league that first year.

The overall up-tempo style of the league, in general, and the Squires' running game, in particular, jump-started Erving's game. His tremendous natural gifts—large hands and exceptional jumping ability—enabled him to do two things well: handle the ball with greater facility and maneuver around larger, slower opponents in midair.

Drives to the basket by Julius Erving became things of beauty. He either dunked

the ball emphatically, or twisted around or above opponents and used his outsize mitts to put backspin on the ball and spin it into the hoop. Erving's style emphasized athleticism and creativity.

His nickname, "Dr. J," Erving recalled, came from an old playground chum who would talk about Erving "operating" on the opposition.

"Julius was the most ferocious dunker I've ever seen," said Kim Hughes, a former Nets (1975–81) teammate. "He always made the basket when he went up to dunk. Even when he was fouled. And he could dunk on anyone. It seemed like every time we played the Kentucky Colonels, he would go up against Artis Gilmore (1971–88) at least once a game and dunk on him."

And suddenly, almost overnight, it became cool to dunk, particularly in the ABA.

In the mid-1970s, the NBA was still a pretty conservative league. Phoenix Suns forward Connie Hawkins (1967–76) was sometimes admonished by NBA refs to curtail his showboating when he palmed a basketball prior to making his move. But in the ABA, players like George McGinnis (1971–82) and Darnell ("the Doctor of Dunk") Hillman (1971–80), both of the Indiana Pacers, and Larry "Dr. K" Kenon

(1973–83), of the New York Nets, were making a name for themselves with the jam.

The absorption of four of the ABA teams (New York, Denver, San Antonio and Indiana) as well as a number of ABA players into the NBA prior to the 1977–78 season finally infused the elder league with a little panache. Erving was still the best dunker in the league, but in the next few years, Philadelphia teammate Darryl Dawkins (1975–89), Utah Jazz guard Darrell "Dr. Dunkenstein" Griffith (1980–91), Phoenix and Atlanta forward Dominique "the Human Highlight Film" Wilkins (1982–99) began to elbow Dr. J out of the spotlight.

By the time former University of North Carolina guard Michael Jordan (1984–93, 1994–98, 2001–present) came to the Chicago Bulls for the 1984–85 season, the game had shifted subtly from one of plodding fundamentals to that of explosive athleticism and speed.

The Perfect Player

Jordan, a 6' 6" guard with spectacular leaping skills, exceptional speed and, most important, an intense desire to excel, found a league almost tailor-made for his abilities. He was not the most imaginative dunker ever (Erving, the Christopher Columbus of midair, will hold that title in perpetuity), nor was Jordan the highest leaper (Wilkins and 6' 9" Larry Nance, who played with Phoenix and then Cleveland from 1981 to 1994, could go higher).

But Jordan combined his leaping and dunking ability with exceptional instincts on offense to become the greatest scorer since Wilt Chamberlain. Opposing players feared his dunks, to be sure. But what they feared more was being destroyed offensively

by Jordan, who was far too quick for bigger players to guard and much too strong for smaller players to check. Worse, Jordan's best moves, particularly after he won his first scoring title in the 1986–87 season, were inevitably played out on national television, and then again and again on sports highlight shows every evening.

The NBA, understanding full well where its bread was buttered, catered to the dunk phenomenon even as Jordan joined the league. The Slam Dunk Contest, once a quaint affectation of the ABA, became a heavily hyped event at the NBA All-Star Game. (Ironically, after participating a few times, Jordan opted out. No matter, there were plenty of leapers to go around.)

When Jordan retired from the league for the second (but not the last) time in 1998, sportswriters and fans searched frantically for "the new Jordan," while at the same time conceding that there was, in reality, no such animal. The Lakers' Kobe Bryant (1996–present), an acrobatic 6' 7" guard, seemed a likely candidate, as did Jordan's fellow North Carolina alum, Vince "Half-man, Half-amazing" Carter (1998–present), a 6' 5" guard for the Toronto Raptors. Carter was the better leaper; Bryant the better overall player. Neither really approached Jordan's dominance.

Lakers center Shaquille O'Neal is the most powerful dunker since Chamberlain. O'Neal's dunks, however, lean more toward the Darryl Dawkins–like power slams. The 7' 1" "Shaq" isn't into finesse under the rim.

But, in fact, even Michael Jordan couldn't be the new Jordan. After un-retiring yet again, and playing in the 2001–02 season, Jordan, at 39, wasn't the leapingest, dunkingest guy in the league anymore, either. The league is still waiting.

The Greatest Dunk of All?

Neophyte NBA watchers saw Toronto's Vince Carter, 6' 5"
playing for the United States in the 2000 Olympics, slam over
France's 7' 2" center Frederic Weis in a game. That, everyone now says, is the greatest slam ever.

Come on. That's not even the first time something like
that has happened. In 1978, University of Louisville guard
Darrell "Dr. Dunkenstein" Griffith (6' 5") dunked over a
6' 8" Soviet player during a preseason exhibition.

"Hey, where'd that guy go?" Griffith said to a teammate as they were running back down the court.

"Man," the teammate said, "you jumped over the
dude."

As a pro, Griffith used to do something a sportswriter
termed "rocking the baby." He would take off from about
the foul line with the ball at his waist, rock the ball from
side to side, then lift it over his head and dunk.

The Doctor's Dunks

In 1977, in Game 6 of the NBA Finals, Sixer forward Julius
Erving, trying to rally his team, dunked over Portland center
Bill Walton (1974–87). The Sixers lost the game, but Erving
scored 40. In the same series, in the first moment of Game
1, Erving took the opening tap, cupped the ball in his hand,
took off from about 15' away, and windmill dunked, sending
the Philadelphia crowd into a frenzy. Philly did win that
game.

The Double-Pump Dunk

Dominique Wilkins would regularly double pump in midair
and dunk. Try doing that just standing on your living-room
floor to see how amazing that is. In his famous Game 7 duel
with Larry Bird (1979–92) in 1988, he did it three times,
once with Celtics forward Kevin McHale (1980–93) literally
hanging on to his arms.

Don't Foul Wilt

In the 1960s, there were actually people who tried to stop
Wilt Chamberlain from dunking. They paid a price. Figuring
Wilt was a lousy foul shooter, Boston forward John Havlicek
(1962–78) once tried to intentionally foul Wilt before he
completed his dunk by grabbing his dunking arm. Wilt just
pulled Havlicek along, like a father lifting up his kid, and
dunked the ball. Havlicek wisely let go just before Wilt
dunked him.

*Left: Michael Jordan in-flight theatrics can bring
down the house.*

*Facing page: Jordan in mid-air about to slam
one down.*

Right: The indispensable Carter, hand through the hoop, two more spectacularly delivered points.

Below: Shaq unsuccessfully tries to rip down the rim against the Jazz in this 1998 playoff match.

It's a dunkers league. The best in the NBA is Shaquille O'Neal, who scores almost half his points that way. His best move is to spin into the lane and blast the ball down on some guy's head with amazing quickness. It ain't pretty, but it works. The best little guy is Vince Carter, who can dunk with authority with either hand. The Clippers' Elton Brand is adept at getting inside position on his man and slamming the ball home.

PLAYERS TO WATCH

The Backboard Busters

These are the three most legendary backboard smashers of the NBA: Darryl Dawkins. Gus Johnson. Chuck Connors.

Chuck Connors? The guy who starred as Lucas McCain in *The Rifleman* television series?

Yep.

In 1946, however, Chuck Connors (1945–48) was not yet a television acting star. Rather, Connors was an exceptional two-sport athlete (baseball and basketball) from Seton Hall who had signed to play with the Boston Celtics after a brief career in the old National Basketball League.

At 6' 7", Connors was a reserve forward-center for the Boston Celtics. As he related many years later, the team was playing its first game on its home court on November 5, 1946, at the Boston Arena. Connors didn't actually dunk the ball. He sailed in for a layup and grabbed the rim, pulling it down and shattering the glass backboard, much to the chagrin of Connors and the annoyance of the fans. It took more than an hour to replace the backboard, as the spare was in another arena. Thus, Chuck Connors became the first player to shatter a backboard in the NBA, even if it was only in warm-ups.

The Bullets' Gus Johnson still holds the all-time record for smashed backboards in the NBA with three career

shatters. Johnson, a 6' 6" forward who played for the Baltimore Bullets from 1963 to 1972, then spent a year with the Phoenix Suns and ended his career on the bench for the 1972–73 ABA champion Indiana Pacers, was one of the strongest and most athletic players of the 1960s. He was a high school teammate of the 6' 11" Nate Thurmond, but it was Johnson who was the star in those days.

Johnson shattered one backboard each in 1963 at Oakland, in 1968 at St. Louis and in 1971 at Milwaukee. Give Gus credit: he always broke backboards on the road.

The record for most backboards broken in a year is held by the Sixers' Darryl Dawkins. On November 13, 1979, he shattered a backboard against the Kansas City–Omaha Kings in Kansas City. Then, 22 days later, he repeated the feat on December 5, 1979, against San Antonio at the Spectrum, which was then the Sixers' home court.

The next year, the NBA took the fun out of it all by inventing the collapsible rim. Now, when too much pressure is put on the rim, it just folds down.

Above: Shattered glass is all that remains after Darryl Dawkins, backboard destroyer, crushes another one in 1979.

4 The Alley-Oop

Beating the Defense by Throwing the Ball Over It

ORIGIN: **The mid-1940s**

THE FIRST: **Jesse Renick**
to Bob Kurland, Phillips 66ers

THE ALL-TIMERS:
Renick to Kurland (Phillips 66ers)
Bob Cousy to Bill Russell (Boston Celtics)
Greg Lee to Bill Walton (UCLA)
Magic Johnson to Michael Cooper
   (Los Angeles Lakers)
Anybody to Michael Jordan (Chicago Bulls)
Kurland, Russell and Walton, as well as Magic, are all in the
Hall of Fame. Jordan is pending.

THE TECHNIQUE:

The passer usually stands at the top of the key or a little
beyond it. The receiver either works his man off a pick,
or fakes a move to the foul line and then cuts sharply
back to the basket.

The passer then throws a pass that must be in the
vicinity of the front rim of
the basket. The receiver
jumps, catches the ball and
either lays it in or dunks
it. The passer must be
aware of the jumping limitations of the man catching
the ball. Lob passes do not
have to be thrown above
the rim. A good lob pass is
thrown at the rim to better
enable the person who is
supposed to catch the ball to
get a grip on it and dunk it.

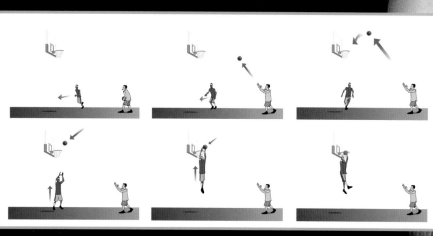

Try to throw the ball the
same way every time. An arched pass takes a millisecond longer to reach its target than a pass on a straight
line. That millisecond can be enough to throw even an
exceptional leaper's timing off.

*Above: Tracy McGrady
is one of the modern
masters of the alley-oop.*

*Bill Russell with
the two handed
catch and reverse
jam.*

The "lob shot" didn't begin with David Thompson (1975–84) or, further back, Bill Russell (1956–69). It probably began with one of the greatest players who never played in the BAA/NBA: Bob "Foothills" Kurland, a 7' All-American from Oklahoma A&M. Kurland graduated from A&M in 1946, and the pro landscape was, at least to him, pretty bleak.

"Well, from my point of view, there were an awful lot of pickup teams out there," recalled Kurland recently. "You had leagues in the Midwest and East, and they were paying guys out of paper bags. It didn't seem like a very good situation at the time. You know, George Mikan and I were probably the two biggest names to come out of college in the 1940s. George got drafted by Chicago, and when that team folded, he had to sue them to get his money. That made me a little nervous."

So Kurland signed up with the Phillips 66ers, a powerful Amateur Athletic Union (AAU) squad that he made more powerful. The 66ers were the cream of the AAU crop, the most dominating AAU squad in league history. Overall, they won 11 AAU titles in their history. Kurland helped the 66ers to three AAU championships in the six years he played (1946–52), and the 1947–48 team was probably the best AAU team of all time.

The 66ers went 62–3 that year, with wins over national champion Kentucky and several college all-star teams. In Madison Square Garden in April 1948, at the Olympic Trials, Kurland unveiled a wondrous new shot: the lob. A guard, usually veteran Jesse Renick, would simply toss the ball in the vicinity of the basket, and the 7' Kurland, who was inevitably much taller than his opponent, would catch the ball and drop it in.

Sometimes, Kurland would dunk the ball. In those days, it was called "flushing" the ball into the basket.

"I wouldn't say we worked on that shot," said Kurland in an interview recently. "At least not in the context of using it as part of our regular offense. But I was one of the few guys who could dunk, and when Jesse threw it up there, I just dunked it in. It was a way of getting the ball to me over the defense."

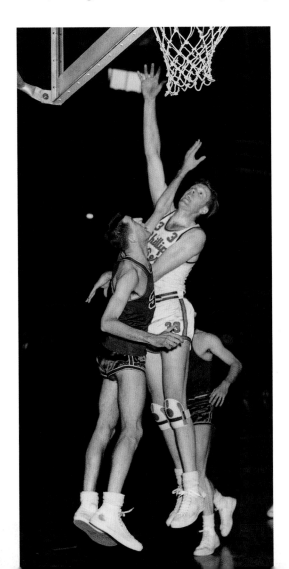

Left: Bob Kurland of Phillips 66ers was an early practitioner of the alley-oop.

MARCH 24, 1973, NCAA CHAMPIONSHIP GAME, UCLA VS. MEMPHIS STATE

It was the game for the national championship, and to date, no one had figured out how to stop UCLA and its stellar center, Bill Walton. Frankly, the underdog Tigers hadn't, either, but figured that since Walton was probably going to get his points anyway, they would play the 6' 11" redhead straight up. That was a mistake roughly on the scale of General George Armstrong Custer's decision to ride into Little Big Horn. Walton scored an NCAA record 44 points on 21 of 22 shooting that night as UCLA cruised to an 87–66 win. A majority of the passes into Walton were lob passes from guard Greg Lee. The grace and athleticism involved in the move was never better showcased.

Right: Bill Walton shoots for two of his record 44 points against Memphis State in the final game of the NCAA tournament.

A New Shot

Well, the sportswriters in Madison Square Garden were enthralled by Kurland's move that night. That may not have been the definitive birth of the "lob" or, as it would later be called, the "alley-oop," but it was for sportswriters.

But it didn't exactly sweep the nation. With the exception of George Mikan, Kurland was much more agile than your average big guy. For the most part, he was about the biggest big man around, so the alley-oop remained a rare beast even after 1946.

But a few years later, the center for the University of San Francisco, who was also a collegiate high-jumping champion, brought the alley-oop back into the college basketball lexicon.

All-American Bill Russell, at 6' 9", was not as tall as Kurland, but Russell was an explosive leaper. He and teammate K. C. Jones often collaborated on the alley-oop while both were in college. In fact, their most unstoppable collaboration came when Jones would stand out of bounds under his own basket and toss the ball to Russell over the backboard. It was an unstoppable move—until the NCAA made a rule prohibiting it.

Later, when Russell matriculated to the Boston Celtics, he and Celtic guard Bob Cousy would turn the trick.

In Cousy's superb book *Cousy on the Celtic Mystique*, the Boston Hall of Famer conceded, "One of our favorite tactics was what we now call the alley-oop. I used to love those things. I'd save it for maybe twice a game. Maybe just once. If it was not a good opponent, maybe we'd use it when we were up by 20.

"With Russell being able to jump so

TEAM DUNKS (2000–01 SEASON)
Los Angeles Lakers: 454
Portland Trail Blazers: 385
San Antonio Spurs: 368
Los Angeles Clippers: 365
Denver Nuggets: 356
Source: Harvey Pollock

Below: Flying high above the rim Bill Russell often caught the pass from Bob Cousy for a quick and spectacular two points.

much higher and being much more agile than anyone else, the alley-oop was always there. Half the time, given Russ's speed advantage, he was standing there waiting. You didn't even have to put it up that high."

Cousy and Jones both used the alley-oop at the end of a fast break, while Renick and Kurland usually applied it in a half-court setting. It was a slightly different approach, but the result was usually the same.

Up through the 1950s and 1960s, the alley-oop was a weapon used exclusively by a guard passing the ball to a center. The New York Knickerbockers of the early 1970s, for example, used the alley-oop play with center Willis Reed (1964–74), a future Hall of Famer, curling off a pick to take a pass from guard Walt Frazier (1967–80), another soon-to-be Hall of Famer, for a dunk.

But as the 1970s unfolded, the alley-oop became a weapon used by forwards as well. Julius Erving, the high-jumping forward for the Virginia Squires and the New York Nets, often made use of the alley-oop, as did 6' 9" Indiana Pacer forward Darnell Hillman, the so-called Doctor of Dunk.

In the case of these players, and many others, the ABA's three-point line was a key factor in facilitating the alley-oop. Defenses had to play a team's three-point shooters fairly honestly, which pulled players away from the basket and opened up the middle.

The Greatest Performances Ever

The alley-oop got a bigger workout in the college ranks during the 1970s. In 1972, North Carolina State started a 6' 4" sophomore forward named David Thompson. Thompson had a 44-inch vertical leap, which, coupled with his speed and agility, gave him a physical advantage over virtually everyone N.C. State faced.

PLAYERS TO WATCH

Anybody and everybody. In terms of degree of difficulty, if you will, Tracy McGrady of the Orlando Magic is the best. Part of it is because the Magic don't have great passers at the guard position, so McGrady is always reaching back or trying to grab the ball at odd angles to throw it down. Carter is good at this, as well. The best passers for the alley-oop are the Rockets' Steve Francis and Seattle's Gary Payton.

Above: With a 44-inch vertical leap David Thompson regularly played above the rim.

One of Thompson's teammates was 5' 5" guard Monte Towe. Towe, who later played two years in the pros (1975–77), was a good shooter and an enthusiastic defender, but he was also a terrific passer. He and Thompson had the alley-oop worked out to a science. The sight of a 6' 4" guard leaping above centers 5" and 6" taller than he to catch a pass and drop it softly into the basket was amazing. Thompson, perhaps one of the greatest college players ever, was named to the Hall of Fame following his pro career.

That same year, Bill Walton, a junior at UCLA, had the greatest scoring night of any player in the history of the championship game of the NCAA tournament, and it was almost exclusively via the alley-oop pass.

Walton was 6' 11" and, like Russell, extremely agile. UCLA's opponent that night was Memphis State, and the Tigers tried to play Walton straight up. UCLA's response was to lob the ball into Walton again and again, and let the big fella drop the ball in.

Walton hit 21 of 22 shots from the field, and 2 of 5 free throws for 44 points, still an NCAA record for points in a championship game, as UCLA won, 87–66.

Bruin guard Greg Lee had 14 assists that night, and Lee's backcourt running mate, Larry Hollyfield, had 9. The dunk was not allowed in college basketball at the time, so Walton converted passes from Hollyfield and Lee in a number of ways. Sometimes he dropped the ball in, sometimes he caught the pass in low and shot a turnaround and sometimes he caught the ball and banked it in. But it was an amazing performance any way one looked at it.

When Thompson became a professional with the Denver Nuggets, he was moved to guard by then-coach Larry Brown. He and

Above: Gonzaga's Anthony Reason jams the alley-oop pass from teammate Dan Dickau.

other backcourt stars like Darrell Griffith of the Utah Jazz began the practice of converting alley-oop passes from the backcourt.

In the 1980s, Griffith was great, but the best guard-guard alley-oop combination in the NBA was in Los Angeles, where guard Earvin "Magic" Johnson would regularly lob a pass into fellow guard Michael Cooper. When the two hooked up on the "Coop-a-Hoop" at home, the crowd would go wild.

Cooper, who played in the league from 1978 to 1990, in addition to being a tremendous leaper, also had great hands. After a while, Johnson got to be so accurate with the pass that Cooper could just jump up and guide the ball in with one hand.

Michael's Move

By the time the Chicago Bulls drafted Michael Jordan, the alley-oop was a regular weapon for most teams in the league, even squads without terrific leapers. Generally, by the 1990s, such was the athleticism of the league that almost any player above 6' 4" or so could catch a lob pass and convert it.

But Jordan, in this, as in many other things, was a few steps ahead of the crowd. His extraordinary leaping ability and large hands enabled him to go after many passes that would otherwise go awry. In a playoff game against New York in 1992, Jordan got behind the defense and took a lob pass from a teammate. The ball was poorly thrown, and Jordan had to reach back almost behind his head to get the ball. But he did, and he grabbed it and slammed it through.

The Chicago crowd was ecstatic but Jordan, in his inimitable way, had turned a poor pass and probable turnover into an exciting play.

There are at least as many great practitioners of the alley-oop pass in the NBA as there are teams in the league in the present era. Most clubs have one or two players who can get up near the basket and score. They come in all sizes, from 7' 1" Shaquille O'Neal to 6' 3" Houston "Jumping Jack" Steve Francis (1999–present). In terms of explosiveness, 6' 5" Toronto guard Vince Carter, 6' 5" Lakers swingman Kobe Bryant and 6' 6" Celtics forward Paul "The Truth" Pierce (1998–present) are the tops in the league.

Right: L.A. Clippers' Quentin Richardson scores on an alley-oop pass from Elton Brand.

Above: Full extension and a long reach is often needed to put away the alley-oop pass; as demonstrated here by Jason Kidd.

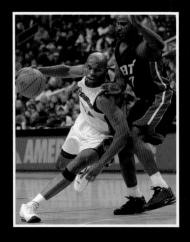

5 The Drive
Taking the Ball to the Hoop with Flair

ORIGIN: 1890s

THE FIRST: Nat Holman

THE ALL-TIMERS:
John Wooden (NBL, 1932–38)
Oscar Robertson (1960–74)
Nate Archibald (1970–84)
Earvin Johnson (1979–91, 1995–96)
Jason Kidd (1994–present)
Except for Kidd, every one of these
guys is in the Hall of Fame.

THE TECHNIQUE:

Dribble the ball to the basket with the dribbling hand farthest from the goal, angling your body slightly to protect
the ball. A few feet from the basket, push off with the
foot opposite from your shooting hand. Keep your body
between your defender and the ball.

If you are right-handed, push off with your left leg. If
your are right-handed, your shooting hand and right leg
should go into the air at the same time. As you jump
toward the basket, cup the ball in your outstretched
hand. Flip the ball into the basket, either off the backboard or directly in. Remember to follow through by
snapping your wrist upward.

*Above:
Jerry
Stackhouse, a
modern mas-
ter of the
drive and
finish.*

If you are fouled, throw the ball toward the basket anyway. There's always a chance it will go in, and you have
a three-point play. Remember to keep your head up when
dribbling, or you risk crashing into a defender and
receiving a charging foul.

*John Wooden, an All-American at Purdue for 3
years, and Player of the Year in 1932.*

Watching early basketball players drive to the basket was a lot like watching a well-played rugby scrum, particularly during the first two decades of the sport.

That's because the double dribble was legal in professional leagues until the mid-1930s. Players would dribble down the court with both hands, head down. Very often, since fouls were rare in the pro ranks in those days (and the games were much more physical than they are in today's NBA), a player would literally head-butt opponents out of the way as he dribbled, sometimes swatting at opponents who tried to take the ball away.

It was a primitive way to play, and it was unattractive to watch. In the early days of pro basketball, many leagues discouraged dribbling. One rule at the time, which would not be rescinded until 1915, prohibited the person dribbling from taking a shot.

Dribbling was not a good way to advance the ball, so many teams rarely dribbled at all. Instead, they would pass the ball around the court. The object was to spring a man free under the basket for a close-in shot like a layup, or set a player up for a long set shot.

The drive changed all that. The first player to actually drive to the basket is lost to antiquity, but Nat Holman (1916–33), who played in a number of professional leagues, was the best of the early players.

The First Flopper

Holman graduated from the Savage School of Physical Education in New York City in 1917. The next year, he was playing professionally. Actually, according to most accounts, Holman was a pro while still in high school, a distinction that was not uncommon in those days of many different pro leagues in various parts of New York City, New Jersey, Long Island and upstate New York.

Holman was a clever ballhandler whose principal strength as a dribbler was drawing fouls. He was almost certainly one of the first, if not the first player, to drive to the basket or just dribble across the court, initiate contact with an opponent and sprawl backward, with a stunned look on his face. Opponents of his day swear that Holman didn't even make contact with the opposing player many times; he would just reel away from the other man if his opponent was close.

Needless to say, in the 1920s, most refs had never seen such a maneuver, which we call "flopping" today, and Holman's act drew a number of sympathetic whistles. In a well-publicized game between Holman's New York Whirlwinds and the Original Celtics in 1921 for the unofficial World Championship, Holman led the Whirlwinds to a crushing 40–27 defeat of the Celtics, scoring 22 points—all on free throws.

But far from being angry at Holman's tactics, Original Celtics manager Jim Furey knew a great player when he saw one. Two

weeks after the Whirlwinds' victory, Holman signed with the Original Celtics.

The Original Celtics (so-called to distinguish themselves from many other teams of that era who called themselves the Celtics) were formed in 1918 by New York entrepreneur Furey and his brother, Tom. Henry "Dutch" Dehnert, sweet-shooting forward Johnny Beckman, 6' 5" "giant" Joe Lapchick, hefty (225 pounds) George "Horse" Haggerty and savvy forward Bernhard "Benny" Borgmann were among the most famous Celtics.

The Celtics, elected to the Hall of Fame in 1959 as a team, were the first team to play together as a unit over the course of many years, thanks to Furey's concept of signing the men to long-term contracts. As a result, they played cohesive, smart basketball and were usually light-years ahead of most teams they faced.

The India Rubber Man

It sounds like the name one would give a superhero, but Johnny Wooden wasn't any such thing. Rather, he was a tremendous basketball player.

Wooden (NBL, 1932–38) was a three-time All-American at the University of Purdue from 1929 to 1932, and he led the Boilermakers to the national championship in 1932. The year after his graduation, he signed a contract to play for the Indianapolis Kautskys in the former National Basketball League. The team was named after Frank Kautsky, who owned several grocery stores in Indianapolis. Wooden would go on to play six years professionally with the Kautskys and other squads.

Above: Kenny Sailors of the Denver Nuggets blasting to the hoop.

The Kautskys were one of the best pro teams in the state, and Wooden, who played professionally from 1932 to 1940, was their best player, earning $50 per game. This was in a league where most players earned $15 to $25 per game.

Wooden was a great all-around player who could do a lot of things well—but, boy, could he go to the hoop! He was called "the India Rubber Man" at Purdue because of his habit of driving to the basket, scoring the goal and then caroming off walls and poles as his momentum carried him off the court. At Purdue, the team would have two student managers at either end of the court to catch Wooden before he pinballed out of the arena.

Wooden and players like him carried the concept of going to the basket to the next level. Johnny Wooden, the famed India Rubber Man, would become Coach John

Above: Jerry West wards off Oscar Robertson in a match-up of two of the greatest.

Wooden. He would lead the University of California at Los Angeles to ten NCAA championships in 12 years from 1964 to 1975. Wooden was the first player enshrined in the Basketball Hall of Fame who would later also be enshrined as a coach as well.

Fat Freddie and the Big O

"Fat Freddie" Scolari (1946–55), of the Washington Capitols, and Bob Davies (1945–55), of the Rochester Royals, were among the first to turn drives to the basket into an art form. Scolari, a savvy 5' 11" guard, really was fat, as he possessed a paunch, but he was also quick as a whip. Davies, a collegiate star at Seton Hall, was the best all-around guard of the 1940s. His drives to the basket were graceful and innovative. Davies, for example, wasn't a great leaper, but if a larger player blocked his way, he had the wherewithal to angle his body in such a way as to enable him to have a clear shot at the goal. There were other players who did this, but Davies was the best of his generation.

The Tank

Adrian Dantley was a 6' 5" forward who weighed 210 pounds, almost all of it muscle. Good thing—because Dantley's principal weapon was an all-out drive to the hole. This was a guy, folks, who wanted to be fouled, because he could usually get the shot off and make it, setting up a three-point play opportunity. Because of his squared-off, powerful body, Dantley was called "the Tank" and "the Baby Bull." Dantley was regularly one of the top scorers in the league, and twice during his career, he scored more foul shots than field goals in a season. The first was in 1983 and 1984, when Dantley connected on 813 free throws and 802 field goals. He averaged 30.6 points per game and led the NBA in scoring. This was the only time in league history that a player led the league in points by scoring more free throws than field goals.

Dantley also accomplished the feat in the 1987–88 season for the Detroit Pistons, scoring 44 field goals and 492 free throws to average 20 points per game. Dantley's career free-throw percentage, by the way, was 82 percent.

In the late 1950s and 1960s, Oscar Robertson, a guard who played professionally from 1960 to 1974, was huge for a guard: 6'-5" and 201 pounds. Worse, for opponents, he was absolutely fearless.

Above: Oscar Robertson pushes the rock on his way to the hole.

Right: Larry Bird taking it to J.R. Reed in 1991.

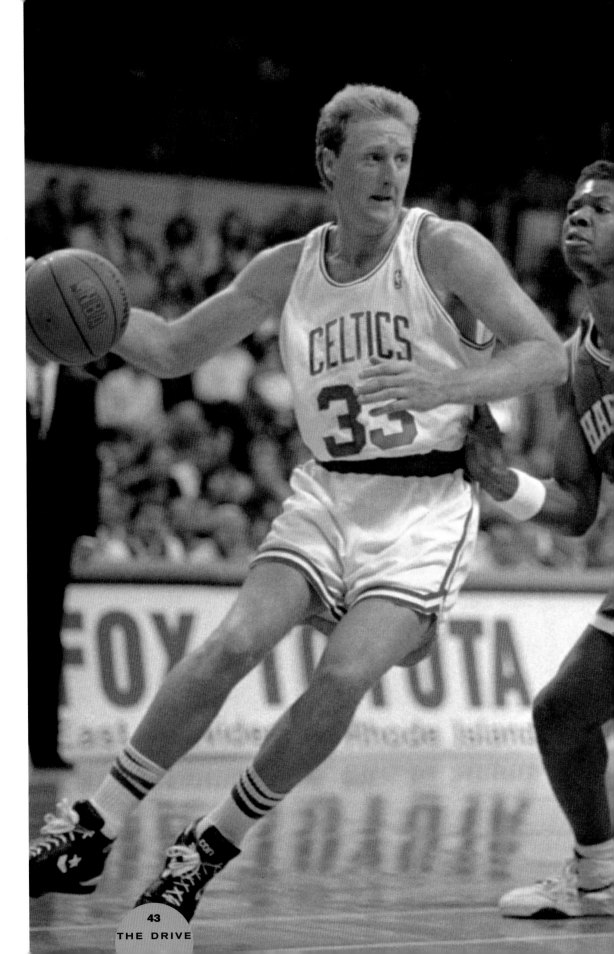

"The Big O," as Robertson was called, was primarily a passer through most of his career. He was also a very good shooter who never passed up a chance to drive to the hoop. Robertson's strength and passing abilities were a nightmare for opponents. He could overpower any guard in the league. If they played off him, he would shoot the jump shot. If they played him tight, Oscar would take a huge first step, dribble around his man and drive to the basket.

At that point, most opponents were at his mercy. Robertson had this move where he would angle his hip into a center in midair, draw the foul and flip the ball into the basket for a potential three-point play. Or, he could draw the big man to him and drop a pass off to his own big man, usually Wayne Embry (1958–69) or, from 1970 to 1974, Kareem Abdul-Jabbar of the Milwaukee Bucks.

Other players were almost as good. The Lakers, Jerry West (1960–74), the Indiana Pacers, Billy Keller (1969–76) were also excellent drivers.

Then there was Tiny.

Nate "Tiny" Archibald (1970–84) was the epitome of the scoring, ballhandling guard. At 6' 1", 160 pounds, Tiny looked frail next to the giants of the NBA in the 1960s

PLAYERS TO WATCH

Stack is the man. The Wizards' Jerry Stackhouse is not shy about taking the ball to the hole. Stackhouse is big enough, at 6' 6", to take the punishment and strong enough to put the ball into the basket even if he's hit. The New Orleans Hornets' Jamal Mashburn is a vastly underrated driver, with an excellent first step.

SELECTED THREE-POINT PLAY CONVERSIONS (2000–01 season)
Stephon Marbury, New Jersey Nets
38 baskets scored, 33 foul shots converted
Steve Francis, Houston Rockets
33 scored, 28 converted
Andre Miller, Cleveland Cavaliers
32 scored, 27 converted
Kobe Bryant, Los Angeles Lakers
49 scored, 38 converted
Allen Iverson, Philadelphia 76ers
45 scored, 33 converted
Paul Pierce, Boston Celtics
75 scored, 53 converted
Source: Harvey Pollock

and 1970s. But driving to the hoop and drawing fouls was how he made his money.

Archibald could drain the 15' jumper, but his strength was his incredible speed and quickness. His first coach, former Celtic Bob Cousy, told Archibald as a rookie that he should be able to get any shot he wanted, such was his speed and agility.

That was usually true. In the 1972–73 season, Archibald led the NBA in scoring with a 34.0 average and assists with an 11.4 mark. It was something no player had ever done before nor has ever done since. It was an amazing performance and a dominating one that admittedly took a toll on Archibald. The next year, he battled injuries and missed 47 games. Archibald recovered the year after, but never hit either of those statistical marks again.

The last several decades have seen variations on the Archibald theme. The NBA's decision to adopt the three-point line has aided those players who take the ball to the basket by spreading some players to beyond the three-point line. Some, like the Lakers' Earvin "Magic" Johnson (1979–91,

Left: Nate Archibald was a master of the drive, here seen out-maneuvering Norm Nixon of the Lakers.

The Evolution of the Basketball

The drive became more refined over the decades in no small measure because the basketball itself became easier to handle. The first balls used in pro leagues at the turn of the 20th century were four pieces of leather sewn together. The seams were raised like those of a football, and when the basketball hit the floor on the seam, it would often career crazily away from the dribbler.

In addition, after a few minutes of fast action, the sewn seams would begin to spread, causing the ball to become slightly lopsided. Thus, drives to the basket were limited to only a few dribbles, lest the ballhandler lose the ball altogether.

But by the late 1930s, the ball was being sewn together by machine, making a much tighter cover. By 1952, the basketball was completely molded and inflated, eliminating problems with the seams altogether.

1995–96), Adrian Dantley (1976–91) and Paul Pierce (1998–present), of the Boston Celtics, are drivers in the mold of Oscar Robertson: physically strong men who overpower their opponents. Pierce, in particular, has an explosive first step that enables him to blow past opponents.

Players like Stephon Marbury (1996–present), of the Phoenix Suns, Mike Bibby (1998–present), of the Sacramento Kings, and Jason Kidd (1994–present), of the New Jersey Nets, are more finesse guys.

Left: Despite Karl Malone's excellent D, Charles Barkley goes to the rack.

Below: Stephon Marbury is furious on the drive as Damon Stoudamire finds out here.

Left: Even the intimidating Olajuwon can't stop Nick Van Excel on his way to the hoop.

Kidd is perhaps the best of both worlds. At 6' 4", 212 pounds, he is tough and durable. He is the best passer off the drive in the league. Although the Nets were swept by the Los Angeles Lakers in the 2002 NBA Finals, Kidd was the best passer on the floor in every game. Kidd hasn't specifically taken the drive to another level, but what he has done is made dishing off to other players more fashionable these days.

6 The Foul Shot

It's the Little Things That Count

ORIGIN: 1894–95

THE FIRST: A player named Simonson for the Brooklyn YMCA in 1896 was the first to do it in a game featuring professional players.

THE BEST:
Bill Sharman (1950–61)
Rick Barry (1965–80)
Calvin Murphy (1970–83)
Larry Bird (1979–92)
Mark Price (1986–98)
All but Price are in the Hall of Fame.

THE TECHNIQUE:
There are several techniques to shooting foul shots, but the most popular is the one-handed shot. Set up with your feet just behind the line and square your shoulders. Take a deep breath to relax. Bend your knees slightly. The ball should be in the "waiter's position" in your hand—that is, resting on your fingertips and not in the palm of your hand.

As you shoot, extend your entire body. Remember to follow through by extending your elbow and snapping your wrist. That allows the ball to roll off your fingers, creating backspin.

When the referee hands you the ball, especially if you are tired, stand a few steps behind the line and step to the line to receive the ball. This will enable you to set yourself better.

Shooting underhand uses a surprisingly similar stance. Set your feet just behind the foul line and square your shoulders. Hold the ball loosely in both hands below your waist. Bend your knees and shoot the ball by tossing it toward the basket with both hands. When shooting, bend your elbows slightly and snap your wrists upward.

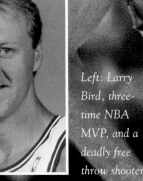

Left: Larry Bird, three-time NBA MVP, and a deadly free throw shooter.

Steve Nash's proficiency at the free throw line adds to his standing as one of the best players in the NBA today.

Initially, in Dr. Naismith's game, there were no foul shots. Infractions, according to Naismith's original rules, were punished by relinquishing the ball to the other team. But eventually, Naismith decided that a foul shot worth one point would be awarded for more egregious errors, such as striking or pushing another player. That amendment in the rules came after a year or so of trial and error. For

Jerry West getting ready to release his free throw in a 1970 game against Atlanta.

a while, foul shots and baskets from the floor were both worth a point. Then both were worth three points. Eventually, to give goals scored from the floor more importance, two points were assigned to those baskets, and one point to a foul shot.

Who shot the first foul shot is pretty much anyone's guess, but the first player to score a free throw in a recorded game was a fellow named Simonson from the Brooklyn YMCA, who scored his team's only point in a 16–1 loss to the Trentons, of New Jersey, led by Fred Cooper and Al Bratton.

The Brooklyn YMCA was an amateur club, but the Trenton fellows were believed to be the first pro basketball team ever.

In the beginning, players shot free throws from a line set 20 feet from the basket. That was moved in to the regulation 15-foot free-throw line in the late 1890s.

For many years, teams followed a rule devised by the Amateur Athletic Union of letting the best free-throw shooter on the team take all the foul shots in a game. Then in 1910, the Troy Trojans, starring standout pro Ed Wachter, pushed for a rule change that would require the person fouled to take the shot. The New York State League, of which the Trojans were a member, adopted the rule in 1910.

Most professional leagues held out until 1915. The thinking was that requiring the person fouled to shoot the free throw would open the game up to excessive fouling late in the contest as teams would move to foul the poorest free-throw shooter on the floor. That didn't really happen, and colleges and high schools similarly changed the rule to require the foulee to shoot the free tries in 1924.

Free throws were originally shot two-handed, either a push shot from the chest or by throwing them underhanded from a

MARCH 21, 1953, EASTERN CONFERENCE SEMIFINALS, BOSTON VS. SYRACUSE

That night, the Boston Celtics eliminated the Syracuse Nationals from the NBA playoffs, two games to none, with a 111–105 win in a game that took four overtimes to complete. In that contest, Celtic guard Bob Cousy scored 50 points, the most points by a player in the league that year. Cousy also hit 30 of 32 free throws. His 30 successful free tries is still an NBA record for the playoffs and the regular season.

Cousy made two free throws with seconds left to tie the game in regulation, 77–77. In the first overtime, Cousy hit four free throws in a row to tie the game, 86–86. Cousy made two free throws in the second overtime, which ended up tied at 90–90. With time running down in the third overtime, Cousy hit a 25-foot push shot to tie the game at 99–99 and force a fourth overtime. Cousy scored nine of Boston's 12 points in that stanza, including five of five free throws, and Syracuse finally ran out of gas. Cousy hit 17 consecutive free throws in the fourth quarter and in the overtimes, one of the great clutch performances in NBA history.

For those in Boston and Syracuse, the contest was no doubt riveting. But for everyone else in the league, it was mostly a free-throw contest. The play was very deliberate, and every time Boston got even a minuscule lead, Cousy would simply dribble down the time. The Syracuse players would foul, and he would go to the free-throw line. The game was exciting because Cousy made the free throws, but also because Syracuse players kept making shots to keep their team in it. But it was bad for basketball, and even then most owners and coaches knew it, which led, a few years later, to the introduction of a shot clock. (Well, Red Auerbach didn't think it was so bad.)

crouch. Percentages in the first 40 or 50 years of the game were never very high, usually around 70 to 75 percent. "Fat Freddie" Scolari (1946–55), the Washington Capitols guard who led the BAA/NBA in free-throw percentage in the league's first year, 1946–47, hit 81.1 percent of his shots, and was the only player above 80 percent in the league.

But that was more because of the basketball itself than because of the players' abilities. Don't forget, in the first part of the 20th century, the ball was just four large strips of

Bob Feerick had been Red Auerbach's pal when both men had served in the Navy, and when Red was assembling his squad in Washington in 1946, he recruited Feerick. "Sailor" Bob accomplished something in the second year of the BAA that no one has done since: he led the league in both foul shooting and field goal percentage. Feerick was a smart, quick backcourtman who was also the fourth leading scorer in the league that year. His free-throw shooting was very good: he hit 189 out of 240 shots for a .788 mark, just ahead of Max Zaslofsky's .784.

His field goal shooting was not so hot. Feerick won the field goal percentage title with a less-than-scintillating .340. No NBA player would ever shoot as badly as Feerick and still win the accuracy crown.

There were a couple of reasons for Feerick's poor shooting. One was the god-awful places in which these players played. Uline Arena, Feerick's home court, was poorly lit and drafty, and there were few places, if any, that were much better.

Of course, the other problem was that a majority of these arenas were also hockey rinks. "They were all just so damn cold," noted Harry "Buddy" Jeannette (1938–50) in an interview years later. "Warming up was impossible."

The other problem was that the balls were lumpy and lopsided. How Feerick hit almost 80 percent of his foul shots was probably one of the more amazing feats in those early days.

leather sewn together with a stitched slit into which an inflated bladder was inserted.

Teams rarely replaced the ball as the game wore on, which meant that after an hour or so of hard dribbling and shooting the ball began to flatten out.

Manufacturing improvements in the 1930s and 1940s made the basketball easier to handle and shoot. After Scolari shot .811 in the BAA/NBA's first year, foul-shooting percentages improved by leaps and bounds, and three years later the best players in the league were all shooting well over 80 percent.

Wanzer Hits 90 Percent

In the 1951–52 season, the Rochester Royals' Bobby Wanzer (1947–57), a 6' guard who played in the same backcourt as Bob

Davies for many years, hit 377 of 417 free tries, a .904 percentage. It was the first time in NBA history that a player had made more than 90 percent of his free throws.

The first of the consistently great NBA free-throw shooters year after year was Bill Sharman (1950–61), a 6' 1" guard with the Celtics who was one of the great shooters from the floor, as well. In 1959, he made 56 consecutive free throws. In 1956, he made 55 in a row. In the 1959 season he led the league with a then-record .934 percentage. Sharman led the league in free-throw shooting for seven of his 10 years in the NBA, including an NBA record five consecutive times.

Sharman's accomplishments were laudable. The problem in the late 1940s and early 1950s, before the advent of the 24-second clock in 1955, was that free throws were beginning to strangle the game.

For instance, on March 26, 1949, the New York Knickerbockers dethroned the defending champion Baltimore Bullets in a tough three-game series that featured one of the most physical playoff games in NBA history. The game, the third and final tilt in the best-of-three series, was played at the old Lexington Avenue Armory in New York. It was won by the Knicks 103–99, and featured 100 personal fouls, 11 player disqualifications and 118 foul shots. There were no fights in the game. What was happening was that any time either side got even a minuscule lead, they would start to stall. And the other side would foul.

It was brutal. The Knicks hit 51 of 64 foul shots, while Baltimore hit 47 of 54 free throws. Knicks reserve Ray Lumpp had this line in the box score: 3–14–20. That's three field goals, 14 (of 15) from the free-throw line, for 20 points. Harry "the Horse" Gallatin had four field goals, was 13 for 17 from the line and had 21 points.

"This is hard to believe, but the last six minutes of that game took 48 minutes," said Knick coach Joe Lapchick a few years later.

In 1954, facing elimination in the play-offs, the Knickerbockers locked up with the Celtics in the Boston Garden on March 20. The game was foul-filled and close the entire way. The Celtics won, 79–78, as Sharman dropped in a smooth 17-footer with seconds left to seal the win. It was only Bill's fifth field goal, but he had dropped in a stunning 16 of 16 free throws to finish with a game-high 26 points. The best line score of the game, however, belonged to Knicks guard Carl Braun: zero field goals, 14 of 16 free throws for 14 points.

In a way, these kinds of games were a good thing. The league realized that something had to be done, and introduced the 24-second clock in 1955. Now, teams didn't have to foul to get the ball back. All they had to do was play good defense.

Calvin's Game

Of course, there have been great free-throw shooters in the era after the introduction of the 24-second clock. Calvin Murphy (1970–83) has the highest career free-throw percentage for one season in NBA history with a .958 mark in the 1980–81 season. That was also the year Murphy hit 78 free throws in a row for the Houston Rockets.

Murphy held on to the record for 12 years until Michael Williams (1988–99), of the Minnesota Timberwolves, broke it in 1993 by hitting 97 in a row. Ironically, Mahmoud Abdul-Rauf (1990–present), then a guard for the Denver Nuggets, also broke Murphy's

Left: A game can easily hinge on one team's free throw proficiency as here the Net's Keith Van Horn sets up with 0.4 seconds remaining in the game.

record that same year by hitting 81 in a row.

Mark Price, a 6' 1" guard who played in Cleveland, Washington, Golden State and Orlando from 1986 to 98, holds the record for the highest career free-throw percentage with a .904 mark. Rick Barry (1965–80) is the only other NBA player in league history to have a career mark of 90 percent or better. Barry is at exactly .900 for his career. He led the league six times.

"It is absolutely beyond me why modern players don't practice free throws more," said Hall of Famer Barry in an interview a few

THE BEST BIG MEN FREE-THROW SHOOTERS

Super Stats

On February 26, 1949, George Mikan scored 53 points in a win over the Baltimore Bullets. The 53-point night against Baltimore was notable in that "Big" George hit 19 of 20 free throws. This was not an aberration. Mikan was a very good free-throw shooter, not just for a big man, but for a basketball player in general. Mikan was a career 78 percent foul shooter and a career 79 percent shooter in the playoffs.

There isn't another Hall of Fame caliber big man who comes even close. Kareem Abdul-Jabbar, for example, is a career 72 percent foul shooter, which is considered excellent for a big man. Willis Reed at 75 percent and Robert Parish at 72 percent are two other excellent foul shooters from the center position. If you're wondering, Wilt Chamberlain was a 51 percent career foul shooter, while Shaquille O'Neal is at 56 percent.

The Real Pro Free-Throw Record?

Michael Williams of the Timberwolves set the NBA record for consecutive free throws with 97 over a two-year span that ended in November of 1993. It remains an impressive record, but the unofficial professional mark was set in 1934–36 by a guard for the Indianapolis Kautskys of the NBL: Hall of Famer John Wooden, who hit 134 in a row. The Kautskys were named after Ed Kautsky, a local businessman who owned the team.

"The record was set over the course of two years," recalled Wooden recently. "I don't remember much about it, except that when I hit 100 in a row, Mr. Kautsky gave me a $100 bill after the game, which was a lot of money in those days."

Wooden, the former Purdue All-American, generally made $30 per game. And he was one of the league's stars.

Although Williams's record was impressive, Wooden set his mark under much more difficult circumstances.

"Most of the games were played on weekends, and all the players had second jobs," said Wooden of his NBL days. "We traveled by car, and we had to deal with dark gyms, home court refereeing and other things."

By the way, while the history books list his accomplishment as 138 free throws in a row, Wooden admits, "As far as I can recall, it was 134. But it was a long time ago."

If coach Wooden says 134, we'll go with 134.

Left: With an 84 percent career free throw percentage Michael Jordan has cashed in on many a foul on his way to winning scoring title after scoring title.

Above: Larry Johnson at the line in a playoff game against the Indiana Pacers.

Above: Karl "the Mailman" Malone's concentration can be seen as he sets up for a free throw.

years ago. "It's the one place where you can be the most selfish person in the world and still help your team."

Larry Bird (1979–92), the Celtics 6' 9" forward, was the tallest player to lead the league in free-throw percentage more than once: he did it four times in his career. Only Barry and Sharman led the league in free-throw percentage more times than Bird. During the 1987–88 season, 6' 11" Milwaukee center Jack Sikma (1977–91) became the only center to lead the NBA in free-throw shooting, hitting 92.2 percent of his free throws.

There are some who say that in the 21st century free-throw shooting has become a lost art. In the old days of the 1960s and 1970s, players played a more fundamental game, which included making their free-throws.

Well, that's really not true. Most years, the NBA will have one or two players in the low 90s, percentage-wise, with the rest of the leaders packed behind them. That hasn't differed much from the 1970s or 1980s. The only exception was the "Golden Year" for free throws, when six players, led by Reggie Miller's .918 percentage, shot better than 90 percent from the line. That was the year Larry Bird missed 20 free throws (161 for 181) and finished 10th in the league.

PLAYERS TO WATCH

The Pacers' Reggie Miller regularly hits 80 percent of his freebies. The Wizards' Rip Hamilton and the Mavericks' Steve Nash are up there, as well. No Rick Barrys or Larry Birds in the league anymore, though.

7 The Layup

The Easiest Shot of All, Sometimes

THE ORIGIN: Soon after the game was invented in 1891

THE FIRST: Amos Alonzo Stagg, Springfield College

THE ALL-TIMERS: A tough call. If you can't shoot a layup, you won't be playing this game very long. Stagg is in the Hall of Fame

THE TECHNIQUE:

Right-handed players dribble to the basket from the right side. As you approach the basket, bring your right leg, arm and hand up at the same time while pushing off your left foot and jumping into the air. Your right arm and leg should go up at about the same time. Shoot the ball with your right hand off the backboard, and bank it into the basket. Remember to follow through. Left-handed shooters should do exactly the opposite.

If approaching the basket from the front, as opposed to the side, aim for the front of the rim and gently push the ball over the rim and straight into the hole. It is more accurate, however, to try approach from the side and use the back-board as often as possible.

Don't rush the shot, unless time is running out. You should be protecting the ball with your body, so unless you're driving on a seven-footer, be patient. And concentrate! A majority of layups are missed because players think they are too easy. Throwing a pumpkin-sized ball at a target 10 feet off the ground is always difficult, no matter how close you are

Above: Jason Kidd soars past David Robinson for an easy layup.

Right: Dolph Schayes of the Syracuse Nationals driving for a layup.

The gimmie. The bunny. The pooch. The cripple. Those are some other names for layups over the years. But if layups are so easy, how come players miss them all the time?

The answer is that it's tougher than it looks. The layup is taken when a player is closest to the basket, but there is often a defender or defenders guarding him, and with all those bodies so close to the bucket, laying it in is not so easy.

From 1891 to 1895, it was even more difficult, because there were no backboards. Players had to cradle the ball in one hand

Above: Johnny Kerr of the Syracuse Nationals flying high through the air for a layup against the Fort Wayne Pistons.

SEPTEMBER 10, 1972, MUNICH, GERMANY, THE OLYMPIC BASKETBALL FINALS, USA VS. USSR

After 39 minutes and 57 seconds, a pair of free throws by U.S. guard Doug Collins had put the United States ahead, 50–49 of their archrivals, the Soviet Union, in this physical gold-medal game. With three seconds left, the Russians inbounded the ball, but play was stopped with a second left while officials tried to clear the court of spectators. The Russians tried a long desperation pass that was deflected as time ran out. The U.S. players began celebrating their hard-fought win.

But literally, almost five minutes later, Robert Jones, secretary-general of FIBA (the International Basketball Federation), ordered the teams back onto the court. Jones had absolutely no standing in the game, except as a spectator (a similar situation would be if, say, NBA Deputy Commissioner Russ Granick came to the scorers' table of a Celtics-Sixers playoff game in Boston Garden and ordered a replay of the final moments). The Soviet coach insisted that he had called a time-out after Collins' free throws and Jones insisted the final seconds be replayed.

The two teams went back out onto the floor, and another long pass was deflected by U.S. players, and once again the team celebrated.

But a Soviet assistant coach noted that 50 seconds, not three seconds, had been put back on the clock, and he demanded the clock be reset again. Jones agreed and ordered the teams back onto the court. At this point, Olympic coach Hank Iba should have pulled his team off the court and back to the locker room. But he didn't.

This time, Ivan Edeshko threw another length-of-the-court pass and Soviet forward Alexander Belov outfought two U.S. players, guard Kevin Joyce and forward James Forbes. After losing his balance momentarily, Belov faked and laid the ball in. The Soviet "victory" was the first time the United States had been beaten in Olympic competition in 36 years. Belov's layup remains the most well known shot in the history of international hoops.

Russia's Alexander Belov leaps high to hit an extra chance basket and give Russia a 51-50 controversial win over the U.S. team in the last seconds of the 1972 Olympics.

The Finger Roll

The finger roll is the layup's stylish cousin. Wilt Chamberlain (1959–73) said in his last book, *A View from Above*, that he invented the finger roll in 1958, and he may have, because to shoot a finger roll, you have to be able to jump high enough to just roll the ball off your fingers into the basket. And you have to have hands big enough to be able to control the ball.

But a few years before Wilt, Nat "Sweetwater" Clifton, who played first for the Harlem Globetrotters and then in the NBA from 1950 to 1958, was also observed rolling a ball off his fingers into the basket, so some hoop historians have given him the nod.

Clifton, Chamberlain and Julius Erving (1971–87) were among the best at the finger roll. But the all-time smoothest was George "The Iceman" Gervin (1972–86). The Iceman, a 6' 7" guard, had huge hands and superb body control. He could drive to the hoop and, palming the ball in one hand, finger-roll it toward the basket from much farther out than almost any other player. Gervin could also do something few other players could accomplish: he could bank finger rolls off the glass. Pretty amazing.

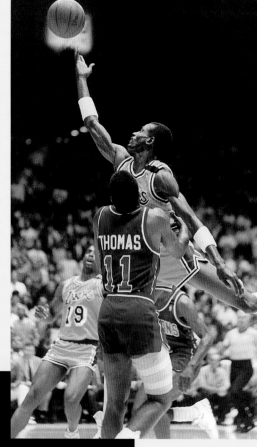

and sort of loft it at the basket. Nonetheless, the layup has been a part of basketball since its inception in 1891.

Amos Alonzo Stagg, who is better known for his considerable contributions to the game of football, was also a big hoops fan. He graduated from Phillips Exeter Academy in New Hampshire in 1884 and from Yale

Above: Michael Cooper's finger roll was a deadly scoring weapon. Shown here against Isiah Thomas and the Pistons.

Left: Jordan's finger roll draws a foul from Cleveland's Larry Nance—can anyone say 3-point play?

PLAYERS TO WATCH

The most fundamentally sound player when it comes to making layups is Gary Payton of the SuperSonics. He is the most graceful player going to the hoop today. The other player to watch is Jason Kidd of the Nets, who is the best at shooting layups with his opposite hand, along with the Mavericks' Steve Nash. The Bucks' Sam Cassell is one to watch.

University in 1888. He worked as a teacher at Springfield College in 1891, when Dr. James Naismith invented the game. Stagg played in the first public basketball game on March 11, 1892, scoring the only basket for the faculty in a 5–1 loss to the Springfield underclassmen.

It's hard to say if Stagg's bucket was a

layup, but in a publication in the 1930s, he recounted his lone basket as coming from under the hoop after a struggle with a number of other players.

Fred Cooper was the best player on the Trentons. (Formed in 1896, this New Jersey squad is recognized as the first professional basketball team.) He, along with his pal, Al Bratton, had devised a way to move the basketball up the court without dribbling, by passing it between themselves. Cooper was also a scorer. He preferred to shoot from close in to the basket, lofting soft, two-handed shots from a few feet out. In the Trentons' first professional game, November 7, 1896, Cooper was the leading scorer in the team's

16–1 win over the Brooklyn YMCA with three baskets (six points).

Since then, the layup is the layup is the layup, as Shakespeare might have said. There hasn't been much overall improvement or refinement of it. It is at once the most fundamental of offensive moves and the most unchanging. Which is probably as it should be.

Left: Bill Bradley going up for two against John Havlicek in this 1970 game between the Knicks and the Celtics.

Above: Grant Hill is extremely active around the hoop.

8 The Set Shot
So Out, It's In

ORIGIN: December 1891

THE FIRST: William H. Davis, Springfield College

THE ALL-TIMERS:
Bobby McDermott (1933-50)
Max Zaslofsky (1946-56)
Carl Braun (1947-62)
Larry Costello (1954-68)
Michael Cooper (1978-90)
Mario Elie (1990-present)
McDermott is in the Hall of Fame.

Left: Mario Elie is the number one set shooter of the 1990s.

Max Zaslofsky was an excellent set shooter.

THE TECHNIQUE:
Stand with your body square to the basket. Balance the ball on your fingertips. (Note: you can either balance the ball in both hands, or balance it on one hand with your "off" hand as a guide. Either way is acceptable.) Push off with your feet, but don't jump, as you aim the shot. After you release the ball, push your arm or arms out straight and lock your elbows. Follow through with your wrist or wrists.

Try to find a spot on the court with which you are comfortable shooting. That spot or spots should be where you shoot a majority of your set shots. Concentrate, but also be aware of where your defender is. The set shot is an easy shot to block, so it's important to get as open as possible.

Once mothballed as a hopelessly old fashioned move by the mid-1960s, the set shot has returned with a vengeance as professional players use the three-point line more and more.

The set shot was developed in the 1890s as players began attempting shots farther and farther from the basket. Using one hand to shoot a layup was acceptable, but from any place farther out, the conventional thinking (until Hank Luisetti, at least) was that you needed two hands to accurately shoot the ball.

We know who the first player to successfully convert a set shot was, because William H. Davis (some accounts say Lyman W. Archibald, but more lean toward Davis) was the first man to score in the first official basketball game in December of 1891. And Davis, according to accounts, threw in a "push shot" from 25 feet out.

The set shot began as a static field goal attempt. That is, players stopped at a spot on the floor and launched the shot. Since nobody jumped, the key was to spring a man off a pick to give him room to shoot. At times, players would dribble to a spot and let the shot fly, but they would have to dribble, stop, set themselves and then shoot. Such a sequence could take several seconds, by which time defenders could easily get into position to contest the attempt.

Even when a player popped out from behind a pick, he wasn't necessarily open enough to shoot. Thus, early basketball games, both college and pro, featured lots of picks and moving without the ball and very patient offensive patterns. A team might hold the ball for three or four minutes—or more—before taking a shot. It is easy to see why scores were so low in those days.

The Greatest Ever?

There were a host of great set shooters in the early days of both pro and college basketball. "Bobby" McDermott was almost surely the best. McDermott was a 5' 11" guard with movie-star looks and an explosive temper who moved from high school to the pros, and he became the best all-around player in pro basketball in the 1930s and 1940s.

There is a lot of fuss these days about high school kids going to the pros. Well, McDermott didn't bother to graduate high school; in 1933, his senior year in high school in Queens, New York, he was already making money playing in the New York–Penn League as the best player in the league.

McDermott was a deadly combination of quick and fast. He was a terror on defense, as

The Pocket Popper

One of the great pro ball players of the early part of the 20th century was Barney "Mighty Mite" Sedran, a 5' 4" Hall of Famer who played in a number of leagues in upstate New York in the 1910s and 1920s.

Sedran was a great scorer, and his signature was an amazing set shot, one of the best of his era. In 1916, Sedran once scored 17 field goals in a game, which was amazing enough for that era. More interesting, though, was that the baskets in this particular gym had no backboards (a not unusual occurrence in the 1910s). So Sedran had to swish 'em all.

Sedran gave an interview to the *New York Times* in April of 1952, telling a story about the old New York Whirlwinds. In 1922, 30 years before the interview, Sedran and three of his teammates, Marty Friedman, Chris Leonard and Dick Leary of the Whirlwinds, were hired to be "ringers" in a big, winner-take-all match between teams from Springfield and Windsor, VT. The two Vermont communities annually played the contest, which was usually heated and upon which large sums of money were bet. Windsor, the home team that year, had hired the Whirlwind quartet to ensure the win. Sedran and his mates were to get $30 per man, a nice sum in those days.

Sedran and Friedman took a train to Windsor. Leonard and Leary were to join them later.

"But when we got there, we found out the Springfield manager had paid Leonard and Leary 40 bucks each to stay home!" laughed Sedran.

The laugh was on Springfield. Sedran and Friedman were enough, as Windsor won the game.

his hands could flick out and strip an opponent of a basketball in the wink of an eye. He was also a reckless driver who went to the hoop with abandon.

"But his greatest asset," said Hall of Famer Al Cervi, who played against McDermott, "was his shooting. I've seen them all, and McDermott is still the best shooter I've ever seen. His range was unbelievable. Beyond three-point range, for sure."

Like Babe Ruth's home runs, stories of McDermott's range grew over the years, until he was reportedly launching shots from midcourt. His range was perhaps not that amaz-

Is Mario Elie still in the league? Well, if not, the Spurs' Danny Ferry is the last of a dying breed. The Celtics' Walter McCarty will shoot a sort of set shot from three-point land. He takes a little hop. That counts as a set these days.

PLAYERS TO WATCH

ing, but he was a very difficult player to stop. Cervi recalled that McDermott, to intimidate the opposition, would shoot 15, 20 and 25 long set shots in warm-ups, and rarely miss any of them.

In 1949, McDermott was voted the greatest basketball player of the first half-century, a vote that was later amended after everyone had gotten a better look at George Mikan. In 1988, McDermott, who died in 1963, was elected to the Hall of Fame.

The Mighty Max

Max Zaslofsky (1946–56) possessed a sort of fadeaway set shot that was difficult to block but extremely accurate. He would launch the shot from between 25 to 30 feet out. A graduate of St. John's University, Zaslofsky was a canny 6' 2" guard who led the NBA/BAA in scoring during the 1947–48 season and was really the only set shot specialist to ever lead the league in that category.

And more than many set shot artists, Max was a streak shooter. In the 1947–48 season, he led the Chicago Stags to the BAA/NBA semifinals. In the quarterfinals against the Boston Celtics, Max was easily the dominant player. In the first game against Boston, Max scored 26 points as Chicago won, 79–72. The Celtics won the second contest in Boston, 81–77.

Back in Chicago, "The Touch," as Zaslofsky was called then, scored 31 points. Late in the contest he crossed the midcourt line, stopped well in front of the man guarding him and launched what sportswriters swore was a 35-foot shot that drew nothing but net.

The next time down the court, Zaslofsky again crossed the midcourt line, again dribbled only a few feet deeper into the frontcourt and again launched a bomb. *Swish!* He repeated the feat a third time, and as the

Above: Max Zaslofsky of the Stags leaps to score in a game against Washington in 1949.

Far left: One of the few remaining set shooters, Danny Ferry is a throwback to a different era.

Chicago crowd roared, Boston coach John "Honey" Russell disgustedly threw a towel up in the air. Chicago won the game, 81–74. "The Touch" had struck again.

But the league was changing. Joe Fulks was jumping as he shot. Kenny Sailors was using only one hand to put the ball in the basket. The set shot was too static and too easy to defend, unless a team had a big center that would force opponents to sag into the post. The advent of the 24-second clock in 1954 made it harder to play a deliberate game.

By the 1960s, few players were shooting sets. By the 1966–67 season, only 6' 1" guard Larry Costello (1954–68) was shooting the set shot, and he had the luxury of shooting it while opponents sagged on teammate Wilt Chamberlain in the low post. The set shot was dead, replaced by the more exciting, and far more accurate, jump shot.

Return of the Bombers

Only for a little more than a decade did the jump shot reign. In the 1979–80 season, the NBA, hoping to open the game up a little more and add some pizzazz to it, decided to legalize the three-point shot. This was the same NBA who had scoffed at the ABA's decision to legalize the shot while it was in existence from 1967 to 1976. But now, the league needed a shot in the arm, and the three-pointer (along with Larry Bird and Magic Johnson) was one way to do it.

THE NBA'S BEST SET SHOOTERS IN THE 1940S
Bob Feerick (1945–50)
.362 career field goal percentage
Max Zaslofsky (1946–56)
.343 career field goal percentage
Buddy Jeannette (1938–50)
.341 career field goal percentage
Stan Miasek (1946–53)
.330 career field goal percentage
Fat Freddie Scolari (1946–55)
.321 career field goal percentage

NBA players, for the most part, didn't shoot from 28 feet out. Some, like Celtic forward Larry Bird (1979–92), just took a few steps farther out to cross the line and shot jumpers. But other players had to shoot set shots. The advantage of shooting a set shot from 28 feet out (as Bobby McDermott would have said) is that shooting from a set position enables a player to use his legs as well as his arms and wrist to shoot the ball. A player got a little more oomph in the shot.

Lakers forward Michael Cooper (1978–90) shot 34 percent in his career from three-point range during the regular season, but upped that to almost 40 percent in the play-offs. And "Coop," for the most part, shot the three-pointer flat-footed, old-school style. In the 1990s, 6' 5" swingman Mario Elie (1990–2002) was a tremendous three-point shooter from the set position.

With the three-point line clearly around to stay for a while, NBA fans will continue to see at least some players spotting up like Max Zaslofsky or "Buddy" Jeannette did in the old days to launch a shot while stationary. And that's fine. It's nice to see the old techniques are still useful.

Larry Bird was one of the masters of the set shot.

Above: The match-up here between Michael Cooper and Larry Bird pits two of the best set shooters of all time against each other.

48-MINUTE MEN, 2000–01

These men hated to come out. They led the league in 48-minute games: (Note: this includes players who played at least 48 minutes in overtime games.)

Chris Webber, Sacramento Kings: 8
Antoine Walker, Boston Celtics: 6
Kobe Bryant, Los Angeles Lakers: 6
Gary Payton, Seattle Super Sonics: 6
Michael Finley, Dallas Mavericks: 6

9 The Bank Shot
Using the Glass

ORIGIN: **1895**

THE FIRST: **Christian Steinmetz,
University of Wisconsin**

THE ALL-TIMERS:
Leroy "Cowboy" Edwards
(NBL: 1935–43),
George Mikan (1946–56)
Sam Jones (1957–69)
Jo Jo White (1969–81)
Tim Duncan (1997–present)
Steinmetz, Mikan and Jones are in the Hall of Fame.

*Big George Mikan
banked his hookers off
the backboard.*

*Inset: Tim Duncan goes
up for a shot over
Stomile Swift of the
Memphis Grizzlies.*

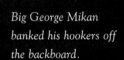

TECHNIQUE:
Follow the same tips you would for a jump shot, only aim
for the square behind the hoop rather than the rim. This
enables you to shoot the ball with varying degrees of
force, and if you put too much into it, the backboard can
absorb your mistake.

Don't try to shoot from too steep an angle, or the ball
will miss the basket entirely.

For the first four years that basketball was a sport, there were no such thing as a bank shot. That's because there were no such things as backboards. Although Dr. James Naismith tacked up his peach baskets to a balcony, which gave each goal a sort of natural backboard, the original design for baskets was to hang them 10 feet from the ground at the end of a pole. There was therefore nothing behind the basket off which a player would have been able to bank a ball.

That changed fairly quickly due to fan pressure. No, fans of the 1890s didn't clamor for a backboard, but what had begun to happen was that fans sitting behind the baskets would use long poles to interfere with opponents' shots. Teams began installing backboards to prevent that practice.

In fact, the reason glass backboards eventually became popular was that wooden backboards created obstructed views. Fans sitting behind those backboards began to complain to promoters that they couldn't see. And since no promoter in the early part of the 20th century had any interest in reducing the number of seats available to sell, they had to come up with a way for fans to see from behind backboards. Thus was born the clear backboard.

Still, players in many parts of the country didn't use bank shots because in many parts of the country, particularly the East Coast, the backboard was set back a foot or more from the basket. Remember, this was initially a deterrent to fans from interfering with play, not a specific feature of the game. In the Midwest, however, the baskets were just nailed to balconies or walls, which meant that players out there played with backboards all the time.

The Father of Wisconsin Basketball

Christian Steinmetz was a 5' 9", 137-pound forward who played for the University of Wisconsin from 1902–05. In photos of him, he's holding a basketball that looks like a medicine ball. Yet in the four years he played for Wisconsin, Steinmetz was the most explosive scorer in the country, at any level.

Steinmetz rang up numbers that wouldn't be seen until Wilt Chamberlain came along more than 50 years later. You don't think so? Try this: he scored 45 points in Wisconsin's 45–16 win over Sheboygan; 34 points in the Badgers' 34–14 win over Dubuque; 40 points in an 80–10 win over Beloit College and 50 points in a win over the Sparta Club in 1904.

Steinmetz possessed a fearsome set shot, but he was also a good foul shooter and layup artist. It's impossible to determine how many layups he banked in as opposed to long sets, but Steinmetz, by all accounts, could score

MAY 11, 1980, NBA FINALS, GAME 4, LOS ANGELES VS. PHILADELPHIA

Julius Erving could jump—that has never been debated. But no one realized until May 11, 1980, that he could actually fly.

How else to explain what even now is known as "The Move"? Dribbling toward the right baseline, Erving took off just outside of the three-second lane on the right side, with the basketball palmed in his right hand. Laker forward Mark Landsberger, however, had positioned himself to take away the middle of the lane, where Erving was most dangerous. So Erving jumped toward the baseline. Laker center Kareem Abdul-Jabbar came over to help Landsberger and took away the baseline as well, so Erving jumped out of bounds and twisted his body under the basket. Laker guard Earvin "Magic" Johnson recalled thinking at that moment that Erving's move had trapped him on the baseline. Johnson remembers thinking that the only thing Erving could do was pass the ball out to a Philadelphia teammate.

Erving did no such thing. He *remained in the air*, went under the hoop and banked the ball, with a little reverse English, off the backboard and into the basket. Landsberger, by the way, had come back to earth well before all this was finished.

"I could not believe my eyes," said Johnson. "It's still the greatest move I've ever seen in basketball, the all-time greatest."

from just about anywhere on the court and by various means, including the bank.

This isn't to say that Steinmetz was the foremost practitioner of the bank shot in the country, but he was known to be the smartest, most fundamentally sound player of his era, and his shots included a lot of layups off the backboard.

The first ballplayer to be actually known for banking his shots was Leroy "Cowboy" Edwards (NBL, 1935–43), a 6' 7" center whose principal weapon was a hook shot that he banked off the backboards.

The Cowboy was a member of the varsity squad of the University of Kentucky before opting to drop out of school and pursue a professional career. For the most part,

Edwards concentrated on offense, and thus became adept at the banked hook shot. (The pivotman has also been credited with having inspired the 3-second rule.)

So did 6' 10" George Mikan (1946–56) of the Chicago Gears and Minneapolis Lakers. Mikan, like Edwards, could shoot hook shots with either hand. Many of the opponents of the Minneapolis Lakers swore that Mikan had a built-in advantage at home, unlike Edwards: the rims at either end of the court were tilted slightly up so that when Mikan banked his hooker off the backboard, the elevated front rim would "catch" the ball.

For the record, Mikan and his coach, Johnny Kundla, have repeatedly denied that the rims were ever treated in such a way, to no one's surprise.

Set shooters, for the most part, didn't shoot bank shots, but when the jump shot came along, a number of players became known for their predilection for angling shots off the backboard and into the hoop,

FOUR-POINT PLAY LEADERS
(A MADE THREE-POINTER AND FREE THROW),
CAREER:
Reggie Miller: 19
Michael Adams: 11
John Starks: 10
Mitch Richmond: 9
Glen Rice: 7

Right: One of the fastest players in the league during the 60s, Sam Jones was a deadly marksman with the bank shot.

which gave them an angle at the hoop around a defender's arms.

Sam and Jo Jo Show the Way

The most famous banker in the 1960s was Celtics guard Sam Jones (1957–69). Jones was a 6' 4" backcourtman from North Carolina College who didn't start for the Celtics until Boston guard Bill Sharman retired after the 1960–61 season. Initially, Sam was known more for his defense.

Boston coach Arnold "Red" Auerbach liked to have Sam guard the opponent's best scorer, which freed up Boston point guard Bob Cousy to concentrate on offense.

When Cousy eventually retired at the

The Bank Is Open!

In Kareem Abdul-Jabbar's autobiography, *Kareem*, former teammate Cazzie Russell (1966–78) used to call for the ball by yelling, "the bank is open!" since Cazzie often banked his jumpers in.

end of the 1962–63 season, Jones got a chance to show his stuff. Two years after Cousy retired, in the 1964–65 season, Jones averaged 25.9 points per game to finish third in the league in scoring, primarily using the bank shot. It was the first time in 10 years, since Cousy had finished third in the league with a 21.2 average, that a Celtic had finished in the top five.

Jones's principal strength, besides his shooting eye, was his otherworldly speed. He was one of the fastest players in the league, and could get to a spot on which to launch his bank shot in a heartbeat. He would just beat people down the floor.

Jones retired in 1969, and the next season, the Celtics drafted a 6' 3" guard from the University of Kansas, Joseph Henry "Jo Jo" White (1969–81). White did not have the speed of Jones, but equaled him in heart and shooting ability.

Jo Jo had an odd way of shooting in that he would sort of snap the ball into shooting position with his right wrist and fire away. More even than Jones, White was a bank-shooting machine. His favorite spot was from both the right and left of the foul line and, if White was open, that was as automatic a two-pointer as there was in the league.

As the 1970s gave way to the 1980s, the bank shot as a weapon began losing its cache, which is something of a surprise. As Jones often pointed out, one can shoot a bank shot too hard and have it still go in. A bank shot artist also had an easier target. While many shooters aimed for the rim, a bank shooter could aim for the square behind the basket, which was easier to see and easier to hit.

Nonetheless, the bank shot didn't exactly flourish in the 1980s or 1990s. Players opted to swish their jumpers. Certainly, many players still banked in their layups, but the rest of the offensive arsenal for most players didn't include a banker.

So it is something of a pleasant surprise to watch San Antonio's 6' 11" forward-center Tim Duncan (1997–present) bank jump shots from the foul line off the backboard these days.

Duncan is possibly the only player who banks shots in regularly. Shaquille O'Neal uses the glass when he's in low, as does the Hornets' Eldon Campbell. But mostly, NBA players have forgotten the backboard can be used for anything. The Clippers' Elton Brand has been known to use the glass a bit, as well.

PLAYERS TO WATCH

Duncan, whose career field goal average is better than 51 percent, banks jump shots, turnarounds and hook shots. It is interesting to note that Duncan is a native of the Virgin Islands, which is where he learned to play the game. Apparently, in the Virgin Islands it's still okay to use the backboard when they shoot.

Teresa's Big Banker

The greatest shot in the short history of the Women's National Basketball Association (WNBA) Liberty guard Teresa Weatherspoon's 50-foot bank shot that won a game in the WNBA Finals in 1999.

The heavily favored Houston Comets had already won Game 1 of their best-of-three series with the Liberty in New York. With just 2.4 seconds left, the Comets had a 67–65 lead, which had the home crowd in Houston's Compaq Center delirious with joy.

The Liberty were not dead yet, however. With Houston's Tina Thompson guarding her closely, Weatherspoon took the inbounds pass, dribbled up the court for as long as she dared, and launched a shot with less than a second left from 50 feet out.

A heartbeat later, *Boom!* The ball banked off the glass and into the net, as Houston players and fans looked on stunned. Weatherspoon was buried by her ecstatic teammates.

It was, admittedly, only a short respite for the Liberty. Houston would wrap up the 1999 WNBA title the next time out, but the Comets could not eclipse "T-Spoon's" amazing effort.

Right: The New York Liberty's Teresa Weatherspoon is mobbed by her teammates after hitting a last-second shot beyond half court for a 68-67 in Game 2 of the WNBA Finals.

Part 2

The Ball-handling Moves

The Artful Pass

Getting the Rock to the Person
Who Will Do the Most Good with It

ORIGIN: Practically when the game
was invented in 1891

THE FIRST: Whoever gave it up in
that first game in Springfield,
Massachusetts

THE ALL-TIMERS:
Jack McCracken (NA),
Dick McGuire (1949–60),
Bob Cousy (1950–63, 1969–70),
Oscar Robertson (1960–74),
Larry Bird (1979–92),
Earvin "Magic" Johnson (1979–91,
1995–96)
John Stockton (1984–present)
All but Stockton are Hall of Famers.

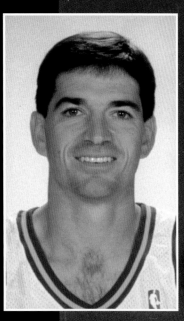

*Bob Cousy
was a magi-
cian with the
ball.*

*Inset: John
Stockton is
headed to the
Hall of Fame
in large part
because of his
tremendous
passing ability.*

THE TECHNIQUE:
There are several different types of pass, but all involve
the same fundamentals. First, control the ball with the
tips of your fingers, not the
palms of your hands. Start
the ball at your chest. Spread
the fingers of each hand on
each side of the ball. Push
the ball out from your chest
and, at the same time, extend
your arms fully. Snap your
wrists out so that the backs
of your hands are facing each
other. Remember to follow
through with the palms of
your hands away from your
body.

For a bounce pass, the technique is the same, only aim at
a spot about three-quarters of the way between you and
your teammate. Always aim for the numbers on your
teammate's jersey. If your teammate is about 6' 6" or
taller, aim slightly higher, as many big men have trouble
bending too far over.

When Dr. James Naismith invented basketball in 1891, the first rule he laid down on paper was this: Rule #1: The ball may be thrown in any direction with one or both hands.

That's it. Even before he spelled out how to score, or how to start the game, Dr. Naismith wanted to make sure that passing was an integral part of this new game he'd invented.

And in fact, very soon after the game was invented, it became clear that passing the ball made more sense than dribbling it. A thrown ball was the fastest way to get from point A to point B. And finally, a passer had many more options than a dribbler.

That first rule is still in the official NBA rule book in its original form. And the concept of passing has remained unchanged for 111 years.

The first passer was obviously the fellow who tossed the ball to William R. Chase, the Springfield College student (reportedly) who scored the only goal in the first-ever basketball game, which ended with a score of 1–0.

APRIL 5, 1984, LOS ANGELES LAKERS VS. UTAH JAZZ

Everybody in the place knew it was going to happen. Lakers center Kareem Abdul-Jabbar was only a few points from breaking former Laker Wilt Chamberlain's all-time record for points scored in a career, a milestone believed unreachable less than a decade earlier.

But there was no doubt that, sooner or later, the graceful Abdul-Jabbar would set a new standard. And Laker guard Earvin Johnson wanted to be the man to deliver the pass.

Sure enough, with about eight minutes left in a game against the Utah Jazz, Johnson fired a pass into Abdul-Jabbar, who shrugged off Jazz center Mark Eaton's forearm smash to his back and lofted a soft shot into the net. It was undoubtedly Johnson's most famous assist.

The Captain and Big Ed

The first players to be known for passing, or perhaps more accurately, to be known for developing a style of passing, were Fred Cooper, captain of the Trentons, and teammate Al Bratton. The Trentons were one of the first professional teams in the history of the game. Cooper formed the team in November of 1896, and the Trentons won 19 of the 20 games they played that winter.

Cooper was a native of England. He and his brother, Albert, came to the United States with their parents in 1885 when Fred was 11 and Albert seven.

Fred Cooper joined the YMCA soon after he arrived in America, and there he met Al Bratton when both were on the soccer team. Both also became interested in basket-ball, as it was called then.

Left: Magic Johnson dishes around Larry Bird in the 1987 Finals.

Cooper, with Bratton, worked out a system whereby they would advance the ball down the court using a series of short, snappy passes. At that point, players usually advanced the ball by passing, but not in a cohesive way. A player would receive the ball and stop, looking for another teammate to pass to, or try to dribble the ball farther. Either option gave the defense plenty of time to recover.

Cooper and Bratton would literally race down the court, passing the ball between them, avoiding opponents trying to intercept the pass.

A few years later, Ed Wachter, of the Troy, N.Y., Trojans, and his brother Lew, improved upon that technique slightly. Wachter, a 6' 2" center who played professional basketball for a number of teams in a career that spanned more than two decades, was one of the innovators of basketball in its early days.

At the turn of the 20th century, Ed and his brother Lew developed a way of passing the ball on the bounce to a teammate that

SELECTED ASSIST TOTALS

TEAM ASSIST LEADERS 2000–01:

Utah Jazz:	2,111
Minnesota Timberwolves:	2,083
Toronto Raptors:	2,004
Denver Nuggets:	1,970
Portland Trail Blazers:	1,963

Source: Harvey Pollock

was difficult to intercept or block because of its low trajectory. There may have been other players in other parts of the country who bounced balls into teammates' hands. But the Wachters did it on a regular basis and as part of a cohesive strategy.

As basketball evolved into the 1920s and 1930s, canny ballhandlers like Nat Holman of the Original Celtics, AAU star Jack McCracken, and others emerged as passing stars. In addition to the chest pass and bounce pass, players also used one- and two-handed underhand passes, hook passes and roll passes to move the ball. Except for the hook pass, these passes are largely out of use now.

The Pivotmen

As the legend goes, the original Celtics were playing a game in Chattanooga, Tennessee, in 1923, against a team called the Railites. The Celtics were clearly controlling play and had a large lead, but the Railites were frustrating some of their offensive patterns by placing one of their players at the foul line in sort of a one-man zone.

During a time-out, the Celtics discussed what to do about the fellow. Eventually, it was decided that hefty forward Harry "Dutch" Dehnert would stand in front of the player with his back to him, and make passes from that point. Thus was born the give-and-go pass, and concurrently, the concept of

pivot play as we know it today.

(Note: clearly, prior to 1923, players stationed themselves in and around the key and took passes and passed off. But Dehnert and his teammates were also the first team to do this regularly and add refinements over the next few years.)

Dehnert took passes from the other players that night and fed cutting Celtics. The process worked so well that the team immediately began working on improving the concept. Since the Celtics never had time to actually practice, the only time they could work on the give-and-go was in games. But most of the teams they played were so outclassed that the Celtics could usually afford to try new things in the latter stages of a game, when they were way ahead.

McCracken was perhaps the best passer of the 1930s. A graduate of Northeast Missouri State College in 1932, he was a superior all-around athlete who had been introduced to basketball in high school. He led his Oklahoma City High team to the finals of the National High School Championship Tournament in 1929.

McCracken was an excellent shooter and rebounder and a determined defender, but his quickness and passing eye made him stand out. He was a forward and one of the first frontline players in the game to be noted as a strong passer. Previously, guards were the best passers on the team, with some centers being strong passers from the high post.

McCracken played only one year in the professional ranks before opting to play Amateur Athletic Union (AAU) ball with Denver and the Phillips 66ers. He led Denver teams to two AAU championships in the 1930s.

Above: Bob Cousy in action for Holy Cross in 1950.

Tricky Business

As the NBA emerged from its infancy, a number of ball players began earning a reputation as playmakers who were head and shoulders above the rest. This was true, for the most part, because the Celtics' Bob Cousy (1950–63, 1969–70), the Rochester Royals' Bob Davies (1945–55) and the New York Knickerbockers' Dick McGuire (1949–60) were slick passers and gutty performers when the game was on the line.

All three had begun to stretch the envelope of the conventional mode of passing by attempting more and more daring throws. And now, five decades later, the inference seems to be that these guys were firing passes behind their backs, between their legs and past their

ears every other time down the court.

In fact, all three men understood before they even came into the professional ranks that attempting risky passes against bigger, faster and quicker opponents than they faced in the collegiate ranks was an invitation to disaster. A canny defender like Rochester's Al Cervi (1937–53), or a quick one like Ralph Beard (1949–51), of the Indianapolis Olympians, was simply not to be trifled with.

"There was a perception that all I did was throw the ball behind my back," recalled Cousy in his 1988 book, *Bob Cousy and the Celtic Mystique*. "In reality, nothing could be further from the truth. That was perhaps 10 percent of my game. The other 90 percent was very conservative."

But Cousy, McGuire and Davies all made it a point to find a player with a crowd-pleasing pass at least once in a game, prefer-

Above: Nate "Tiny" Archibald drives around Phil Ford opening up his teammates for a quick dish from within the paint.

Doubling the Record

The Knickerbockers knew they had a good one in Dick McGuire early in the season. The Minneapolis Lakers came to town on December 14, 1949 and went down to defeat, 94–84. Big George Mikan pumped in 38 points, but all anyone could talk about was the rookie from St. John's.

McGuire was called "Tricky Dick" McGuire because of his fancy dribbling and his great passing.

That afternoon, McGuire collected a league-record 16 assists, sending passes to Carl Braun (26 points) and Connie Simmons (19 points).

What was amazing about this record was that it doubled the previous mark set the year before by Johnny Logan of the St. Louis Bombers.

"If any single player dominated the fracas," wrote Lou Effrat of the *New York Times*, "it was the dashing McGuire. Dick scored but six points, but his passing was superb."

ably when the issue was either settled or at least close to being so. This was, after all, something of an entertainment sport, even before ESPN.

And let's face it, fans remembered Cousy's behind-the-back fancy stuff when they were popping beers after the game. The five or six bounce passes that led to layups and the six or seven pinpoint entry passes into center Bill Russell (1956–69) were appreciated, but for the most part forgotten.

Fast-forward to the 1980s. The most fundamentally sound passing point guard of that era was Lakers guard Earvin "Magic" Johnson (1979–91, 1995–96), and he would be the first to admit it. The Lakers very effectively marketed "Showtime" in the 1980s as a high-speed dunkathon replete with crazy passes from Johnson. Certainly, the highlight films bore this out. But for every lookaway bullet to Kurt Rambis (1981–95) underneath, there were probably a half-dozen or more solidly fundamental, two-hand passes to Kareem Abdul-Jabbar in the low post.

Similarly, the best fundamental passer of the past half-century, Oscar Robertson (1960–74), and his spiritual successors, Nate "Tiny" Archibald (1970–84) and John Stockton (1984–present), are almost dismissed by the casual fan. Well, Robertson probably never threw a lookaway pass in his life. Yet no one who played in the league at any time during Robertson's tenure would say that the man was anything but outstanding. What he wasn't was flashy.

Similarly, Archibald was just as economical. More than Oscar, Tiny tended to pass off in midair, as he was driving to the hoop, and at times did something relatively unconventional. But for the most part, Tiny's game was tight.

Stockton's one concession to the peanut gallery is his "slap pass," whereby he dribbles toward the hoop, and at the last moment drops his hand behind the ball and pushes it toward a teammate. Good thing. If he didn't do that every once in a while, he'd never be on the highlight shows.

Larry Legend

One of the most creative passers of all time is not a guard. It is Boston Celtics forward Larry Bird (1979–92), who was nicknamed "Larry Legend" even as he was playing. You want showtime? Bird restored the underhand pass and was virtually the only player to use

Above: Veteran John Stockton passes the rock over up-and-comer Steve "Franchise" Francis.

Above: Dr. J flips a pass back over his head to an awaiting teammate.

it consistently in his era. With his large hands and powerful wrists, Bird could also send slap passes much farther than Stockton. His over-the-shoulder slap pass to Kevin McHale in the 1986 playoffs is still on most highlight films.

Bird had to be a little more creative than most guards because in many cases he was creating offense off of set plays. Johnson, for example, was overwhelming in the open court, as was Oscar Robertson and Stockton. Bird was not as good as they in a fast-break situation (although he was very good). What he was good at was creating a pass to get past the man defending him and also beat the man defending his intended target. Again, we're talking the NBA. To be able to do that consistently, without incurring excessive turnovers, is a very difficult feat. But you must admit: Larry made it look easy.

This is not to say that there are no great passers in the NBA these days. First of all, Stockton is still playing, and is finally beginning to receive the accolades he deserves. Think about it: the man is 40 and he's still playing. Why? Because he's smarter with the

ball than 99.99 percent of the players in the league. Heck, 99.99 percent of the players in the world.

Mike Bibby (1998–present), of the Sacramento Kings, is a playmaker in the Cousy-Davies pantheon. Bibby is an excellent passer who can also hit jump shots in traffic. Likewise, the Nets' Jason Kidd is beloved by many old-timers. Kidd will give the crowd something to cheer about from time to time, but he knows the priority is getting the ball to the open man.

Point guards in the professional ranks are much more daring than their mid-century counterparts. The problem is, they tend to generate many more turnovers. Cousy often laments that there are very few, if any, real playmakers in the league.

His point is that fellows like himself, Oscar, Magic and Tiny made sure the ball got to where it was supposed to. There is no sense trying to throw an alley-oop pass from half-court unless one is absolutely sure it can be converted. Many of the guards of the 21st century enjoy trying to beat the defense with a fancy pass. But more often than not, that pass does not make its mark. Those are the ones you usually don't see on the highlight shows.

PLAYERS TO WATCH

The Kings' Mike Bibby, John Stockton of the Jazz, the Cavaliers' Anfre Miller and Seattle's Gary Payton are the best fundamentally sound passers in the NBA. The strength of these players is that they make the right pass at the right time and don't turn the ball over. The best of the mid-sized players is the Celtics' Antoine Walker. He posts up low and is the best at hitting a cutter, sometimes with a behind-the-back number.

Above: Jason Kidd always finds a way to get the ball to an open teammate.

11 The No-Look Pass
The Fancy Way to Move the Ball

ORIGIN: About 1930

THE FIRST: Inman Jackson, Harlem Globetrotters

THE ALL-TIMERS:
Bob Cousy (1950-63, 1969-70)
Dick McGuire (1949-60)
"Pistol" Pete Maravich (1970-80)
Earvin "Magic" Johnson (1979-91, 1995-96)
Jason Kidd (1994-present)
All but Kidd are in the Hall of Fame

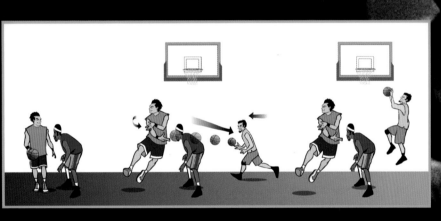

THE TECHNIQUE:

This is a tough one to explain. But, essentially, make sure you know, somehow, that the person you're passing to is indeed in the place you plan to throw the ball. This may take hours of practice, to get to know where your teammates are at a given time. Good peripheral vision is a plus, but the no-look is just that: a pass thrown without looking.

Usually, a no-look pass is thrown with one hand, although one can throw a no-look overhead pass with both hands. Look in the opposite direction and pass the ball. Remember, also, that the intent of this pass is to fool the defense but to still get the ball to a teammate. Don't throw the ball away too many times, or your coach will get angry.

The Pistol confounded defenses with his no-look pass.

Inset: Jason Williams constantly causes opponents headaches with his tricky passing styles.

Former Harlem Globetrotter Inman Jackson is almost certainly the author of the no-look pass, but just as certainly, it probably didn't come in a game situation. Jackson came to Abe Saperstein's barnstormers in 1929. He was a tremendous athlete, extremely well coordinated with large hands. By this time, the Globetrotters were already trying to figure out unorthodox ways to entertain the crowds. The 'Trotters were so talented, they were often far ahead of their opponents after a quarter or two.

Unfortunately, while that was nice for the old win-loss record, founder Abe Saperstein realized that if his team blew out the home side, they probably wouldn't be welcomed back. So Abe had the fellows work up little tricks, or "reems," as 'Trotters called them, to keep the crowd happy and excited, even if the score wasn't particularly close.

Jackson reportedly came up with quite a few tricks, including spinning the ball on his fingertips, dribbling between his legs and looking one way and passing the other.

Some of the tricks, like spinning the ball on a finger, weren't necessarily very good in a game against more talented opponents, like some of the professional teams the Globetrotters would play. But the "eye fake," as the no-look pass was originally termed, was pretty effective.

And, of course, Jackson and his mates had plenty of time to practice it in games against less distinguished fives.

The move didn't seem to catch on right away, at least not in the professional ranks, because, first of all, the Globetrotters had, by the 1930s, earned the reputation as a "clown team," and there weren't a lot of coaches (well, actually, there probably weren't any)

Stephon Marbury often buries teams with his passing abilities.

who thought a move dreamed up by the Globetrotters was legitimate.

But the move caught on in the urban playgrounds of the 1930s and 1940s. And pretty soon, a young Irish lad in New York City named Dick McGuire began using it with great success.

The Real Tricky Dick

McGuire (1949–60) starred at St. John's University and later with the New York Knickerbockers and Detroit Pistons. He was

Time was running down, and the East, led by San Antonio guard George "Iceman" Gervin, had a slim lead, 142–136. The East had the ball, and a player from the squad took a shot. The shot missed, however. All-Star forward Larry Bird, in his first season, controlled the rebound and, without looking, slapped the ball to a wide-open Gervin under the basket. It was a brilliant, spontaneous move and Gervin obliged by looping in one of his patented one-handed jumpers. That gave him a game-high 34 points and locked up the game. It also locked up Gervin's nomination as All-Star Game MVP. But it was Bird's pass that clinched it.

known as "Tricky Dick" when Richard Nixon was still a gleam in the collective eyes of the Republican party. And McGuire came by the name honorably. His no-look passes, in addition to almost never ending up in the third row, were extremely accurate. He was also a tremendous dribbler and crowd-pleaser.

Many NBA-watchers consider McGuire as perhaps the greatest "pure" playmaker in NBA history, in that his philosophy was geared toward making the unit he directed as effective as possible, regardless of how many points he scored.

Of course, McGuire's perennial opponent, Celtics guard Bob Cousy, also used the no-look to great advantage. Cousy was blessed with exceptional peripheral vision, as was McGuire, but in the hyperbolic sportswriting era of the day, that gift was soon morphed into a more bizarre explanation of Cousy's facility with the no-look. Supposedly, Cousy's eyes were so large that his eyelids could not cover them. This little chestnut was quickly tossed out of the reality arena after one looked at any photo of Cousy to see that his peepers were about the same size as anyone else's. Still, it would have made a great science-fiction novel.

Above: Pete Maravich extends off the ground in order to create room for either a quick dish or a shot at the goal.

NBA FINALS ASSIST RECORDS (CAREER)

Earvin Johnson: 584	
Bob Cousy: 400	
Bill Russell: 315	
Jerry West: 306	
Dennis Johnson: 228	
Michael Jordan: 209	
Scottie Pippin: 207	
John Havlicek: 195	
Larry Bird: 187	

NBA FINALS ASSIST RECORDS (INDIVIDUAL)

Earvin Johnson, Los Angeles vs. Boston, June 3, 1984: 21	
Earvin Johnson, Los Angeles vs. Boston, June 4, 1987: 20	
Earvin Johnson, Los Angeles vs. Chicago, June 12, 1991: 20	
Bob Cousy, Boston vs. St. Louis, April 9, 1957: 19	
Bob Cousy, Boston vs. Minneapolis, April 7, 1959: 19	
Walt Frazier, New York vs. Los Angeles, May 8, 1970: 19	
Earvin Johnson, Los Angeles vs. Boston, June 14, 1987: 19	
Earvin Johnson, Los Angeles vs. Detroit, June 19, 1988: 19	

Source: *NBA Encyclopedia*

While both Cousy and McGuire's respective careers were winding down in the early 1960s, the heir apparent to the no-look was already practicing his craft as a diminutive 13-year-old.

Pistol Pete

Peter Press Maravich (1970–80) was born in 1947, in Aliquippa, Pennsylvania. His father, Press, had a typical coach's career, which meant the Maraviches bounced around a lot. By the time he graduated from high school in South Carolina, Pete Maravich was an explosive scorer, a near-legendary dribbler and a tremendous passer.

Maravich played his collegiate basketball at Louisiana State University and there he rewrote college basketball's scoring records. He was only the second man to average more than 40 points per game (the first being Furman's Frank Selvy) and by the time he graduated from LSU, he became the only man to average more than 40 points in a career (44.2, to be exact).

And yet, although people enjoyed watching Maravich shoot, almost as many bought tickets just to see him pass.

Maravich had a host of tricks in the pass department: an on-the-run, between-the-legs number that he usually snapped off on a fast break, the behind-the-back pass, the behind-the-head pass, and the no-look or lookaway pass.

In fact, Maravich nearly succeeded in making the no-look commonplace, so often did he throw it in those collegiate days. He didn't succeed, though, because, unfortunately, his teammates were only human. Maravich would come blowing down the court, dribbling between his legs and behind his back. At some point he would let loose with a pass—maybe—to a teammate.

But the Pistol, as he was called, wasn't really a playmaker. He was a scorer, and his mates were never sure what he was going to do. And of course, it was a better than even bet that Pete would go to the hoop himself.

Maravich got better in the professional ranks. But he came into the league trying to make the play that pleased the crowd first, which made him less effective as a team player. It wasn't until he was in the league a few years that Maravich began to play under control. When he did that, he was nearly unstoppable.

Above: Penn State's Sharif Chambliss makes a no-look pass around Wisconsin's Dave Mader.

Ernie D's Game

Ernie DiGregorio (1973–78) was, with Maravich, the master of the no-look pass in the 1970s. Ernie D, as he was called, was only 5' 11", and relatively slow afoot, but he could deliver the rock. His most sensational pass came in college, when he threw a no-look, full-court, behind-the-head pass to teammate Marvin Barnes in the NCAA semifinals against Memphis State in the 1973 NCAA tournament. DiGregorio's defensive shortcomings (not as great as many coaches made them out to be) prevented him from having a long pro career. But he was always fun to watch.

Earvin "Magic" Johnson (1979–91, 1995–96) made the no-look pass appear easy. Johnson dished blind assists to either side of him, and even behind him, and more often than not, those balls seemed to find their mark.

Johnson didn't have gigantic eyeballs, or even eyes in the back of his head. What he had was a well-constructed fast-break offense with which to work. Back in the 1950s and 1960s, Cousy, McGuire, Slater Martin (1949–60) and later Lenny Wilkins (1960–75), K. C. Jones (1958–67) and others had refined the fast break considerably.

Above: Tom Gola fakes out a leaping Elgin Baylor by passing the ball around his back.

Above right: Magic Johnson getting rid of the ball as he's guarded by Jordan in the 1991 Finals.

Above: Allen Iverson in the air dishing off to a waiting teammate.

But the Lakers developed the fast break in the 1980s into a fearsome beast called "Showtime." It was a carefully orchestrated offensive system, and because of that, Johnson knew where his teammates would be. Thus, his no-look passes often found their mark.

Besides unleashing the ball on the break, there are many passers who have used the no-look pass in a set offense. Many of these are centers. Johnny "Red" Kerr (1954–66) was an exceptional passer from the high post. He fed teammates via no-look passes from between his legs and over his head.

Center Wilt Chamberlain was a tremendous passer who once led the NBA in assists in 1967. His technique was usually to hold the ball in one giant hand and drop it to a cutter in the lane. But when Bill Sharman came to coach the Lakers in the 1971–72 season, Wilt and Lakers guard Gail Goodrich (1965–79) devised a give-and-go play whereby Goodrich would lob the ball to Wilt in the low post. Goodrich would cut down the lane and Wilt would fire a no-look pass behind his back to Goodrich for a layup.

Portland center Bill Walton (1974–87) was an excellent passer and often fed no-look passes to his teammates. His favorite target was Blazers forward Bobby Gross (1975–83). By the time Walton was traded to Boston in 1985, he and Celtics forward Larry Bird had a competition to see who could throw the most exciting pass. These two players, among the best passers at their respective positions in pro history, at times passed opponents dizzy. In the 1986 playoffs against the Milwaukee Bucks, Walton won the bet that day, firing a no-look, over-the-shoulder pass to Bird for an easy layup.

In the NBA of the 21st century, most teams have three or four players who have

Other Passes: The Inbounds Pass

So, you think the inbounds pass is no big deal, don't you? Take the ball as it comes through the net and throw it in, right? Piece of cake.

Well, no less a personage than Arnold "Red" Auerbach believed that the inbounds pass was one of the most crucial steps in setting up an offense, at least after the advent of the 24-second clock.

And if you think that's a lot of hooey, ask Bill Russell. In the 1965 playoffs, seventh game, against the Philadelphia 76ers, five seconds left, Russell tried to lob the ball inbounds over Wilt Chamberlain's head, and the ball hit the guide wire above the basket and bounded back out of bounds. Philadelphia ball, with the Sixers trailing, 110–109.

And as we all know, the Sixers blew their chance when Boston forward John Havlicek stole the inbounds pass from Hal Greer.

The inbounds pass is to a basketball offense what cocking a hammer is to firing a gun. And the greatest inbounds passer in NBA history was Celtics forward Larry Bird. Bird's instinctive sense of how far to test a defense was what made him great. No one was better at throwing the "football" (a long-range downcourt pass) after a made basket than Larry Bird. Few players even tried it. Bird, particularly in key situations, was never afraid to use it. Conversely, if that pass was not there, Bird would not force the issue unless the situation was dire. There may have been instances when Larry Legend lost the ball on an inbounds throw, but not too many.

the skills to fire no-look passes to teammates. If there is one factor that has improved exponentially in the league in the last two decades, it is the ball-handling and passing skills of bigger men. Dallas Maverick Dirk Nowitzky (1998–present) is seven feet tall. Yet he routinely handles the ball on the fast break, and can deftly deliver a no-look pass with athleticism that players like Johnny Kerr and even Chamberlain could only aspire to.

Even Shaquille O'Neal, a 7' 1", 320-pound giant, can dish the no-look. And in fact, O'Neal has done so on Lakers fast breaks, which must look terrifying to opponents. Even though the no-look pass is becoming more commonplace, it remains an exciting way to deliver the ball.

PLAYERS TO WATCH

The best and worst is Jason Williams of the Memphis Grizzlies. When Williams is on, he's amazing. When he's not on, it's not pretty. These days, when Williams isn't making the play, he's learned, somewhat, to tone his act down. But this guy is the best. Boston's Walker is another player who throws a good no-look, most of the time.

Above: Brian Shaw of the Lakers is trying to create something from nothing as he squeezes a no-look pass between two Timberwolves' defenders.

12 The Behind-the-Back Dribble

Tricky but Effective

ORIGIN:
Probably 1938

THE FIRST:
Hank Luisetti, Sanford University

THE ALL-TIMERS:
Bob Davies (1945–55)
Bob Cousy (1950–63, 1969–70)
Isiah Thomas (1981–94)
Jason Kidd (1994–present)
Again, everybody but Kidd is in the Hall of Fame.

Hank Lucetti was an excellent ballhandler and shooter who played for Stanford University in the 1940's.

THE TECHNIQUE:

The key to dribbling behind one's back effectively is to make sure that you don't lose a step. Dribble forward with your "strong," or best dribbling hand. As the ball comes up to your hand, cup your hand to the side of the ball, and, still moving forward, guide the ball behind your back and bounce it to your other hand.

Pick up the ball with that hand and resume dribbling. If you cannot perform this move without losing a step, practice until you can. The move is most effective if you also change directions.

If you have to stop, or if you have to back up to complete this move, then don't do it in a game. Stopping to dribble behind your back gives the defender plenty of time to recover and reset himself, and you have lost the element of surprise.

Inset: Damon Stoudamire moves his dribble with finesse and agility.

For some reason, the behind-the-back dribble, when it began to emerge in the 1940s, was the ugly stepchild of outside-the-box moves. In Red Auerbach's seminal and still instructional 1952 book, *Basketball for the Player, the Fan and the Coach*, he warns those who attempt the behind-the-back dribble that, in addition to being tough to control, it tends to earn the playmaker attempting it the nickname "hot dog." And nobody, Red asserted, wants to be called a "hot dog."

Well, not then, anyway.

But the originator of the behind-the-back dribble wasn't Bob Cousy. It wasn't Dick McGuire. It wasn't even Bob Davies, although a lot of hoop historians credit him with it. Davies himself admitted that he got the idea from Luisetti after seeing *Campus Confessions*.

Six decades after he starred at Stanford University, Luisetti is seen today as a basketball player who changed the structure of shooting, by opting to launch balls at the basket with only one hand.

That is certainly true. But Luisetti was not a just a shooter. He was a great ballhandler, passer and rebounder, as well. In fact, Luisetti's former Stanford teammate Howie Dallmar (1946–49) ended up playing professionally with the Philadelphia Warriors and Jumpin' Joe Fulks (1946–54), the man who took Luisetti's one-handed technique and went airborne with it.

Of course, the comparisons between Fulks and Luisetti were obvious, and Dallmar was clearly the man to make them, having played with both. But, as Howie admitted a few times, it wasn't even close. Luisetti was a much better all-around athlete and basketball player than Fulks.

Howie's Mistake

Once, Dallmar made the mistake of making those comments to a sportswriter when Fulks was in earshot. Fulks wouldn't talk to him for days afterward.

Luisetti was clearly a heck of a ballhandler. The film Luisetti was in that Davies caught in a moviehouse in the late 1930s was called *Campus Confidential*, a little ditty about college life in that era starring Betty Grable. Finding a print of it now would be tough. Dwight Chapin, the veteran hoopologist from the *San Francisco Examiner*, has seen it and reports that it falls considerably short of *Gone with the Wind*.

But in the movie, Luisetti is seen dribbling behind his back as he drives down the court. And an 18-year-old Davies saw the

1938, *CAMPUS CONFESSIONS* IS RELEASED

The movie was a forgettable little three-reeler, starring Hank Luisetti, several of his Stanford teammates and the lovely and talented Betty Grable. The subject matter is lost to the ages, and it was not nominated for any Oscars. But across the country, an 18-year-old high school senior named Bobby Davies went to see the movie and was mesmerized by a scene in which Luisetti dribbles a basketball behind his back, as a kind of show-offy stunt.

Davies, though, didn't look at it that way. He went home and began to try it. He practiced for literally years before attempting a behind-the-back dribble in a game. When he did, as a sophomore at Seton Hall, at least one of the Hall's priests literally fainted as the crowd went crazy. The behind-the-back dribble was here to stay after that.

Below: Brent Barry performs a behind-the-back dribble to elude Gary Payton.

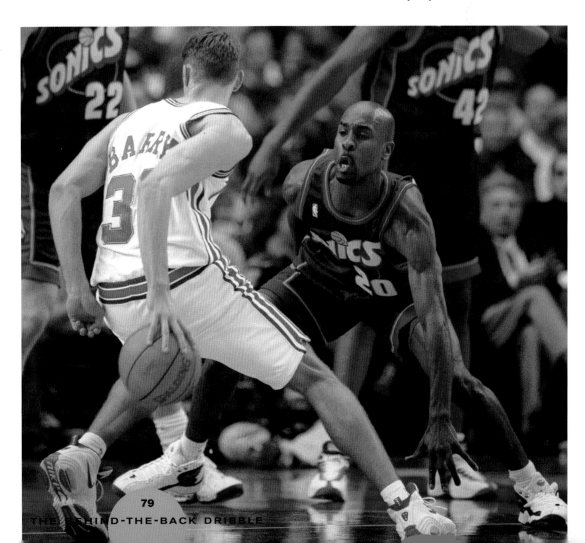

Above: Washington Mystics guard Kiesha Brown dribbles behind her back and past Detroit Shock guard Elaine Powell.

NBA TEAM-HIGH LEADERS IN ASSISTS, 2000–01:		
These players led their respective teams most often in assists:		
Andre Miller, Cleveland Cavaliers: 75 times		
Jason Kidd, Phoenix Suns: 72 times		
Mike Bibby, Vancouver Grizzlies: 70 times		
John Stockton, Utah Jazz: 67 times		
Gary Payton, Seattle Super Sonics: 67 times		
DOUBLE-FIGURE ASSIST LEADERS, 2000–01		
These players led the league in games in which they hit double-figures in assists:		
Jason Kidd, Phoenix Suns: 38 times		
John Stockton, Utah Jazz: 31 times		
Gary Payton, Seattle Super Sonics: 28 times		
Mark Jackson, Indiana Pacers: 25 times		
Nick Van Exel, Denver Nuggets: 25 times		
TOP TURNOVER-PRODUCERS IN THE NBA, 2000–01		
Jerry Stackhouse, Detroit Pistons: 326		
Antoine Walker, Boston Celtics: 301		
Jason Kidd, Phoenix Suns: 286		
Andre Miller, Cleveland Cavaliers: 265		
Steve Francis, Houston Rockets: 265		
Source: Harvey Pollock		

flick and went home and tried the move in his room. Luisetti made it look easy, but Davies admitted in an interview years later it took him several years to actually work out the move so that he could use it in a game. Supposedly, the first time Davies did it, when he was a sophomore at Seton Hall, a priest fainted in the stands.

Well, the priest may have fainted, but

The Alternate Origin

There is also another origin story of the behind-the-back dribble. Inman Jackson, the great star for the Harlem Globetrotters, often dribbled behind his back and between his legs to entertain crowds when the 'Trotters were barnstorming, according to the late Dave Zinkoff, a former publicist for the team. This was probably during the mid- to late 1930s, as near as anyone can tell.

But Jackson was usually not moving when he went behind his back, as the dribble was usually part of the Globetrotters' pregame show.

everyone else was galvanized. Bob Cousy in particular a few years later was seen doing it often while an undergraduate at Holy Cross, although his coach, Alvin "Doggie" Julian was none to happy about.

When Cousy finally began playing professionally, his coach, Arnold "Red" Auerbach, didn't like the move much, either. Auerbach told Cousy to knock off the fancy stuff or he'd be sitting on the bench. Although Cousy didn't knock it off entirely, he did tone it down for Red.

Actually, a number of old-timers recall that when Davies first uncorked the move in a game, it provoked great controversy.

"Well," said Hall of Famer Arnie Risen, a former teammate of Davies, "if you've ever tried to do it, you have to palm the ball to do it. And that's obviously illegal. So there was a lot of discussion as to whether or not it was legal. But eventually, the refs just allowed it."

The odd thing about the growth in popularity of the behind-the-back dribble was how fast it happened. Cousy, Davies and a handful of other guards had the behind-the-back dribble all to themselves in the 1950s and early to mid-1960s.

Then, all of a sudden, everyone was doing it. High school kids were dribbling behind their backs in the 1970s. Forwards were doing it. Centers were trying it, although usually not doing as well as their smaller teammates.

"Pistol" Pete Maravich (1970–80), the master ballhandler from LSU, was clearly one player who fueled the behind-the-back fire in that era. But he was abetted by television, which in the decade of the 1960s and 1970s was becoming more of a factor in broadcasting both professional and college games. The televised schedule was still only one game a week, two at most. And there were no real highlight shows as of yet, and for the most part, even national news shows did not have live-action highlights as viewers know them today.

But in some ways the dearth of games highlighted the ones that did get on television even more. As a collegian, Maravich was on television several times in his career, and when he graduated to the professional ranks in 1970, ABC televised his first regular-season game against the Milwaukee Bucks.

Robertson vs. Maravich?

That game was heavily hyped because Maravich would supposedly be matched

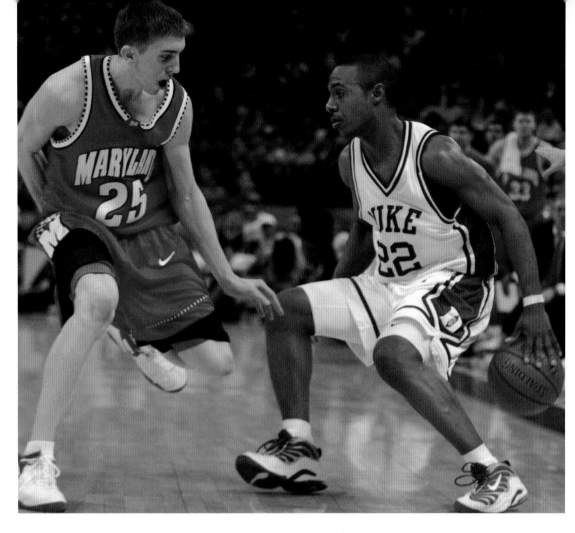

Above: Jason Williams dribbles behind his back as he works against Steve Blake in the ACC Championship game in 2000.

By the 1980s, the behind-the-back dribble, which had been an innovative, radical, almost sinful move when it was introduced in the late 1930s, had become a part of virtually every guard's repertoire. Certainly, some players, such as Isiah Thomas, of the Detroit Pistons, could perform the feat better than others. In fact, Thomas was one of the few players who could complete a behind-the-back dribble on a dead run, without slowing up a whit. Certainly, it was a difficult physical feat to accomplish, particularly when a player was on a full run and guarded by an NBA athlete.

But just as certainly, it was a most common weapon, used mostly for changing direction while protecting the ball from a defender.

In fact, the heyday of the behind-the-back dribble as an exciting, crowd-pleasing move seems to have been several decades past. Just about everyone, including Shaquille O'Neal (1991–present), can execute a behind-the-back dribble in 2002. And while the more artful ballhandlers, such as Jason Kidd, Steve Francis (1999–present), Damon Stoudamire (1995–present) and John Stockton now make it look ridiculously easy, that is merely a reminder that watching the NBA is watching a group of the most well-coordinated humans on the planet.

Nicknames

For some reason, clever ballhandlers got some of the more interesting nicknames in the history of professional basketball. For instance, Johnny Wooden of the Indianapolis Kautskys was the "India Rubber Man." How cool is that? Here are some other diminutive dynamos and their nicknames:

Bob Cousy—The Houdini of the Hardwood
Dick McGuire—Tricky Dick
Bob Davies—The Harrisburg Houdini (there seems to be some repetition, as well)
Pete Maravich—The Pistol or Pistol Pete
Earl Monroe—The Pearl
Earvin Johnson—Magic
Donald Watts—Slick

Then there's Fred J. Scolari, who was called, well, "Fat Freddie."
And Tyrone Bogues, who is called "Muggsy."
And Daron Oshay Blalock, also known as "Mookie."

against Bucks guard Oscar Robertson (1960–74), the former University of Cincinnati star whose records Maravich broke while performing at LSU.

Fat chance of that. Maravich, a rookie for the Atlanta Hawks, didn't start, and Hawk coach Richie Guerin was way too smart to match a rookie, even a rookie as talented as Maravich, against one of the all-time greatest players in the league. There were a few isolated matchups in the contest, when Maravich had to switch onto Oscar because of a pick, but for the most part, there was no big battle, because Robertson would have buried Pete at that point in Maravich's career.

PLAYERS TO WATCH

The Sonics' Payton and Stockton, of the Jazz, are the best, because they never lose a step when they go behind their back. Close to them is Steve Nash of the Mavericks. The Clippers' Andre Miller, when he does it, is also very good.

ORIGIN: The 1920s

THE FIRST: Max Kinsbrunner, St. John's University

THE ALL-TIMERS:
Charlie Scott (1970–80),
Walt Frazier (1967–80),
Isiah Thomas (1981–94),
Kobe Bryant (1996–present),
Tim Hardaway (1989–present),
Allan Iverson (1996–present).
Frazier and Thomas are in the Hall of Fame.

Walt Frazer was an extremely agile dribbler.

Inset: Allan Iverson's quickness makes him almost unstoppable.

THE TECHNIQUE:
The crossover involves switching your dribble from one hand to another while facing your opponent. If you are dribbling to your right and want to make a quick move to the left, step back with your left foot and bounce the ball from your right hand to your left. The lower you can bounce the ball, the quicker the crossover. Remember, guide the ball with your fingertips and do not let it move up into your palm.

If you are being guarded tightly, dribble the ball low to the ground. If you are moving the ball downcourt and need to cross over, you can remain upright.

The crossover dribble is now one of the most explosive and heavily used methods of beating one's opponent in the professional leagues. In the NBA of the 21st century, literally every player on every roster can execute a crossover dribble with some degree of facility. The crossover has become the principal move by which many professional players get by their opponents as they drive to the basket.

The move itself goes back to college basketball's Jurassic era. It was an odd thing. The colleges outlawed the double dribble, a move by which players either dribbled the ball with two hands or dribbled, stopped, and dribbled again in 1908. By 1915, all amateur leagues, including the Amateur Athletic Union, eliminated the double dribble.

The pros didn't until the 1930s (various leagues in various years got around to it). So while professional players were muscling their way up the court by dribbling with two hands, collegians and other amateurs were moving completely away from that concept.

In fact, because of the ban on the double dribble, more and more collegians began dribbling with either hand. And frankly, many began to realize that switching hands while being guarded by an opponent was an excellent way to get around that defender.

While there is no way to definitively pinpoint the first crossover dribbler, Max "Mac" Kinsbrunner, the 5' 8" guard who originally played for the St. John's "Wonder Five" from 1927 to 1931, was clearly one of the first players who used the crossover dribble regularly.

Right: Throughout the 1970's Charlie Scott was the man to watch with his crossover faking out defenders left and right.

News accounts of Kinsbrunner's prowess in dribbling the ball with either hand often mentioned how he could easily transfer the ball from one hand to the other.

It's important to note that, for the most part, Kinsbrunner did not use the crossover, or "switching dribble" as it was called then, to drive to the basket. Basketball in general before the shot clock was a game of extended stalling when one team managed to gain even a small lead.

So Kinsbrunner's principal reason for crossing over was to keep the ball away from the other team when St. John's had a lead. He would occasionally flick a pass to an open teammate for a layup; and if he completely befuddled the opposition, he would drive to

FEBRUARY 25, 1977, NEW YORK VS. NEW ORLEANS

When some players get into a zone, they have maybe five or 10 minutes of that feeling of invincibility, that just about everything they throw at the hoop will go in.

Well, on February 25, 1977, "Pistol" Pete Maravich of the New Orleans Jazz was in that zone just about the entire game.

Maravich hit 26 of 37 shots that night and added 16 of 18 free throws for 68 points, the ninth-highest total in NBA history to that point. The Jazz, courtesy of a red-hot Maravich, jumped out to an early lead in the contest and never looked back, winning 124-107.

In the third quarter, Maravich was in the zone of zones. With future Hall of Fame guard Walt Frazier trying to stay with him, the Pistol dribbled to the head of the key, crossed over from his left hand to his right, crossed back over from his right hand to his left, and crossed over a third time with his left hand to his right. At that point, he shot a 10-foot fadeaway jump shot over Knicks center Bob McAdoo and forward Lonnie Shelton, who had moved up to help Frazier. Nothing but net.

The "triple-cross" was the move of moves on a legendary night. One final note: Maravich was in foul trouble in the second half, was rested by coach Elgin Baylor in the third quarter, and actually fouled out of the game with 1:18 left. Who knows how many points he might have got if he had been able to play the whole game?

the basket. But for the most part, his game was stalling with the ball.

Finally, The Pros Catch On

The professionals, even as the double dribble was being outlawed, began to eventually catch on, of course. Kinsbrunner played several years for the New York Jewels and brought his ballhandling skills to the professional ranks. Great playmakers like Freddie Scolari (1946–55), Al Cervi (NBL, NBA, 1937–53), Bob Cousy (1950–63, 1969–70), Kenny Sailors (1946–51) and Bob Davies (1945–55) became skilled practitioners of the crossover, particularly as a stalling tactic.

The crossover that NBA fans know today—that hard, low power move that virtually every guard in the league can execute—came along in the 1970s. Again, it was a collegian who led the way. Charlie Scott, the 6' 6" guard at the University of North Carolina, was one of the first players to give the ball that hard bounce when transferring the sphere to his other hand. Scott was an excellent leaper and an acrobatic driver, so once he got an opening to the basket, he could usually finish the move with a basket.

While Scott (1970–80) was thrilling crowds in the Atlantic Coast Conference in the late 1960s, a young guard with the New York Knickerbockers was also refining the crossover into a stunning midcourt move.

Walt "Clyde" Frazier (1967–80) was one of the best guards in the NBA by his second year, 1968–69. And by the next year, he was one of the league's best players. An accomplished defender, a surprisingly strong rebounder for a backcourtman and a confident performer in the clutch, Clyde developed a devastating crossover dribble that was

particularly difficult to anticipate in the open court.

Like Scott, Frazier's crossover employed a hard bounce once the transfer was made. In fact, Frazier's crossover was so good that he could often freeze opponents by shifting his shoulders and faking a crossover.

It's important to note that playmakers like Oscar Robertson (1960–74), K. C. Jones (1958–67) and Larry Costello (1954–68) were accomplished ballhandlers who often used the crossover dribble. It wasn't an alien concept in the 1960s. The point is that Scott, Frazier and, later, "Pistol" Pete Maravich (1970–80) pushed the crossover envelope a little farther out.

The 1980s and 1990s saw this move become more and more refined. One of the best crossover dribblers of the 1980s was the Pistons' Vinnie Johnson (1979–92), who used the crossover to free himself as he drove down the lane.

The modern practitioner of the crossover, the acknowledged master, is Tim Hardaway (1989–present). At 6', 190 pounds, the compact Hardaway is perfectly suited, physically, to carrying out the crossover.

In fact, it helps to be low to the ground. Hardaway often stands out on the perimeter, moving the ball back and forth between his hands, constantly keeping his opponent off balance as to which way he will drive. The

crossover, in the 21st century, has replaced, in large part, the use of the head-and-shoulder fake by guards and small forwards who are trying to carve out an opening to the basket.

In addition to Hardaway, former water-bug playmaker-scorer Kevin "KJ" Johnson (1987–01), of the Phoenix Suns, the Sonics' Gary Payton (1990–present) and the Sixers' Allen Iverson (1996–present) are the best modern crossover pros. The Lakers' Kobe Bryant (1996–present) is a good example of a larger man who can also employ the crossover in the open court.

Iverson, unlike some of these other stars, uses sheer speed to get the job done, rather than deceptiveness. He simply flies down court, crossing over to beat already shell-shocked opponents.

The (Legal) Double Dribble

There was no crossover dribble, for the most part, from 1891 to the 1920s in professional basketball. That's because most professional leagues in the United States allowed players to double dribble, either by dribbling the ball with both hands at once, or dribbling, stopping, and then restarting their dribble. The technique is exactly as ungraceful as it sounds.

In the early era of basketball, inventor James Naismith envisioned the dribble almost as a last resort for moving the ball. He did not want players to carry the ball, à la football or rugby, because that would invite tackling. But clearly, if a passer's options were stifled by a good defensive scheme, the man with the ball needed a way to advance it on his own.

So Naismith didn't pay much attention to dribbling, other than to rule that a player could dribble with both hands and that interrupting his dribble and then restating it was not a violation.

Interestingly, although the rules were eventually amended in the 1930s to outlaw the double dribble, what really killed this particular move was the pass. Very quickly, teams in the early part of the last century that featured players passing the basketball instead of dribbling it were obviously getting the ball down the court faster and more efficiently. The double dribble as a strategy began to fade from pro basketball even before it was eventually outlawed. But prohibiting it was still a good idea.

The Super Staller

Marques Haynes was almost certainly the greatest dribbler of all time. And, contrary to popular myth, it didn't come naturally. Haynes was born in Sand Springs, Oklahoma, on October 3, 1926. As a young boy, he would accompany an older sister to her high school basketball practice. While the girls practiced, Haynes would stand on the sidelines, dribbling a ball endlessly until practice was over.

Haynes was one of the smaller boys in his neighborhood, and often wasn't picked for the neighborhood basketball games. So once again, he stood on the sidelines, dribbling a ball until someone got hurt or had to go home for lunch or dinner.

Ironically, when Haynes finally made his high school team as a junior, his coach was not a fan of the dribble. So Haynes was not a dribbler throughout his high school career.

He won an athletic scholarship to Langston University in Oklahoma in 1942, and was a two-sport star, playing guard on the basketball team and quarterback on the football team. But his Langston coach, "Zip" Gayles, was another coach who hated "showboats," so Haynes played it straight.

But he played in an exhibition against the Globetrotters in his senior year. When Langston handed the 'Trotters a 74–70 defeat, Haynes so impressed Globetrotters head honcho Abe Saperstein so much that Haynes was offered a job a few months later. Haynes, after getting his degree, joined the team in 1946.

Haynes had not lost his touch, mostly because he continued to work on his dribble in practice even if he didn't use it much in games. For the first few months of his first year with the Globetrotters, Haynes was on one of the Globetrotters' several "farm," or "tryout," teams. These were sort of minor-league Globetrotters teams that could feed the regular Globetrotters squad if a regular was injured or had to miss a game.

In one of his first games, Haynes's squad was playing a team in Mexico, and a Mexican referee ended up fouling out all but Haynes and two of his teammates. With eight minutes left in the game, Haynes's team was up by

Above: Harlem Globetrotter Marques Haynes was a magician with the ball, sliding between defenders quickly and easily.

three points. Haynes took the ball out and dribbled away all but 15 seconds of that eight minutes, ending his show by feeding a wide-open teammate for a layup. A few days later, he was with the first team.

Haynes's secret, besides literally thousands of hours of practice, were large, powerful hands. He could dribble inches from the floor, and, more importantly, move quickly downcourt while he was doing it. Possibly 5' 3" guard Tyrone "Muggsy" Bogues (1987–02) keeps the ball lower to the ground than Haynes could, but it is debatable.

Haynes's pro career lasted from 1946 to 1992, with several other pro touring teams besides the Globetrotters, including the Harlem Magicians, which Haynes formed. He played in more than 12,000 games and traveled more than 4 million miles. He is now a businessman in Oklahoma and was elected to the Hall of Fame in 1999.

Nobody crosses over in the NBA like Kobe Bryant of the Lakers. He is so big, with those long arms, and so quick, that when he does a "double-cross" that is, crossing over from his right hand to his left and then, in the same move, back to his right hand, a defender has difficulty staying with him. The Rockets' Steve Francis and Allen Iverson, of the Sixers, are masters of the midcourt crossover. Both come down at full speed and change hands—and direction—in one quick, explosive move.

PLAYERS TO WATCH

Right: Tim Hardaway looks for an opening against Damon Stoudamire.

ORIGIN: Around the 1910s

THE FIRST: Barney Sedran and Max Friedman, the "Heavenly Twins", Newburgh, NY Tenths

THE ALL-TIMERS:
Bob Cousy and Bill Russell of the Boston Celtics (1956-63)
Oscar Robertson and Wayne Embry of the Cincinnati Royals (1960-66)
Larry Bird and Robert Parish of the Boston Celtics (1980-92)
John Stockton and Karl Malone of the Utah Jazz (1985-present)
Sedran, Friedman, Cousy, Russell, Robertson and Bird are in the Hall of Fame.

THE TECHNIQUE:
The play involves two players, including a ballhandler. The player with the ball heads in the direction of a teammate. As he does so, the teammate sets himself with the middle of his chest lined up with the shoulder of the player defending the dribbler. This is the pick.

Once the defensive player makes contact with the player setting the pick, that player should spin on the foot farthest from the basket and head toward the basket. This is the roll. The ballhandler has several options. If his defensive man switches, the setter of the pick is now behind both defenders and the ballhandler can hit him with a pass for a layup. If the dribbler's defensive man tries to go behind the pick, the dribbler has an open shot.

Always remember to take what the defensive man, or men, gives you. Don't anticipate you'll get a layup. An open shot is also acceptable.

Above: With the help of John Stockton, Karl Malone has mastered the easy two points off of a Stockton pass.

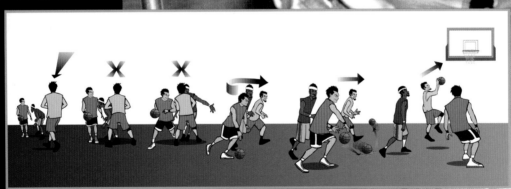

Bill Russell was 1/2 of the Russell Cousy pick-and-roll tandem.

The pick-and-roll is one of those plays that evolved during the barnstorming days of pro basketball. It is one of a number of two-man plays that grew out of the two-man games that barnstorming teams would regularly impose on other squads.

The reason was simple: barnstorming clubs didn't have time to practice. They were almost always playing. And when they weren't playing, they were traveling. And when they weren't traveling, they were eating or sleeping.

So set plays involving all five men were, for the most part, unavailable because they were difficult to practice in a live game. But the two-man game, or the "Buddy System," as many old-timers called it, was a more viable option. While the same five players didn't often barnstorm year after year, there were often a core of players who played together for many years.

And even the Buddy System didn't evolve out of practice. The best way to explain it is that players would simply "try things" while they were playing. Players who played with each other for years and instinctively knew each other's moves would raise an eyebrow, or nod their head, and the other player would cut to the basket and take a pass for a layup.

The pick-and-roll evolved in this manner. And to be honest, Barney Sedran (various leagues, 1911–26) and Max Friedman (various leagues, 1909–27) may not have been the absolute first players to work this out, but they were by far the best of their era.

Friedman, a 5' 8" guard-forward, was usually the passer. Sedran, a miniature 5' 4" guard, was usually the scorer. Friedman was a

APRIL 14, 1967, NBA FINALS, GAME 1, SAN FRANCISCO VS. PHILADELPHIA

The Warriors, with superstar Rick Barry, were knocking on the door in Game 1 of the 1967 Finals, hoping to steal the home-court advantage. With the score tied, and 13 seconds left, Barry and center Nate Thurmond executed a perfect pick-and-roll, with Barry dishing to Thurmond after Thurmond's man, Philadelphia 76ers center Wilt Chamberlain, had switched off on the San Francisco forward.

Except that Wilt, somehow, got to the basket the same time Thurmond did, and clobbered Nate. Even former 76ers don't deny that Wilt got away with a little extra contact.

Still, as Barry would admit a few years later in his autobiography, *Confessions of a Basketball Gypsy*, he was sure that Thurmond would at least get to the line.

"But," said Barry, "the whistle never blew. I couldn't believe it. Thurmond couldn't believe it."

And the Warriors eventually lost the game in overtime, 141–136.

The moral: Sometimes, even when the pick-and-roll works, it doesn't work.

1908 graduate of Hebrew Technical Institute in New York City, Sedran a 1911 grad of City College of New York. Both men turned pro after their college years.

The two became teammates as members of the Newburgh, N.Y., Tenths, of the Hudson River League (HRL), and led that squad to the HRL title in the 1911–12 season. They were smart, they were athletic and they worked in tandem so well that they were called the "Heavenly Twins."

The two men practiced both the give-and-go—in which Sedran would usually pass to Friedman and cut, taking a reverse pass for a layup—and the pick-and-roll—in which Sedran would set the pick and Friedman would hit him with a pass. These two plays

Left: New York Knick's Walt Frazier is stopped by Los Angeles Lakers' Wilt Chamberlain as Jerry West begins a pick-and-roll.

were sort of variations on the same offensive theme.

There is no record of when or under what circumstances the two men used the pick-and-roll, but former original Celtic Nat Holman (various leagues, 1916–33) said the "Heavenly Twins" were the best he had ever seen at the two-man game.

Holman should know. He, Friedman and Sedran were teammates on the New York Whirlwind team that beat the original Celtics 40–27 in what was billed as the "World Championship" game in 1921. And

POINTS IN THE PAINT, 2000–01

These teams scored the most points in the lane:

Seattle Super Sonics: 3,748
Los Angeles Lakers: 3,616
Sacramento Kings: 3,570
Los Angeles Clippers: 3,506
Utah Jazz: 3,474

Least points allowed:

New York Knicks: 2,460
Utah Jazz: 2,634
San Antonio Spurs: 2,784
Indiana Pacers: 2,804
Detroit Pistons: 2,900

Utah's differential (most scored, least allowed) of +840 points was tops in the league by a stunning 302 points over the runner-up Lakers (+538). In comparison, the Lakers' point differential was only 18 points better than third-place Seattle. Despite scoring only 2,711 points in the paint, which was next to last in the league, the New York Knicks' differential was +251, seventh best in the NBA.

THE OPENING TAP

This doesn't have anything to do, really, with the pick-and-roll, but it's too good a stat to ignore.

TOP FIVE OPENING TAP WINNERS, 2000–01:

Shaquille O'Neal, Los Angeles Lakers: 62
Ben Wallace, Detroit Pistons: 55
David Robinson, San Antonio Spurs: 55
Jermaine O'Neal, Portland Trail Blazers: 48
Patrick Ewing, Seattle SuperSonics: 46

TOP FIVE OPENING TAP LOSERS, 2000–01:

Michael Olowokandi, los Angeles Clippers: 48
Brian Grant, Portland Trail Blazers: 46
Vlade Divac, Sacramento Kings: 46
Antonio Davis, Toronto Raptors: 43
Jahidi White, Washington Wizards: 36

Holman went on to develop his own two-man game with original Celtic Johnny Beckman (various leagues, 1910–37). Both these fellows are Hall of Famers, also.

Big Bill and the Cooz

One of Bill Russell's most underrated skills was setting screens. Although Russell (1956–69) was a stringbean at 6' 9", 220 pounds, he set excellent picks. And teammate Bob Cousy (1950–63, 1969–70) needed only a quick opening to get the ball to Russell for a dunk.

The polar opposite of Russell-Cousy was Embry-Robertson. Wayne Embry (1958–69) was a 6' 8", 255-pound widebody. He could set picks that loosened an opponent's fillings. Robertson would dribble up the floor, and the man guarding him knew he had better be aware, or an Embry pick would knock him to his knees.

But, of course, that kind of overawareness worked both ways. Guarding Oscar with only partial concentration was also a bad idea, because pick or no pick, he could either blow

---

past a player or pull up for a quick jumper.

When the New Orleans Jazz acquired rebounding forward Leonard "Truck" Robinson (1974–85) prior to the 1977 season, it was ostensibly to gain a rebounder. But Jazz coach Elgin Baylor also wanted to use Truck's hefty 6' 8", 245-pound frame to spring his best shooter, "Pistol" Pete Maravich (1970–80).

The Jazz had, basically, one play in the 1977–78 season, albeit an extremely effective one: the Truck would park himself on the left side of the key, and Maravich would dribble past him, hoping to slam his defender into the Truck.

If he did, Maravich took the shot. If Pete's defender switched onto Robinson, Maravich would lob the ball into Robinson, who would shoot over the smaller defender. It was a relatively monotonous offense, but it also helped generate the best record in the short history (1974–79) of the New Orleans Jazz, 39–43. The Jazz, with Robinson leading the league in rebounding at 15.3, finished only two games out of the playoffs, and if

---

Tommy Heinsohn—A Passing Fool?

The other effective pick-and-roll combination for the Celtics of the late 1950s and early 1960s, believe it or not, was Russell and Tommy Heinsohn (1956–65). In fact, it's time to dispel the myth of "Tommy the Gunner." In four of the first five years of his pro career, Heinsohn was the best passing forward on the Celtics. And the following stat will win you a bet. In the 1959–60 season, he had more assists than Bill Sharman, 171-144 (okay, it was Sharman's next-to-last season, but he was still a starter).

Was Heinsohn Larry Bird? No. But he was more than a shooter for the Celtics, despite what Bob Cousy used to say ("Give Tommy credit. He only shoots when he has the ball."). But that stereotype was a popular and easy perception for local sportswriters, and Heinsohn, named to the Hall of Fame in 1986, had no reason to contradict them. Boston won World Championships in eight of the nine years he wore that green and white uniform.

Maravich hadn't been injured, they might have made the tournament.

The Forward Pass

Both Rick Barry (1965–80) and Larry Bird (1979–92) were excellent passers from the forward position, and both were exceptional at converting the pick-and-roll with their centers. Barry fed a number of big men, and perhaps his best target was 6' 9" Clifford Ray (1971–81), who played for the Warriors from 1974 to 1981.

But the Larry Bird–Robert Parish pick-and-roll was a thing of beauty to watch.

"Robert set the best pick of any player I ever played with," noted Bird.

The two men played from 1980 to 1992. The beauty of the Celtics' pick-and-roll play was that Bird was such a devastating outside shooter that, often, when Parish (1976–97) would jump out to set a pick for him, both defenders would jump out to try to prevent Bird from shooting. Bird would then obligingly fire a pass to the Chief for an emphatic dunk shot.

Above: John Starks caught behind Corliss Williamson as John Barry makes for the beginnings of a classic pick-and-roll.

The epitome of the modern pick-and-roll play is John Stockton and Karl Malone. The two men have been working this play since 1985, when Malone was a rookie and Stockton was a second-year player.

Players over the decades have tried all manner of ways to disrupt the two men, including trying to simply not allow Stockton to run his defender into the Malone pick. But Malone is so big and strong, and Stockton so smart, that unless a defender grabs Stockton around the waist, he's going to find himself trying to climb over Malone.

In a way, the effectiveness of the pick-and-roll as performed by those two players is a testament to the simplicity of the game, even in 2002. Almost a century after it came into existence, the pick-and-roll still works. Beautifully.

John Stockton and Karl Malone, of the Jazz, run the pick-and-roll the same way the Green Bay Packers ran the end sweep: again and again until a team can prove they can stop it, which most can't. The Mavs' Nash and Nowitzki run a nice two-man game, usually at the top of the key, and Paul Pierce and Tony Battie, of the Celtics, have a similar play. In both cases, the pick frees a man for a mid-range jumper, rather than a layup.

PLAYERS TO WATCH

John Stockton drives away from Steve Francis as Karl Malone sets a pick.

Part 3

Most defensive specialists don't really play their opponent for the steal. They play their opponent to take a shot the opponent doesn't want to take, or make a pass from a difficult angle. Steals are sort of the basketball equivalent of a fresh cherry on an ice cream sundae.

Which is not to say there weren't guys who were great at stripping opponents. The original Celtics and the New York Rens, both barnstorming squads that had their roots in the 1920s, had a bunch of good ballhawks on their respective rosters. That's because both teams, after years on the road, knew exactly what their teammates would do defensively, and were adept at switching and forcing opponents to make plays they didn't want to make.

As the NBA evolved, ballhawkers became more noticeable. Both Jim Pollard (1945–55) and Slater Martin (1949–60) of the Minneapolis Lakers were solid defensive players who were also quick enough to snare an errant pass and strip unaware dribblers. Pollard's unusual leaping ability, for example, meant that he could get up in the air and pick off careless passes thrown by foes ignorant of his athleticism. Martin was so quick he could often flick a hand at a dribbler and recover quickly enough to still prevent a ballhandler from penetrating.

With defensive wizard Bill Russell (1956–69) back to erase any mistakes, most of the Celtics of the late 1950s and 1960s accumulated their share of steals. It was a matter of being able to take risks with the Great Eraser (Russell) sitting back ready and willing to discourage any opponent from driving the lane.

The best pilferer of the 1960s and early 1970s was Lakers guard Jerry West (1960–74). West was one of the quickest players to ever play the game and, even better, had

APRIL 15, 1965 NBA EASTERN CONFERENCE FINALS, GAME 7, PHILADELPHIA VS. BOSTON

With five seconds left in this heart-stopper, Boston Celtics center Bill Russell made an unforgivable error. His attempt to lob the ball inbounds under the Philadelphia basket hit a guide wire that supported the basket. (A footnote: in one of his autobiographies, then-Celtics coach Red Auerbach insisted that Philadelphia forward Chet Walker illegally stepped over the inbounds line to harass Russell.) So, with the score Boston 110, Philadelphia 109, the 76ers got the ball back under their own basket. Philadelphia guard Hal Greer is set to inbound the ball. John Havlicek is guarding Walker and, aware that Greer only has five seconds to inbound, begins counting to himself: one thousand one, one thousand two, one thousand three. Havlicek was facing away from Greer, overplaying Walker. But he stole a quick peek over his shoulder at "one thousand four" and saw Greer start to release the ball to Walker. Looking at the tape, it wasn't a very good pass, just a soft lob. Havlicek turned and picked it off. As he dumped it over to Sam Jones, he was mobbed by the fans. And meanwhile, at courtside, Celtics broadcaster Johnny Most was uttering perhaps the most famous words ever heard on radio during a basketball game:

Havlicek stole the ball! It's all over! Johnny Havlicek stole the ball!

Above: The Celtics' Dave Cowens tries to strip Dr. J as he drives to the hoop during NBA playoff action.

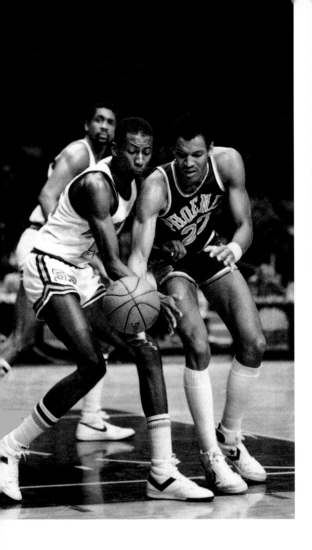

TEAM STEALS LEADERS, 2000–01
Sacramento Kings: 793
Phoenix Suns: 775
Boston Celtics: 769
Golden State Warriors: 742
Philadelphia 76ers: 690

TEAM STOLEN LEADERS 2000–01
(i.e., teams who had the ball stolen from them the most)
Golden State Warriors: 722
Vancouver Grizzlies: 710
Utah Jazz: 699
Atlanta Hawks: 698
Orlando Magic: 695
Source: Harvey Pollock

Far Left: Larry Nance takes the ball from Louis Orr of the Knicks.

Below: Daryl Dawkins of the New Jersey Nets robs Larry Bird.

exceptionally long arms. One of his favorite tactics (and one that inevitably resulted in a foul for any other player who tried it) was to reach across a dribbler's body and tap the ball away behind him, and then pick up the free ball as it bounced the other way down the court.

West was good in the 1960s, but when the Los Angeles Lakers acquired Wilt Chamberlain (1959–73) at center, he became even better. Steals weren't recorded officially by the NBA until the 1974–75 season, but during the first three years of the 1970s, Jerry West would have been among the top thieves in the league.

In one game against Seattle, the year the Lakers won the NBA championship in

1971–72, West had, unofficially, 10 steals. The next night against Detroit, he got, unofficially again, seven more. Maybe 17 steals in two games isn't a record, but it should be.

The best of the frontcourt thieves was 6' 7" forward Rick Barry. Barry was a terrific athlete with tremendous quickness and great hands. In the 1974–75 season, Barry led the NBA in steals with 228, almost 40 more than runner-up Walt "Clyde" Frazier of the Knickerbockers, who was no slouch himself. Until Chicago's Scottie Pippin won the steal crown in the 1994–95 season, Barry was the only forward to do so in league history.

Clyde

Frazier was a superior two-way player who got a lot of ink in New York during the Knickerbocker championship run of the early 1970s. In fact, his nickname, Clyde, was bestowed on him because of his predilection for thefts in the manner of former bank robber Clyde Barrow.

Frazier, more than just about anyone of his era, played opposing teams' passing lanes,

MOST STEALS, NBA FINALS

Four-game series, Rick Barry, Golden State, 1975: 14

Five-game series, Michael Jordan, Chicago, 1991: 14

Six-game series, Julius Erving, Philadelphia, 1977; Earvin Johnson, Los Angeles, 1980; Larry Bird, Boston, 1986: 16

Seven-game series, Isiah Thomas, Detroit, 1988: 20

Five Most Notable Playoff Steals

These are the biggest steals in the biggest games that stand out in the collective history of the NBA.

April 10, 1955: NBA Finals, Game 7, Fort Wayne vs. Syracuse

The 1954–55 NBA championship was secured by a steal by Syracuse guard George King in the seventh game of the NBA Finals with time winding down. The Nationals led the game, 92–91, with seconds left. King had just hit a foul shot to put the home side ahead.

"King wasn't one of our best foul shooters, but he was one of our best ballhandlers," recalled his coach, Al Cervi. "When he was fouled, I felt he'd make that vital shot, and he did."

With time running down, the Pistons pushed the ball up the court. Piston forward George "the Bird" Yardley was driving up the middle of the court, and Cervi admitted recently that his heart was in his throat.

"George Yardley had the ball, and I really was swallowing hard. But Seymour deflected the ball, and King came up with it as the clock ended the game. My Hail Mary had been answered with that play!"

April 10, 1962: NBA Finals, Game 3, Boston vs. Los Angeles

This was supposed to be the series the Los Angeles Lakers would win. Los Angeles had already taken the home court advantage away from Boston on April 8, securing a 129–122 win to tie the series between the teams at one game each. Two nights later, in Los Angeles, Lakers forward Elgin Baylor pumped in 39 points and guard Jerry West had 35, and with three seconds left, the score was 115–115. The Celtics had the ball. West was guarding Celtics great Bob Cousy, and Cousy was attempting to get the ball to Boston guard Sam Jones, but West deflected Cousy's pass, stole the ball and raced in for a layup as the buzzer sounded. No one could ever remember anyone stealing the ball from Cousy, and certainly not in such a crucial situation. "It was the basketball version of a home run in the bottom of the ninth," said West in an interview later. The Lakers won the game and took a 2–1 lead in the series. Nonetheless, eight days later, the Celtics won Game 7, 110–107 in overtime.

May 31, 1984: NBA Finals, Game 2, Los Angeles vs. Boston

The Lakers had wrested the home court advantage from the Celtics on May 27, with an impressive 115–109 win in Boston Garden in the opening game of the Finals. And in Game 2, although the Celtics led most of the way, the Lakers surged in the fourth quarter and took a 115–113 lead with 24 seconds left. The Celtics' Kevin McHale was fouled, but, incredibly, he missed both shots. With 18 seconds left, all the Lakers had to do was run out the clock, but Lakers forward James Worthy lobbed a crosscourt pass to teammate Earvin Johnson. It was picked off by Celtics guard Gerald Henderson. With the incredulous Celtics crowd howling, Henderson sailed in for a layup to tie the game in regulation. In overtime, Boston prevailed, 124–121, and went on to win the series in seven games.

May 26, 1987: NBA Eastern Finals, Game 5, Detroit vs. Boston

The Eastern Finals between the Celtics and the "Bad Boy" Pistons had run about the way everyone had expected. Lots of funny business under the basket, a host of technical fouls and a fight or two. The Pistons seemed a step faster than the older Celtics in the latter part of the series, and in Game 5, Detroit had a 107–106 lead with only four seconds left. With Game 6 slated for the Pistons' home court at the Pontiac Silverdome, Detroit finally appeared to be in control.

With time ticking down, the Pistons' Isiah Thomas had to inbound the ball on the baseline opposite the Celtics' bench near Boston's basket. He tossed the ball to Detroit center Bill Laimbeer. Celtics forward Larry Bird beat Laimbeer to the ball by an eyelash with a smart jump on the ball, intercepting the pass. But that wasn't the end of the play. As he was falling out of bounds, Bird alertly fed a cutting Dennis Johnson for the game-winning hoop. Once again, Johnny Most went bonkers.

And there's a steal by Bird, over to D. J. for the layup and the Celtics have a one-point lead! What a play by Bird! This place is going wild!

June 14, 1998: NBA Finals, Game 6, Chicago vs. Utah

Actually, the Bulls superstar made two amazing plays in the final seconds of Game 6. He hit the jumper to win it, 87–86. Just before that, he got the ball for his team. The Jazz, at that point, were in the driver's seat. Leading 86–85, Utah had possession of the ball with 37 seconds left, and were clearly planning to run the clock down and try to get a good shot with 15 or so seconds left. Jordan anticipated the most obvious play: a pass into Jazz forward Karl Malone. Malone, with his maneuverability and strength, would try to get as close as he could for a basket or a foul, or both. Malone received the ball, and as he was jockeying for position, Jordan snuck around behind him and knocked the ball cleanly out of Malone's hands. The crowd was stunned. And worse, there were 18 seconds left, plenty of time for Michael to be Michael. Which, of course, is exactly what happened.

the areas where opponents would be likely to pass the ball while running a play.

While popular myth posited that Frazier somehow intuitively sensed where the ball would be and made his move, the fact is, Walt Frazier was great because he worked at it. Frazier studied opposing teams' plays and strategies and determined where the basketball might go at a given time. It was then his job to get to the ball before it could be passed to its target. He did that with such facility that some teams would literally pull the man Frazier was guarding completely out of the offense and play the Knicks four-on-four with Frazier conveniently out of reach. This happened several times during the Knickerbockers' first championship year of 1969–70.

In addition to quickness and hard work, sheer speed and athleticism were also becoming more and more important in how defenders played their men. Alvin Robertson (1984–95) and Michael Ray Richardson (1978–86) both led the NBA in steals multiple times. Both were blessed with near-Mach speed. Before he fell prey to drugs, Richardson could literally run down long

PLAYERS TO WATCH

Baron Davis of the New Orleans Hornets is a sneaky little bugger who plays the passing lanes well. Iverson can just flat out strip you at midcourt, as can Jason Kidd. Kidd's other trick is to come around on the blind side of a pivot player and take the ball away. He comes, as Robert Frost might say, on little cat's feet.

passes to intercept them, as could Robertson.

Chicago Bulls star Michael Jordan (1984–93, 1994–98, 2000–present) has combined the strengths of Robertson, Richardson and Frazier into a fearsome defensive package. Jordan is not quite as fast as Robertson or Michael Ray, but he is nearly as quick as Frazier, and as smart.

Three times in his NBA career, 1987–88, 1989–90 and 1992–93, Jordan led the league in both steals and scoring, an unprecedented, amazing feat. Barry is the only other player who had led the league in scoring and steals, and he did it in separate years. What it meant was that Jordan was committing himself to playing hard at both ends of the court, a feat of exceptional endurance and concentration.

It is amazing to say, but in the 1990s, Michael Jordan was almost as intimidating on defense as he was on offense.

The era of big men of superior quickness is upon us, and no one exemplifies that era as well as Hakeem Olajuwon (1984–present). Hakeem "the Dream" began his career as a shot blocker and low-post scorer. He also has hands as quick as most, if not all, guards in the league. In 10 of his first 11 years in the league, Olajuwon led the Rockets in steals. The only year he didn't, the 1990–91 season, he played only 56 games due to an injury. He still had 121 thefts that season. Few centers, if any, can match that degree of defensive excellence for as long as "the Dream" has.

Facing page: Jason Kidd reaches in to steal the ball from Allan Iverson.

Right: Kidd, again, coming around on Michael Jordan.

16 The Reject

Get That Stuff Out of Here!

ORIGIN: The 1890s

THE FIRST: Mike Novak, Loyola
of Chicago

THE ALL-TIMERS:
Bob Kurland (AAU: 1946–52)
Bill Russell (1956–59)
Wilt Chamberlain (1969–73)
Tree Rollins (1977–95)
Manute Bol (1985–95)
Hakeem Olajuwon (1984–present)
Kurland, Russell and Wilt are all in the Hall of Fame.

THE TECHNIQUE:
Jump straight up. Don't fall for fakes. Use the hand closest to the basket when trying to make a block. Follow through only with your wrist. Following through with your entire arm is more likely to generate contact with your opponent.

Also, following through with your entire arm is more likely to knock the ball out of bounds. Following through with just your wrist will give you a better chance to control the ball after it is blocked. Pick your spots. Don't try to block everything, or you will be exhausted after 10 minutes.

Again, study your opponent's moves. If he goes to his left to shoot, try to beat him to that spot. Never swipe at the ball in midair. Even if you miss, an official may think he saw a foul. Keep your arm straight up.

Bob Kurkland, one of the first goaltenders.

Inset: Tim Duncan is today's premier rejector.

Almost as soon as the game was invented, players were taught to put their arms up to deflect passes and shots. The blocked shot, the act of rejecting a field goal attempt, only started when the ballplayers began to get really big.

Ed Wachter (1896–1918) of the old Troy, New York, Trojans, was one of the smartest basketball players of the early era and, at 6' 1", one of the biggest. No record exists of his defensive abilities, but this was a guy who was always trying to find things to do in a game that would be to his advantage. So it's reasonable to assume that Wachter blocked or deflected his share of shots.

The first player to be noted as a major shot-blocker was Mike Novak, the 6' 9" giant from Loyola of Chicago. Novak was probably the first player to actually stand in the lane and reject shots from all players, not just the guy he was guarding.

Above: George Mikan, another early goaltender, blocks a shot by Rochester Royals guard, Bob Davies in 1951.

Above: Kareem Abdul-Jabar (33) swats away a shot by Denver Nuggets Charles Scott.

The New York Knickerbockers had a three-games-to-two lead on the Houston Rockets in the series. Knickerbocker guard John Starks was on a roll, having scored 16 of his team-high 27 points to keep the Knicks in the game. With six seconds left in the game, Houston had an 86–84 lead, but New York had the ball. The Knicks opted to go for broke and freed up Starks deep in the left corner for the three-pointer that would win the ballgame.

Houston center Hakeem Olajuwon, who had been playing with five personal fouls for most of the quarter, took a couple of huge strides and was in Starks's face in an instant. The 6' 11" Olajuwon got a hand on the ball (and, many Knicks fans say, on Starks's wrist) and blocked the shot to preserve the Rockets' victory. Houston went on to win Game 7 and the first championship in franchise history.

The art of shot-blocking really came to people's attention when giants like 7' 0" Bob Kurland (1946–52) and 6' 10" George Mikan (1946–56) began doing something on a regular basis that no one had been able to do before: goaltend the basketball.

Understand that since the game's inception, until the midpoint of the century, there were no prohibitions against goaltending. A player was well within his rights to try to block a ball going into the basket whether it was going up to or coming down into the basket. The catch was, of course, that with a 10-foot hoop, there were few players tall enough to try. Many of those who could do so lacked the coordination to goaltend on a consistent basis, so it wasn't really an issue for the first 50 years of basketball, although Novak certainly did his share of goaltending.

Mikan and Kurland changed all that. Both became adept, in the early years of their college careers, of knocking balls out of the basket before they could go through the hoop. Kurland, in particular, was an absolute master of it when he played for Oklahoma A&M. After goaltending an even dozen shots in one game, a sportswriter called him a "menace to the game."

It wasn't that bad, but clearly there had to be some adjustments to the rules. Thus, in 1944, both the NCAA and the professional leagues outlawed goaltending, which also prohibited players from tipping balls into the basket when they were on the rim of the hoop.

That helped considerably, but the Kurlands and Mikans of the world were clearly here to stay.

The Eagle with a Beard

At the beginning of the 1953–54 NCAA basketball season, the University of San Francisco started a 6' 9", 200-pound sophomore at center. His name was William Felton Russell. He wasn't much of a scorer, but he had great speed, exceptional leaping ability (he was a champion high jumper for the USF track team) and superb anticipation. Coach Phil Woolpert rightfully figured he'd be a good player to have for rebounding.

Years later, in recognition of his formidable stature, NBA forward Tom Meschery, who has also published books on poetry, called Russell "the Eagle with a Beard."

Russell blocked shots, but, frankly, in his sophomore year, this shot-blocking thing was sort of an interesting sidebar. San Francisco was a decent team that year and, in fact, the best player on the team was backcourtman K. C. Jones. The Russell kid was still learning to rebound and his pivot moves needed a little work.

It all coalesced in 1954–55. The Dons, as the team was nicknamed, lost one game, to UCLA (with their new coach, John Wooden), but ran the table the rest of the season, which included a national championship.

Russell was the key. Heck, he was the

Left: Wilt Chamberlain trying to shoot over Bill "the Eagle with a Beard" Russell.

key, the lock and the whole door. No one had ever seen anything like him. He not only blocked the shots of the man he was guarding, he blocked the shots of players his teammates were guarding. He not only blocked the shots of players who drove the lane. He was fast enough, and blessed with enough leaping ability to leave his man, take one or two strides, and explode into the air to reject the shot of a play out by the foul line or in the corner.

Even in those early years, Russell was figuring out that blocking the shot wasn't, or shouldn't be, the end of the play. He began angling his body to block the shot so that he or a teammate could recover the ball. This is a skill so rare that even today, in the 21st

GOALTENDING LEADERS, 2000–01:

Kenyon Martin, New Jersey Nets: 30 (24 defensive, 6 offensive)
Jermaine O'Neal, Portland Trail Blazers: 27 (26 defensive, 1 offensive)
Kevin Garnett, Minnesota Timberwolves: 23 (21 defensive, 2 offensive)
Theo Ratliff, Philadelphia 76ers: 22 (20 defensive, 2 offensive)
Keon Clark, Denver Nuggets: 19 (19 defensive, 0 offensive)

O'Neal's 26 defensive goaltends led the league. Darius Miles of the Clippers had 7 offensive goaltends and 13 overall. There were 752 goaltending calls in 2000–01, including 603 defensive, 149 offensive.

Above: Mark Eaton of the Utah Jazz trying to shut down a shot by Magic Johnson. Thurl Bailey (41) looks on.

century, there are virtually no players who do this at any level on a consistent basis.

Russell dominated college basketball like no player ever had. He blocked 10, 12, 14 shots a game. Still, believe it or not, the perception was that Russell's relative lack of an offensive game would hurt him in the pros. This despite the fact that Russell averaged 23.4 points per game in the 1955 NCAA tournament and 22 points per game in the 1956 playoffs.

Needless to say, Russell, a better athlete than probably 95 percent of the players in the league, found ways to score in the NBA. And he also found ways to dominate on defense. "Most of the players of that era that I talked to believe that Russell would have made any team he played on strong," said George Yardley, who played against Russell in the 1950s. "He was such a dominating player."

The Celtics drafted Russell in 1956, and by the end of the year, Russell had led Boston to the NBA championship. In 11 of his 13 years, Russell's teams won the NBA championship. Extending that back to his collegiate years and the Olympics, Russell played on 16 different squads from 1954 to 1969, and was on the winning side of 14 of them. Unbelievable.

Wilt Chamberlain, who burst into the NBA two years after Russell, was also a formidable shot-blocker. In fact, many of Wilt's fans believe that Chamberlain actually blocked more shots per game than Russell.

But Wilt, like the players of today, often blocked shots out of bounds. And he was also a victim of his formidable leaping ability: many times, he would explode off the court and reject the shot of a player several feet away. It was such a radical move, and appeared to be so amazing, that often referees would nail Wilt for goaltending.

The Specialists

It may have been calculated earlier, but it was former Atlanta Hawk coach Hubie Brown who determined in the late 1970s that a good shot-blocker meant several points a night to a team. Thus, Brown drafted 7' 1" center Wayne "Tree" Rollins (1977–95) to play center for the Hawks. The Tree was a decent rebounder (hey, he was seven feet tall!) and initially a very poor scorer, but he could block shots like nobody's business, more than two a game for his career. That, and the thinly disguised zone the Hawks played, turned the team into a contender. The Hawks improved by 10 games over the previous season and made the playoffs.

Naturally, when something is successful, other coaches want to emulate it, so supersized players, regardless of their offensive skills, started showing up on team rosters. And it worked, somewhat.

The Utah Jazz drafted 7' 4" center Mark Eaton in 1983. Eaton (1983–93) had not even started for UCLA, his alma mater. Jazz coach Frank Layden, however, needed a big man to clog the middle and block shots. Eaton, a scrub at UCLA, became a solid player for Utah, making the All-Star team one year.

As much as Eaton helped his team, and as much as he was clearly a hard working guy, his limitations on offense, particularly in the playoffs, held Utah back. It was not until Eaton retired that the Jazz made their move to the NBA's elite, appearing in the NBA Western Finals in 1993–94 and 1994–95 and the NBA Finals the next two years, from 1995 to 1997.

In 1985, this trend was pushed to its limit when the Washington Bullets drafted 7' 7"

Above: Hakeem "the Dream" Olajuwan rejects Brian Grant's effort.

TOTAL SHOTS BLOCKED BY A GUARD, 2000–2001		
Eddie Jones, Charlotte Hornets: 58		
Jerry Stackhouse, Detroit Pistons: 58		
Ron Artest, Chicago Bulls: 45		
Doug Christie, Toronto Raptors: 45		
Jalen Rose, Indiana Pacers: 43		
Kobe Bryant, Los Angeles Lakers: 43		

Source: Harvey Pollock

MOST BLOCKED SHOTS, NBA FINALS		
Bill Walton, Portland Trail Blazers, June 5, 1977: 8		
Hakeem Olajuwon, Houston Rockets, June 5, 1986: 8		
Patrick Ewing, New York Knicks, June 17, 1994: 8		
Dennis Johnson, Seattle Super Sonics, May 28, 1978: 7		
Patrick Ewing, New York Knicks, June 12, 1994: 7		
Hakeem Olajuwon, Houston Rockets, June 12, 1994: 7		

Manute Bol, a Dinka tribesman from the Sudan, whose exposure to basketball had been extremely limited. And it showed when he ascended into the NBA. Bol scored 298 points in 80 games his rookie year. He passed for a modest 23 assists. But he blocked 397 shots, which led the NBA in the 1985–86 season.

As intimidating as Bol was, and he was certainly intimidating, his relative lack of skills on offense did not help the Bullets turn the corner, record-wise, either. Washington was above the .500 mark only once in Bol's three years there. Subsequent trades to the Golden State Warriors, Philadelphia 76ers and Miami Heat saw Bol's teams in the playoffs two of the next seven years.

To be sure, this was not entirely Bol's fault. Or Eaton's in Utah. But what it showed was that shot-blocking specialists such as Bol or

Eaton were best used as complementary players, if they played significant minutes at all.

Players like Hakeem Olajuwon (1984–present) and Patrick Ewing (1985–2002), who came into the league as defensive specialists and have emerged as great all-around players, were far more effective. Olajuwon blocked 200 or more shots 12 years in a row, and was first or second in the league for six years in a row, beginning in the 1989–90 season. Ewing blocked 200 or more shots in six of seven years running from 1987 to 1994.

Hakeem "the Dream" also developed a variety of skillful moves around the basket. This two-way excellence enabled Olajuwon to lead the Rockets to a pair of NBA championships, in 1993–94 and 1994–95. Ewing, who also matured as a player over the years, brought the Knicks to the Finals in 1993–94 and his teams had several memorable battles with Michael Jordan's Bulls for eastern supremacy.

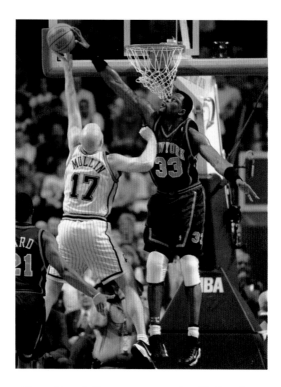

Above: Patrick Ewing goes vertical to block a shot by the Indiana Pacers Chris Mullin.

Tim Duncan is the premier rejector in the league. Duncan will allow a jump shot in the lane from time to time, but layups are verboten. The other very active shot-blockers in the league are Ben Wallace and Jermaine O'Neal of the Pacers. O'Neal is still young and excitable, so he goes after almost everything. Raef LaFrentz of the Mavericks is also very active and underrated.

Above: Tim Duncan reaches across for the block against Seattle Super Sonics Vin Baker.

Right: Duncan, again, denies Los Angeles Lakers Devon George.

Elmore Smith's Big Night

On October 26, 1973, Lakers center Elmore Smith (1971–79) set an NBA record for blocked shots by swatting 14 of them against the Detroit Pistons as the Lakers defeated Detroit, 94–92, on a pair of Gail Goodrich free throws. This was the first year blocked shots were recorded by the NBA, and Smith's feat, while impressive, was admittedly somewhat tainted, seeing as the two greatest shot-blockers in league history, Wilt Chamberlain and Bill Russell, had retired.

But Smith wasn't done. Two nights later, Smith rejected 17 shots against the Portland Trail Blazers in a 111–98 win, a record that still stands.

It was a tough season for Smith, who was trying to take the place of the retired Chamberlain, and while his shot-blocking abilities were unquestioned, Smith was not the rebounder Wilt was. Smith wasn't interested in being the second coming of Wilt Chamberlain, however. A deeply religious, gentle man, Smith's fondest wish was to be able to play his game and go home, a near-impossibility in Lakers land, where expectations were always high. Worse, Smith had been traded to Los Angeles for the popular Jim McMillian, which put him further under the microscope. Finally, the Lakers were being forced to play most of the year without the injured Jerry West, who would play only 31 games in this, his last season.

Smith would spend one more year in Los Angeles before moving on to Milwaukee. A few years after his record-setting game, the 30-year-old Smith retired.

17 The Defenders' Moves

The Guys They Call "the Gloves"

THE ORIGIN: The 1920s

THE FIRST: Harlan Page

THE ALL-TIMERS:
John "Honey" Russell (1918-46)
Slater Martin (1949-60)
K. C. Jones (1958-67)
Tom Sanders (1960-73)
Dave DeBusschere (1962-74)
Bobby Jones (1974-86)
Dennis Rodman (1986-2000)
Russell, Martin, Jones and DeBusschere are in the Hall of Fame.

Left: The Seattle Super Sonics Gary Payton. One tough defender

Slater Martin, one of the best defensive players of the 1950s.

THE TECHNIQUE:
Keep your man within arm's length at all times. Overplay him to prevent him from getting the ball, or to at least force his teammates to make difficult passes to get him the ball. If need be, pick him up all over the court.

Make your opponent work just to get his hands on the basketball. Try to keep your body on him at all times. Don't turn your head while guarding him.

If you can, study your opponent's tendencies. Does he dribble with only one hand? Does he prefer going to the left or to the right? Does he like to set up on a specific spot on the court? If he does, try to ensure that he sets up as far away from it as you can force him to. Forcing him to shoot a few feet from his usual spot is enough, in some cases, to make him miss.

Before there was Gary "the Glove" Payton, of Seattle, there were a host of players who could play their man tight and, in fact, enjoyed "digging in" on defense.

The first player really known for his defensive prowess was Harlan "Pat" Page, a 5' 9" guard who starred for the University of Chicago from 1906 to 1910. Page never played professionally, but he was the quarterback for those old Chicago University powerhouses and led the team to the national championship in 1908. He was elected to the Hall of Fame as a college player in 1962.

Page was hard-nosed and pugnacious. What made him a great defender was the fact that he was left-handed. Dribblers trying to get by him inevitably found themselves protecting the basketball or face losing it. It is an advantage with which they can still confound opponents.

A few years later, Page's professional counterpart, John "Honey" Russell made his debut. Russell was a great player at Alexander Hamilton High School in New York City from 1915 to 1919. So great, in fact, that he also played a lot of pro ball while still in high school, a not uncommon occurrence.

Russell graduated from high school in 1919 and began a full-time pro career. He led the Cleveland Rosenblums to five consecutive American Basketball League championships from 1924 to 1929. Russell was a canny playmaker on offense. On defense, he was tenacious and a very physical ballplayer.

In the rough-and-tumble days of the early professional game, Russell was a handful. He was a player known for being physical, holding players' shorts when they shot, stepping on their feet under the basket, grabbing their arms as they tried to cut. He was generally a big pain for the opposing player, knowing that when they concentrated on him, they weren't concentrating on scoring.

The fact is that throughout hoop history, the moves used by strong defensive players haven't really changed all that much. Things might have been more physical in the early days, but the real factor that separated the men from the boys, defensively, was mental toughness and a willingness to play hard on the defensive end for extended periods of time.

In the 1940s, the top defensive guard in the pros was Al "Digger" Cervi, a Hall of Famer who played professionally from 1938 to 1954. Cervi was a strong set shooter and great playmaker, but, like Russell, was a contentious—and tricky—defender.

"Cervi would show you something different every time you played," recalled former pro Ralph Beard. "He'd knock you on your butt one time down the court and back off you the next time. He was tough to play against."

The best defensive player in the 1950s, and one of the greatest ever, was 5' 11" backcourtman Slater "Dugie" Martin of Minneapolis. Martin was fast and quick, and a solid playmaker, but his defensive prowess was legendary.

Fellow Hall of Famer Bob Davies conceded in an interview years later that Martin was the reason he was shut out from the field in a regular-season game, the only time in his career that it happened.

"He was just all over me," admitted Davies.

Slater "Gloves" Fat Freddie

Another time, in the Western Conference championships in 1953, the Lakers were locked into a battle with the Fort Wayne Pistons. Fort Wayne's "Fat Freddie" Scolari, a savvy veteran himself, had been burning the Lakers in the first four games. Just before Game 5, the last game in this best-of-five

MARCH 31–APRIL 9, 1964, THE NBA EASTERN FINALS, BOSTON VS. CINCINNATI

It was a new era. The Boston Celtics had lost all-time All-Star guard Bob Cousy to retirement. To outside observers, without Cousy, the Celtics were clearly vulnerable. This was the year they could be taken.

The team to do it appeared to be the Cincinnati Royals. At the end of the 1963–64 season, Royals guard Oscar Robertson (1961–1974), averaging 31.4 points per game, a league-leading 11.0 assists per game and 9.9 rebounds per game (seven rebounds short of a triple-double season), won the NBA's MVP award. Rookie forward Jerry Lucas (1963–74) led the league in field goal percentage and was the best rebounding non-center in the league. And in fact, the Royals, although they finished second to Boston in the Eastern Division championship race, had beaten the Celtics seven of 12 times in the regular season.

The Royals dispatched Philadelphia in five games and headed for Boston Garden on March 31 for the big matchup.

It proved to be a big mismatch. The Celtics ripped the Royals, 103–87 and 101–90 in Boston, and then, in what should have been a hectic Game 3 in Cincinnati Gardens, pummeled the Royals, 102–92. The Royals won Game 4, 102–93, before being smoked, 109–95, in Game 5, which eliminated them.

The difference, according to Royals coach Jack McMahon, was Celtics guard K. C. Jones, who picked up Robertson from endline to endline the entire game, every game. He fronted Oscar, overplayed him and generally made it very difficult for the Royals to run their offense. Robertson, who had averaged 31.4 points in the regular season, was held to 28.1, including 20 points in the first game and 24 in the fifth. It was an outstanding example of individual defense and determination on the part of Jones. And two weeks later, the Celtics won their sixth consecutive World Championship.

series, Minneapolis coach Johnny Kundla told Martin to stick to Scolari.

Martin got on Fat Freddie, holding Scolari to one field goal and four points in an easy 74–58 Lakers win.

One of the ways that good defensive players became great defensive players, or perhaps greater defensive players, was to have a big guy back them up. In the 1960s, the Boston Celtics had a fearsome fast break, but their principal strength was their defensive players.

Guard K. C. Jones (1958–67) and forward Thomas "Satch" Sanders (1960–73) were the two best defensive players at their respective positions from about 1961 to 1967. Both were known for guarding their opponents closely and aggressively. K.C. (by the way, that is his name; his mom just decided to use initials) is better known for his straight-up, man-to-man style. "Satch," who had long arms and great leaping ability, was better at playing slightly off his man and blocking his shots or stealing passes.

Regardless, both were extremely effective. If a player got past K.C. or Satch, there was Boston center Bill Russell (1956–69) right back there waiting.

Now, did Russell make these two guys better defenders because of his own defensive abilities? Absolutely. Were these two still

Right: Orlando Magic's Nick Anderson dribbles toward the basket as Latrell Spreewell blocks.

Below: New York Knicks David DeBusschere working his relentless D on Phil Chenier (45) of the Baltimore Bullets.

great in their own right? Again, absolutely. This relentless, punishing defense is the principal reason the Celtics won eight championships in a row from 1958 to 1966.

As he established his reputation in the 1970s, many observers termed Knickerbockers forward David DeBusschere (1962–74) a "throwback" player. That was because in a league that was increasingly relying on athleticism to get by, DeBusschere was, relatively speaking, one of those players who didn't jump very well and who wasn't very fast.

He didn't have to be a jumper or sprinter, however. DeBusschere, who was usually in superior condition, literally imposed his will on opponents. In his biography, *Maverick,* former Knicks forward Phil Jackson (1967–80) recalled seeing DeBee, as he was called, literally taking a player out of the offense minutes at a time by overplaying him and just not allowing that opponent to get to the spot on the floor that the player needed.

DeBusschere was relentless and fearless. Opponents would be denied their favorite spots down the court for as long as the game was an issue. It was an intimidating sight to see his opponents just give up after two or three quarters of pounding.

6' to 7" forward Bobby Jones, who played for Denver and Philadelphia (1974–86), was just as relentless, but not as nasty. Jones was quicker and faster than DeBusschere and a

Above: Shaq is shut down by Dennis Rodman (right) and Luc Longley.

Left: San Antonio Spurs Allan Bristow (30) and Mike Gale double-team Dr. J.

much better jumper. He could be physical with an opponent, but many times, Jones would back off his man and rely on his speed and anticipation to break up an opponent's offensive patterns.

Jones had 1,380 steals and 1,300 blocks in his 12-year pro career, one of the few players in league history to average more than 100 blocks and 100 steals per year in his career.

In sharp contrast to those stats is the phenomenon that is 6' 8" forward Dennis "the Worm" Rodman. Rodman (1986–2000) did not block an extraordinary number of

These Guys Could Guard Anyone

Five defenders who were the best at their positions, and among the best guarding bigger and smaller men, as well.

Frank "Rams" Ramsey, Boston Celtics (1954–64):

A tremendous athlete, "Rams" was known for his scoring. But then-Celtics coach Arnold "Red" Auerbach had no problem matching Ramsey up with either guards or forwards, and sometimes, even centers. In the 1964 Finals, Auerbach matched future Hall of Famer Frank Ramsey, 6' 4", against future Hall of Famer Nate Thurmond, 6' 11", of the San Francisco Warriors. Thurmond was no awkward stiff, but Auerbach and Ramsey realized that Ramsey's quickness and athleticism more than made up for his seven-inch height disadvantage. And Red was right, of course. The Celtics won the series, four games to one.

Kevin McHale, Boston Celtics (1980–93):

He was 6' 11", with long arms that increased his wingspan to that of a player five or six inches taller. From 1980 until a foot injury slowed him down in 1987, Kevin McHale was the most versatile one-on-one defender in the NBA, and perhaps in league history. Philadelphia's 6' 5" forward Charles Barkley (1984–2001) said McHale was the toughest player to score on in the league. So did Milwaukee's 6' 5" guard Ricky Pierce (1982–98). And yet, McHale was just as tough against Houston's 7' 4" Ralph Sampson (1983–92) and the Los Angeles Lakers, 7' 2" Kareem Abdul-Jabbar (1969–89). He was named to the Hall of Fame in 1999.

Dennis Rodman, Detroit, San Antonio, Chicago, Los Angeles, Dallas (1986–2000):

In one playoff run during the 1988–89 season, Rodman guarded Boston's All-Star forward Larry Bird (1979–92), Milwaukee's 7' All-Star center Jack Sikma (1977–91) and Los Angeles Lakers All-Star guard Earvin "Magic" Johnson (1979–91, 1995–96). That may be the most telling tribute to his talent, especially since the Pistons won the NBA title that year. For most of his career, Rodman was asked to guard just about everybody, but his strength was guarding post players. Although only 6' 8", 220, Rodman regularly battled in the low post with the likes of 7' Patrick Ewing (1985–02), 6' 10" Alonzo Mourning (1992–present) and 7' 1" Shaquille O'Neal (1992–present).

Willie Wise, Utah, Virginia, Denver, Seattle (1969–78):

Nobody remembers this guy, because he played in the ABA. But the 6' 6" Wise was, to many observers, the Dave DeBusschere of the ABA: a tough, smart, versatile defender. Wise's defense on the greatest playoff scorer in ABA history, 6'-5" guard-forward Roger Brown (1967–75), helped the Utah Stars win the ABA championship in 1971.

Sidney Moncrief, Milwaukee, Atlanta (1979–91):

Moncrief was only 6' 4", but he was a versatile defender of guards and forwards. He guarded both 6' 6" Julius Erving and 6' 9" Larry Bird, as well as smaller players.

Left: Boston Celtics Kevin McHale, one of the most versatile one-on-one defenders, battles Los Angeles Lakers James Worthy for the rebound.

PLAYERS TO WATCH

Detroit's Ben Wallace has perfected the art of the weak-side shot block. What this means is, he is excellent at coming over and helping out a teammate who might be isolated in the low post. Wallace is also a strong post defender. The Sonics' Gary Payton is still a tough defender, and Kevin Garnett of the Timberwolves is the best of the big men. The best man-to-man defender in the NBA is Doug Christie of the Kings. Christie is one of those guys who can get belly-to-belly with an opponent and make him work just to get from point A to point B.

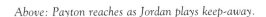

FORCING 24-SECOND VIOLATIONS

These teams forced the most 24-second violations in 2000–01:

Orlando Magic:	77
Boston Celtics:	71
New York Knicks:	65
Minnesota Timberwolves:	59
Miami Heat:	57
Sacramento Kings:	57

And the ones who held the ball too long. These squads committed the most 24-second violations in 2000–01:

Chicago Bulls:	89
Los Angeles Clippers:	75
Atlanta Hawks:	68
Indiana Pacers:	67
Houston Rockets:	65

Source: Harvey Pollock

shots (531 in 14 years) and he did not make a heap of steals (611 in the same span). What he did, better than almost anybody, was play excellent position defense.

If you want to conceptualize how the pros played each other six decades ago, Rodman was the man to watch. All of his nutty hairstyles, tattoos and sartorial choices aside, this guy was a true throwback to the old days. He cared almost nothing about statistics, except his rebound numbers (and how can one fault that?). His career scoring average is 7.3 points per game, and only once in his career did he average double figures. In fact, six times in Rodman's career, he collected more offensive rebounds than points.

Unfortunately, all that was obscured by his odd off-the-court behavior. Too bad, because the Worm was, on the court, as good a teammate as one could want.

Above: Payton reaches as Jordan plays keep-away.

Right:Payton squares himself against the drive by Scottie Pippin.

Part 4

The Offensive Moves

18 The Pivot
Doing the Job in the Paint

ORIGIN: **1924**

THE FIRST: **Henry "Dutch" Dehnert, Original Celtics**

THE ALL-TIMERS:
Dehnert (1920–41)
George Mikan (1946–56),
Wilt Chamberlain (1959–73)
Kareem Abdul-Jabbar (1969–88)
David Cowens (1970–83)
Hakeem Olajuwon (1984–present)
Shaquille O'Neal (1992–present)
All of these men except for Olajuwon and O'Neal are Hall of Famers.

THE TECHNIQUE: **Varied. Most centers know how to play both the high and low post; that is, facing the basket and with one's back to the basket. The best high post position is at the head of the key or farther out, facing the basket, to enable the center to pass to teammates who are cutting and screening or to shoot or drive. A good low-post player will set up on either side of the basket with his back to the hoop. Again, this position enables a player to pass or shoot. The most important thing to remember when playing the low post is to protect the ball by positioning your body between it and your defender.**

And retain your position in the low post. If you have to, lean on the man guarding you, but don't be knocked away from where you've set up.

Above: Shaq, the master of the low post.

Right: Wilt Chamberlain goes up for the shot.

It was one of a hundred or so games the Original Celtics would play on the road that year (1923). And as usual, it was in a strange town hundreds of miles from home. But the Chattanooga Railites had offered the team a pretty good guarantee, and the Celtics would have otherwise taken a train straight from Miami to New York. So a stopoff for a few extra bucks in Chattanooga was probably a good idea.

The Railites (named because the team was sponsored by a local transit company) were about average for the type of teams the Celtics usually played: a couple of halfway decent athletes, a couple of head-knockers, nothing special.

But the Railites had an unusual strategy: they posted one of their players at the foul line in a sort of one-man zone. And the guy kept breaking up the Celtics' passes.

Was it a problem? Not really. The Celtics were pretty much kicking butt and taking names. But it was annoying. And at halftime, Celtic center Henry Dehnert (1920–41) told his mates that he would stand in front of the guy, take passes and feed his teammates. And that's what he did. And thus, the pivot play was born.

Strictly speaking, there were other players before Dehnert who stationed themselves around the key, took passes and either shot or fed teammates. But it wasn't really a regular strategy until the Big Dutchman and the Celtics worked it out.

And initially, of course, one didn't have to be a member of the seven-foot club to play the pivot. Dehnert was six feet tall. But his opponents weren't much bigger, and besides, his role was to pass and set screens, not necessarily to shoot.

Dehnert was, for the most part, a high post player. And in fact, pivot play itself was restricted to the high post for many years. It wasn't until the hook shot became more prevalent that coaches would move their players closer to the basket to maneuver against opponents on the baseline.

Top: Chamberlain scores against Cincinnati Royals' Greg Lucas(16), Happy Hairston(22), and Guy Rodgers (5).
Left: Utah Jazz Karl Malone battles for position against Magic Johnson

The most famous moment in pivotry came early in the 1959–60 season. Rookie superstar Wilt Chamberlain (1959–74) was making his debut in Boston Garden with Philadelphia. It would be the first time he would face the Celtics' big man, Bill Russell (1956–69).

Chamberlain was 7' 1", 240 pounds, a fearsome physical specimen who was already averaging almost 40 points a game up to that point. He seemed unstoppable and his team, the Philadelphia Warriors, were still unbeaten (3–0).

But so were the Celtics (5–0). And they had the most effective defensive force on the planet in Russell. It was a matchup that captured the imagination of basketball fans across the country. Think of what ESPN would have done with this!

Wilt played well, with 30 points and 30 rebounds. But Russell scored 22 points and grabbed 35 rebounds. He also blocked several of Chamberlain's shots. Boston won, 115–106, as the basketball world heaved a sigh of relief. The unstoppable had been stopped. At least that night.

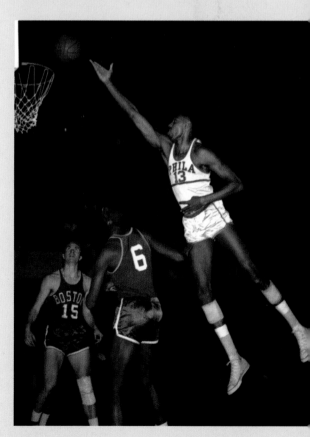

Above: Chamberlain (13) grabbed 30 points and 30 rebounds in a game against the Celtics early in the '59-'60 season.

The Twin Towers, and More

Six years before, the Minneapolis Lakers had been one of the smallest teams in the league. During the 1953–54 season, with the acquisition of former Kansas All-American Clyde Lovelette via the draft, they became the biggest.

Lakers coach John Kundla often played the 6' 11" Lovelette, 6' 10" Mikan and 6' 8" Vern Mikkelson along the front line with the 6' 4" Pollard and the 5' 9" Slater Martin in the backcourt. The backup center was 6' 9" Lew Hitch.

In the playoffs, the Lakers were, if you will pardon the expression, head and shoulders above every other team in terms of rebounds, easily averaging the most rebounds per game.

In Game 5 of the NBA Finals, the Lakers won the game, 84–73, and just destroyed the Nationals on the backboards, 65–37. Mikan led the way with 16 rebounds, Pollard had 14, Mikkelson 12 and Lovelette 10.

This was the last year before the 24-second clock was introduced, and the relatively slow tempo of the pro game made it easy for the Lakers to slow the game down and pound the ball in low.

Although fans talk about the Boston Celtics Hall of Fame front line of Larry Bird, Robert Parish, Kevin McHale and Bill Walton, this edition of the Lakers was the original Hall of Fame front line. Mikan, Pollard, Mikkelson and Lovelette are all in the Hall. Although, frankly, with Walton, McHale and Bird already there, no one will bet against Parish reaching that milestone, as well.

The first team at any level to feature two seven-foot players in the same starting lineup were the Jacksonville Dolphins in the 1969–70 NCAA season.

The Dolphins, who went to the NCAA finals that season, featured 7' 2" center Artis Gilmore and 7' forward Pembrook Burrows III. Gilmore (1971–88) went on to a stellar professional career. Burrows, drafted in the fourth round by the Seattle Supersonics in 1971, never played in the NBA.

Interestingly, Dolphins coach Joe Williams would often use 6' 10" backup center Rod McIntyre on the front line as well, giving the Dolphins a lineup that averaged seven feet all along the front three.

But in the end, in the NCAA Finals, the Dolphins couldn't outplay the quicker, smaller Bruins of UCLA: 6' 9" center Steve Patterson, 6' 8" forward Sidney Wicks and 6' 6" forward Curtis Rowe. The Bruins outrebounded the Dolphins, 50–39, and won the game, 80–69.

Mikan, The Main Man

There were rough-and-tumble centers who rebounded, played defense close to the goal and were effective on tap-ins and getting offensive rebounds. Ed Wachter (various leagues, 1896–1918) comes to mind: a tough six-footer who knew his way around the basket and wasn't afraid to give as good as he got.

But the first player to play almost exclusively in the low post his entire career was 6' 9" center Mike Novak, who played nine years in the NBL (1939–48), and then three more years in the NBA.

Novak was a very big man in the pros in the late 1930s and early 1940s. He was not much of a scorer. He didn't have an effective hook shot and his moves in the pivot were limited. But he set himself under the basket for tip-ins and offensive rebounds and his size alone caused havoc with teams. Novak was the first real low post center in pro basketball.

But the first player to park in the low post and make a living off of pivot play was George Mikan (1946–56), of the Minneapolis Lakers.

The low post was heaven on earth for Big George. For one thing, prior to the 1951–52 season, the lane was only six feet across. (The new rule change widened it to 12 feet.) That meant that the 6' 10", 255-pound Mikan was three feet from pay dirt. With his devastating hook shot, Mikan was the original "Money" before Michael Jordan ever had that name bestowed upon him.

And the Lakers didn't waste him. They slowed the tempo down and pounded the ball in low. If teams double-teamed Mikan, as they inevitably did, he would pass it to a cutting teammate or out to the perimeter for another mate to take a set shot.

But centers were not the only players to post up their opponents. The Lakers, for example, often posted up "Jumpin' Jim" Pollard (1947–55), who could shoot over just about anyone. Red Auerbach, when he was coaching the Washington Capitols

Left: George Mikan in the low post.

low post and score. Both are in the Hall of Fame now.

Other big men, such as 6' 7" Alex Groza (1949–51) of Indianapolis and 6' 8" Dolph Schayes (1948–64), before Dolph was moved to forward, played out on the perimeter and tortured foes with long-range shots. Groza pushed the high post envelope even further than that; he could run up and down the court all day, and worked at beating a larger opponent down the court for easy layups.

When Mikan retired in 1956, the next real low post scoring machine didn't come

(1946–48), used to love to pull 6' 8" center John Mahnken (1946–53) away from the hoop and post up 6' 4" guard Bob Feerick (1945–50). It was a tactic Auerbach used when he came to the Celtics in 1950, and very soon after, many other coaches copied it.

The High Post Players

But there was more than one way to skin a cat, and there was more than one way to play the pivot. Centers with not as much beef as Mikan stayed in the high post, passed and set screens. The Rochester Royals' Arnie Risen (1945–58) and Ed Macauley (1949–59), of the Celtics and St. Louis Hawks, were two of the best at this tactic. Risen was the better passer, Macauley the better screen-setter.

And, if need be, both Risen and Macauley were always able to set up in the

Above: New York Knicks' Patrick Ewing pivots around Shaquille O'Neal
Top: David Robinson tries to work around Utah Jazz' Karl Malone

Five Great Centers You May Not Know Of

Well, we all know about Kareem, and Wilt and Shaq, but here are a couple of post players that have eluded the limelight over the years for one reason or another. (Note: we didn't go back too far into the early days of the pro game, mostly because the men of that era weren't big men in the most basic sense of the word. They were mostly guys 6' 3" to 6' 5" and not the giants we know as centers today. Otherwise, Ed Wachter (6' 2") and Joe Lapchick (6' 5") would be on this list.)

Bob Kurland, 7', Phillips 66ers (1946–52)

Well, obviously, he's not totally unknown, because he's in the Hall of Fame. But the last time he laced them up was in the early 1950s, so maybe a few people have forgotten that "Foothills" as Kurland was known, is one of the all-time greats. He held his own and sometimes outplayed George Mikan when Mikan was a star at DePaul and Kurland manned the middle for Oklahoma A&M (now known as Oklahoma State). And let's remember, it was Kurland, not Mikan, who won back-to-back NCAA championships in 1945 and 1946. Kurland is also the first American to win two Olympic gold medals in basketball, annexing in 1948 and 1952.

Alex Groza, 6' 7", Indianapolis Olympians (1949–51)

This guy was the Dave Cowens of the 1940s: a quick, agile player who faced the basket, but played the center position with aggressiveness and energy. Groza was a star at the University of Kentucky, where he led his team to an NCAA title in 1948, but he blossomed as a pro. Groza could dribble, pass and shoot and with no zones to hinder him, and was hellish to guard. He could hit baskets from outside if an opponent didn't come after him, and if the opponent did, Groza would drive around him. Groza was All-NBA his only two years in the league. But his undoing was that he was identified as one of the college players who accepted money to shave points in the college basketball scandals of the early 1950s. He and several Indianapolis teammates were banned from the league for life.

Arnie Risen, 6' 9", Indianapolis, Rochester, Boston (1945–58)

Another guy that's in the Hall of Fame, but whose contributions to the game have been all but forgotten. "Stilts," as he was called, was an exceptional passer and a rugged rebounder, despite his somewhat thin frame (6' 9", 200 pounds). Risen was also a strong defender and led the Rochester Royals to the 1951 NBA championship. It was the only time in six years in the NBA and a seventh season in the NBL that a team with other than George Mikan at center won a professional championship. Risen also showed himself to be the consummate professional his last two years in Boston. He clearly had to step aside when the Celtics picked up rookie Bill Russell. But he also acted as Russell's mentor and advisor, a gesture Russell graciously acknowledged in his first autobiography. This man, folks, was where the so-called Celtic Tradition began.

Mel Daniels, 6' 9", Indiana Pacers, Memphis Pros, New York Nets (1967–77)

Walter Bellamy is in the Hall of Fame and this guy isn't? Sheesh. This tough, competitive big man (think Alonzo Mourning in the ABA) was the American Basketball Association's first big man. He led the Indiana Pacers to a record three ABA titles and a record five appearances in the ABA Finals. A tireless rebounder, Mighty Mel gave the Pacers a presence in the paint that no team in the league had until the Kentucky Colonels drafted Artis Gilmore in 1971. A two-time ABA MVP, a four-time All-ABA center and the league's first Rookie of the Year, Daniels was one of the all-time great players no matter what league he played in.

Uljana Semjonova, 7' 1", USSR (1967–89)

Sorry. This is not a male-only category. The 7' 1" Semjonova was certainly the most dominating female athlete in the history of basketball, and a case could easily be made that she was the most dominating basketball player of any sex.

No, Semjonova would not have been able to play for the 1964 Boston Celtics. What we're saying here is that she dominated the women's basketball world, as completely, or more completely, than even Boston center Bill Russell.

Semjonova was not a tremendous scorer, although she had career highs of 54 points and 46 points in international play. She was, however, an intimidating shot blocker, once rejecting 22 shots in a game, and many times recording double figures in blocks. She was also a strong rebounder, a great low-post player, an excellent passer and a solid free-throw shooter.

Semjonova was, in short, an excellent all-around center whose principal strength was that, as long as she was at the top of her game, she never lost a game in international play.

That's right. Semjonova played for the Soviet National team, and in 18 years, her side didn't lose. The Russians won 11 European titles (played every other year), three world championships (played every four years) and two Olympic titles. Those are Russell-like numbers, and the casual hoop fan could do worse than read up on this woman's remarkable career.

Right: Kareem Abdul-Jabbar, playing here for UCLA, became one of the greatest post players in the game.

down the turnpike until 7' 2" Wilt Chamberlain made his debut in 1959. Wilt had a power game that did not include a hook shot; he just muscled his way to the hoop and dunked. But Wilt also had a nice touch: he had a fadeaway jumper and a graceful finger roll in his arsenal, as well.

Chamberlain was another step in the evolution of the post game in that he was the first of the really big and agile seven-footers. There had been seven-foot players before Wilt, notably 7' Don Otten (1946–53), who played in both the NBL and the early NBA. But Otten was shaped more in the Mike Novak mold: a big man who camped close to the basket and stayed there all night. As the saying went, after everyone was tired, he was still tall.

Wilt was something much, much more. He could outjump every other player in the league, including the Celtics' Bill Russell. He could outrun every center in the league, with the occasional exception of Russell. And he was, by far, the strongest man in the history of the game to that point.

Chamberlain was such a quantum jump, both physically and athletically, in the center position, that he set records that will never be topped: averaging 50.4 points per game in the 1961–62 season; scoring 100 points that same year; averaging 44.8 points the next season; averaging 30 points per game for a 14-year career; shooting 68 percent from the field in 1966–67, 65 percent in 1971–72 and 73 percent in 1972–73.

Right: Tim Duncan puts one up over Toronto Raptors center Hakeem Olajuwon.

MOST BLOCKED SHOTS PER MINUTES PLAYED, ALL-TIME

This stat, another Harvey Pollock beauty, measures the amount of time between blocks for each player.

Manute Bol (1985–95)	
a block every 5.61 minutes	
Mark Eaton (1982–93)	
a block every 8.21 minutes	
George T. Johnson (1972–86)	
a block every 8.33 minutes	
Shawn Bradley (1993–present)	
a block every 8.80 minutes	
Tree Rollins (1977–95)	
a block every 9.45 minutes	

Above: Olajuwon shoots over Utah Jazz' Karl Malone (32) and Greg Ostertag.

"At one point in the [1961–62] season, I was averaging around 54 points per game," recalled Chamberlain in an interview. "I was concerned; I didn't want to set the bar too high. So I cut back on my scoring a bit as the season wound down."

Think about that: the guy basically eased up!

It was difficult to imagine a player better than Chamberlain in the low post. But in 1969, the Milwaukee Bucks drafted 7' 2" center Lew Alcindor out of UCLA. Alcindor, who eventually changed his name to Kareem Abdul-Jabbar, was not as strong as Chamberlain. But he was actually more graceful, and his hook shot, which he could convert with either hand, became the most devastating low post weapon in the history of the game.

Fourteen years after Abdul-Jabbar's retirement, and 18 years after he terrorized centers with what sportswriters dubbed the "Sky Hook," it is tough to describe how nearly automatic the shot was. Abdul-Jabbar was regularly double-teamed every night, and for most of his career, officials let players hammer him in the pivot. But in his glory years, between 1969 and 1984, Abdul-Jabbar still converted on almost 60 percent of his shots.

Big Red Arrives

In 1970, the Boston Celtics were in dire need of a center to replace departed all-time All-Star Bill Russell (1956–69). The team's decision to draft 6' 8" center David Cowens out of Florida State did not seem to be the answer. Most publications had Cowens listed as a forward, and pre-season predictions had Cowens fighting for a slot on the front line with Celtic veterans Don Nelson (1962–76) and Thomas "Satch" Sanders (1960–73).

Nobody really asked Cowens what he thought, which was unfortunate. "Big Red" as he was known, was determined to play center, and very soon it was clear that what David wanted, he usually got.

Cowens turned the center position on its head. He ran like a deer, all game. He could jump through the ceiling, he had an excellent outside jump shot, he set bruising screens and, when needed, could post up smaller or less agile opponents down low and either drive around them or loft a hook over them.

And he dove for loose balls.

Understand, big men didn't dive for loose balls, for obvious reasons. No big men did this. Not Wilt, not Abdul-Jabbar, not Mikan, not Bill Russell. It was just too far to go. By the time Wilt Chamberlain tried to get down on the floor for a loose ball, a smaller man could easily have gotten there first and picked it up himself.

Cowens not only dove for loose balls, he would dive for loose balls 15 feet away from him. He would dive for loose balls that were almost out of bounds. He would dive for loose balls even when it appeared that an opponent would get possession. It was, for the other team, incredibly intimidating to see a 6' 8", redheaded madman lunging after a ball and sliding like a trained seal along the floor. Who wanted to contest that?

Cowens also switched out on picks. He would switch on a pick 20 feet from the basket, and the sight of him lunging toward an opponent, waving his arms and jumping around, often unnerved whatever poor ballhandler happened to be trying to make a play.

"He's like a 6' 8" Jerry West," said New York Knickerbocker Jerry Lucas (1963–74), in an interview in 1974.

Cowens helped the Celtics to a pair of NBA titles, won the MVP award in the 1972–73 season and played in six All-Star games.

PLAYERS TO WATCH

Shaq calls himself LCL (Last Center Left), and he's almost right. If you let him have any kind of position in the low post, it's a dunk. And with his strength, it's almost impossible not to let him have that position. There are other guys who play the low post well. The Spurs' Tim Duncan is the second-best player in the league when it comes to playing with his back to the basket. And among midsized players, Shareef Abdur-Rahim of the Atlanta Hawks and the Kings' Chris Webber are the two best at getting the ball in the low post and either hitting a turn-around or kicking it out to a shooter on the perimeter.

In the early days of basketball, there were very few gyms devoted exclusively to basketball. In fact, at the turn of the 20th century, most places created basketball spaces by tacking a hoop to the wall. Some of those places, like the basements of churches and schools, held the ceiling up by means of posts. And these posts, of course, were often in the field of play. Some enterprising teams would run unsuspecting opponents into these posts. So many of the veteran barnstorming teams, like the New York Rens or the Original Celtics, would warn their teammates by yelling "High post!" if the post was near the head of the key or foul line, or "Low post!" if it was near the baseline. And that's where those terms came from.

Left: Shaq, who calls himself LCL (Last Center Left) moves the ball as New Jersey Nets' Todd MacCulloch attempts to block.

The biggest improvement of this latest era in post play is how well even big men handle the ball. The Lakers' Shaquille O'Neal (1992–present) is not afraid to electrify the crowd by taking a rebound and dribbling coast-to-coast as the center man on the fast break. A scant 15 years ago, no center would attempt that. Yet O'Neal is only the best of many big men who can do that, including the Spurs' Tim Duncan (1997–present) and David Robinson (1989–present), and the Timberwolves' Kevin Garnett (1995–present).

O'Neal's power game is his bread and butter. But most observers who are not Lakers fans don't see how smooth his footwork is and how well he moves in the open court. In terms of big, mobile centers, Shaquille O'Neal may well be near the end of the evolutionary line. And if he's not, it will be frightening to see someone better.

19 The Scorers
Putting Up the Numbers

ORIGIN: March 12, 1892

THE FIRST: Edwin P. Ruggles, Springfield College

THE ALL-TIMERS:
Nat Holman (1916-33)
Bobby McDermott (1930-53)
Elgin Baylor (1958-72)
Rick Barry (1965-80)
George Gervin (1972-86)
Larry Bird (1979-92)
Michael Jordan (1984-93
1995-98, 2001-present)
Everybody except Jordan
is in the Hall of Fame
Jordan is pending

THE TECHNIQUE:
No single technique. Review films of Larry Bird and Elgin Baylor. Do the best you can. Practice shooting off either foot, with either hand. Understand that the only way to win is to put the ball in the basket.

Never give up on a field goal attempt. If you miss, follow your shot. If you feel yourself being pushed or fouled, shoot the ball anyway. You may draw a whistle.

Above: George Gervin knew how to put the ball in the basket.
Above inset: Allan Iverson gets points any which way he can.

There is a difference between being a shooter and being a scorer, hence this chapter. Shooters can be scorers, but some scorers aren't necessarily shooters. Conversely, some shooters aren't very good scorers. Got that?

A shooter is a guy who can stand out on the perimeter all day long and drain long shots, whether they be set shots or jumpers or even hook shots. Joey Hassett (1977–83) was a shooter. John Roche (1971–82) was a shooter. Trent Tucker (1982–93) was a shooter. None of these guys were big scorers.

Conversely, a scorer is a guy who can do a little of everything well and always seems to find a way to put the ball in the basket. John Havlicek (1962–78) was a scorer. George Gervin (1972–86) was a scorer. Michael Jordan (1984–93, 1995–98, 2001–present) is a scorer.

The absolute first scorer was a fellow named Edwin P. Ruggles. He was a member of Dr. James Naismith's "first team," that class at Springfield College that first played the game in December of 1891.

In March of 1982, several members of that first squad played a bunch of students from the college. The final score was 5–1, and Ruggles scored four of the baskets. Clearly, he understood the game, and understood how to score.

Nat Holman (various leagues, 1916–33) was another of the earliest great scorers, because he could draw fouls while dribbling. In fact, consider this: Nat Holman and World B. Free (1975–88) were a lot alike, in that they were both extremely good at drawing fouls. Holman had a move where he would dribble into a player and bounce away like he had been struck, often drawing sympathetic whistles.

Free, 42 years later, developed a move whereby he would shoot and kick his legs into an opponent. Not surprisingly, opposing fans hated Free in the 1970s and 1980s as much as they despised Holman a few decades previously.

Holman's career overlapped that of 5' 11" guard Bobby McDermott's (1930–53) by only a few years, but Bobby clearly picked up a lot of that Holman acting ability. McDermott, in fact, took Holman's little act a step further: he would get hit (or more often, flop into someone), and reel away.

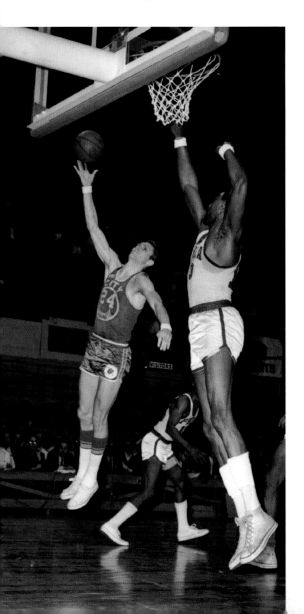

Left: Rick Barry (24) of the San Francisco Warriors, with the hook shot against Philadelphia in 1967.

November 15, 1960, Madison Square Garden, Lakers vs. Knicks

Elgin Baylor's mantra was the same as that of Malcolm X, but the intent was a little less radical: "By any means necessary." Elg, as his teammates called him, could shoot from the outside, bang with just about anybody inside, and score from just about anywhere else in between.

In the early part of the 1960–61 season, Elg just kicked tail one night at Madison Square Garden. He scored 71 points to set a new NBA scoring record, on 28 field goals and 15 free throws. He also had 25 rebounds as the Lakers defeated the New York Knicks. To commemorate the event, Lakers owner Robert Short had cufflinks made up with the number "71" embossed on them and gave them to each member of the team. It was the second consecutive year Baylor broke the NBA scoring record. The year before, he had scored 64 points against the Celtics to break Joe Fulks's scoring record of 63 points, set in 1949.

"Baylor was as unpredictable as he was unstoppable," said Robert L. Teague, a sportswriter for the *New York Times*. "He counted quite a few points on driving layups and tap-ins, but a good number came from angles that seemed impossible."

Baylor had not been happy with his shooting the past few games. (Must be nice: he got 45 against Philadelphia two days before.) So during the afternoon prior to the game at Madison Square Garden, he took extra shooting practice with a few teammates.

Above: Elgin Baylor driving for the hoop against Golden State Warriors' McCoy McLemore in 1965.

Above: Larry Bird the consummate scorer, drives to the basket again.
Right: Here, Barry heads for two points against the New York Knicks.

Then he would find the official and cast a stunned look his way. Sometimes, although not every time, an official would be influenced McDermott's way.

McDermott sometimes took it a step further. If the official didn't start calling the game the way McDermott thought it should be, Bobby would not hesitate to physically threaten a ref. It was one measure to ensure things went your way.

If being a great shooter is about jumping straight up in the air, squaring one's shoulders and arching the wrists, being a good scorer is exactly the opposite. The common thread that runs through all good scorers is the ability to take (and make) difficult shots, twisting one's body hither and yon and releasing the ball at awkward angles.

The Greatest Ever?

Elgin Baylor was perhaps the best at this in the history of the league. He was a 6' 5" forward with tremendous spring and Herculean upper body strength. He liked to shoot with one hand and put backspin on the ball, like a giant cueball. Sometimes, when he was being defensed out of position for a halfway decent shot, Baylor would actually shoot the ball at the backboard and miss on purpose, then try to retrieve the rebound for another shot.

As Celtics legend Bill Russell once said, "Give Elgin credit for even having the imagination to try something like that, let alone accomplish it."

As if his skill level weren't enough, Baylor also had a nervous facial tic that resembled a head fake. It was inadvertent, but it would happen at odd times, and to many of his opponents, it was distracting.

A number of his contemporaries believe that Baylor's feat in the 1961–62 season of

Wilt's Biggest Night

We all know that Wilt Chamberlain scored 100 points on March 2, 1962, at Hershey, Pennsylvania. It remains the greatest single individual effort in NBA history. No player in the league today has a legitimate shot at breaking that record, because no player physically dominated the league so completely as Wilt did that year.

But how the hell did he do it?

"The night I scored 50 in a game, I was exhausted," said Hall of Famer Dolph Schayes (1948–64) in an interview on the 40th anniversary of the game. "I can't imagine scoring 100."

First of all, according to Wilt's former teammate, Al Attles (1960–71), what no one remembers about the Wilt of the early 1960s was that the Big Guy could *Move*, with a capital "M."

"I know he's going to be laughing at me up there, wherever he is now," said Attles recently (Chamberlain died in 1999). "But we used to have races all the time, and he and I were the fastest guys on the [Warriors]. I would say I beat him, but he would say he beat me."

But he was fast. The NBA wasn't on television much when Wilt was younger, so people only saw him later in his career when he was bulked up. But in those first few years, he got up and down the court better than most other players, let alone most other centers.

Also, according to Attles, Wilt was a terrific leaper and very agile.

"And that night," said Attles, "he was hitting his free throws, too."

Chamberlain was 28 for 32 from the line, in addition to his 36 for 63 from the field.

By the way, if you'd like to win a bet, Attles had the best scoring night, percentage-wise, of the evening. He hit all eight of his shots and his only free throw for a perfect night.

Right: Jordan drives passed Shaq.

Left: George Gervin at the hoop, surrounded by 76ers.

averaging 38.3 points per game was even more impressive than Wilt Chamberlain's season average of 50.4 that same year. Wilt, at 7' 2", 240 pounds, was the biggest player on the court every time he played. Baylor, on the other hand, at 6' 5", 225 pounds was often the smallest forward on the court, trying to score baskets against players a half foot taller.

In his autobiography, *Confessions of a Basketball Gypsy*, the 6' 7" Barry admitted that he tried to emulate Baylor's offensive style. Barry wasn't quite the muscleman Baylor was, but he was an excellent leaper who could take shots from odd angles that would often go in. If they didn't, Barry could often draw contact and go to the line. And as a free-throw shooter, Barry had few peers.

John Havlicek was another player who used to be able to turn a lemon of a shot into a lemonade move. Once, Havlicek was driving for a layup against the Phoenix Suns in 1970. Phoenix center Mel Counts (1964–76), a former teammate of Havlicek's, wanted to prevent him from scoring. So Mel wrapped his arms around Havlicek as he drove to the basket, pinning Havlicek's arms to his side.

But Havlicek, arms jammed at his side, flipped the basketball at the net with sort of a two-handed underhand toss. The ball, of course, went in, and Havlicek was also given a free throw, which he converted. This was the lesson Havlicek and other scorers learned at some early point in their career: no matter what, don't be afraid to attempt the shot. The worst thing that can happen is you miss.

In the NBA of the 21st century, body control is now called athleticism, and a majority of NBA players can do what Barry, Free and Havlicek used to.

PLAYERS TO WATCH

Allen Iverson of Philadelphia is one of those players who gets points all different ways: jump shots, three-point baskets, drives to the hoop. He is one of the best in the league at that, along with Kevin Garnett of the Timberwolves. The Celtics' Paul Pierce is another guy who can get buckets in a variety of ways. Iverson sets up his jump shot by driving. Pierce sets up his drive by hitting jumpers. Same result.

CHAMBERLAIN'S STATS BY PERIODS
1st quarter
FG: 7–14, FT: 9–9, REB: 10, AST: 0, PTS: 23
2nd quarter
FG: 7–12, FT: 4–5, REB: 4, AST: 1, PTS: 18
3rd quarter
FG: 10–16, FT: 8–8, REB: 6, AST: 1, PTS: 28
4th quarter
FG: 12–21, FT: 7–10, REB: 5, AST: 0, PTS: 31
Totals
FG: 36–63, FT: 28–32, REB: 25, AST: 2, PTS: 100

Note: Chamberlain set the record for most points in one period, 28, in the third period of the game, then broke that record in the next quarter with 31 points.

Note: The Warriors won the game, 169–147. They had four men in double figures and another man, Chamberlain, in triple figures. And New York Knicks center Cleveland Buckner (1961–63) had his career high that night, with 33 points.

Ice, Ice Baby

At 6' 7", George "Iceman" Gervin was primarily an outside shooter. But he could also drive to the hoop, and his finger rolls, which he would often flip just beyond the reach of much bigger players, were a joy to watch.

Gervin was called "Iceman" or "Ice" when he got to the ABA. Why?

"Because he was just so cool," said former ABA teammate Rolard Taylor.

Gervin had a funny jump shot, in that he held the ball off to the side before he released it. But Ice hit 51 percent of those shots and averaged 26 points per game in the NBA.

Unlike Gervin, or Michael Jordan, or even Rick Barry, Larry Bird's principal asset was not leaping ability or any particular agility. No, Larry was so great because he knew he was great.

Bird took shots from all angles and with both hands. In a 1981 NBA playoff game against the Houston Rockets, Bird shot, missed, followed up the shot, grabbed the rebound as he was falling out of bounds, transferred the ball from his right hand to his left and tossed in a basket.

In an exhibition game in Hartford against the Houston Rockets prior to the 1986–87 season, Bird recovered a rebound as he was falling out of bounds. He spun in midair and, falling away, shot the ball over the backboard. It went in (but it wasn't a field goal, because shots from behind the backboard didn't count). Still, it was a stunning affirmation of Bird's ability to score from anywhere over half court.

And even beyond. During the 1987–1988 season, Celtic coach K.C. Jones told his team that practice would be called off if anyone could make a shot from past half court. Bird

Left: Gervin goes up for two.

didn't even hesitate, launching the ball from midcourt and swishing it to the cheers of his teammates.

The modern scorer is, like Michael Jordan, Vince Carter, Kobe Bryant, Jerry Stackhouse and others, primarily a tremendous athlete. He is a player who can twist and contort his body and get off almost any kind of shot. The aforementioned gentlemen are the best in the league at it. They regularly inhabit ESPN's Sports Center and are also among the top point-makers in the NBA. Because in the end, the scorers all have to, well, score.

Above: Boston Celtic's Paul Pierce (34) drives on Detroit Piston's Corliss Williamson.
Above right: Wilt Chamberlain after scoring 100 points against the New York Knicks on March 2, 1962.

Underestimating Selvy

The Milwaukee Hawks acquired two great rookies, 6' 9" forward Bob Pettit (1954–65) from LSU, and 6' 2" guard Frank Selvy (1954–64) from Furman at the beginning of the 1954–55 season. Pettit was fourth in the league in scoring that season, averaging 20.4 points per game, and Selvy was fifth, averaging 19.0. It marked the only time in NBA history that two rookies from the same team were in the top five scorers in the league.

This was a reverse of the previous season for the two men. Pettit had been the second-leading scorer in the NCAA the year before, and Selvy the leading scorer. For most of the 1953–54 college season, the two men were neck-and-neck for a while. On February 13, 1954, Pettit had a big game against Georgia Tech, scoring 46 points.

In his autobiography, Pettit recalled that he was aware that Selvy and Furman were playing Newberry College the same night. Pettit figured that if Selvy hit between 30 and 32 points, he, Pettit, would take over the scoring lead. The next day, Pettit opened the newspaper and had to look again to make sure he had read the story correctly: Selvy had dropped 100 points on Newberry. So much for the scoring race.

Selvy ended up averaging a then-record 41 points per game, with Pettit second in the country with a 31.4 average.

20 The Garbage Men's Moves

The Guys Who Do All the Dirty Work

THE ORIGIN: Sometime in the 1940s

THE FIRST: Vern Mikkelsen (1949–59), Mineapolis Lakers, was the best known early player.

THE ALL-TIMERS:
Mikkelsen, Rudy LaRusso (1959-69)
Bailey Howell (1959-71)
Tom Washington (1968-73)
Wendell Ladner (1970-75)
Charles Oakley (1985-present)
Ben Wallace (1996-present)
Mikkelsen and Howell are in the Hall of Fame.

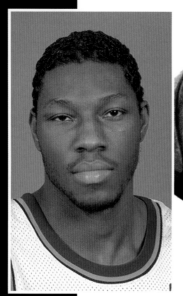

Right: Bailey Howell could battle under the boards with the best.
Left: Ben Wallace, an upper-echelon putback player.

THE TECHNIQUE:
It's mostly desire. In fact, of all the chapters in this book, the "technique" and evolution of this particular category has been pretty flat over the years. If Vern Mikkelsen were reincarnated as a player in 2002, he would almost certainly be just as effective as he was in 1952. In fact, he would make the All-Star team.

You don't have to be fast, or quick, or, in Wendell Ladner's case, even particularly tall. You just have to want to mix it up underneath and contribute. It's about playing hard and eschewing the credit, more than anything learned.

However, the unwritten rule in the NBA and WNBA is, always clip your nails. And if you want to keep your nose intact, no elbows above the neck.

Rebounding and scoring off missed shots: it's a dirty job, but someone has to do it. And if a team has such a someone, they usually win more than they lose.

This is a chapter about a lot of players the casual pro basketball fan will know little about. That's because the duties of the so-called "garbage man" are not particularly telegenic. Even if Wendell Ladner or Rudy LaRusso had played in the 1990s, you would not have seen them on ESPN too often, if at all.

The whole concept of a "garbage man" began in the 1940s, with Minneapolis Lakers forward Vern Mikkelsen (although no one really called it that for several more years). Mikkelsen was a 6' 9" center, who graduated from tiny Hamline University and was drafted by the Lakers.

The Lakers, of course, already had a big man: 6' 11" center George Mikan. Although they had Mikan, the rest of the team was relatively small. For the Lakers' first year in the NBA, the 1948–49 season, the next tallest regular on the Laker roster was 6' 5" forward "Jumpin'" Jim Pollard, who also doubled as the Lakers' backup center.

Lakers coach John Kundla initially wanted to use Mikan and Mikkelsen in a double-post offense. As attractive as that seemed, it didn't work very well for the Lakers. Instead of creating scoring opportunities, Mikan and Mikkelsen seemed to get in each other's way. Kundla quickly decided to refocus the offense with Mikan at the center of it.

Mikkelsen, then, had to learn to play forward. He had to learn to be a part of a team that ran more plays for other starters, specif-

ically Mikan and Pollard. That he did it without complaint speaks volumes about his professionalism and desire to win, rather than to accumulate statistics.

There may have been players before Mikkelsen who accepted similar roles, but they were few and far between. Big scorers in pro basketball were scarce, and big scorers who played up front were rarer still. Mik, as Mikan often called his teammate, was one of the first, and one of the best, helping the Lakers to four NBA championships and winning a spot in the Hall of Fame in 1995.

Roughhouse Rudy

In 1959, Mikkelsen played his final season. He was scoring as well as ever, but his

May 4, 1968, ABA Finals, Game 7, New Orleans vs. Pittsburgh

Tom "Trooper" Washington (1968–73) was a 6' 7" forward who was possibly the worst shooter from more than five feet out in the American Basketball Association. Yet in the first year of the league, Washington led the ABA in shooting percentage with a .523 average and was also one of the best rebounders.

The secret to his field goal success was an awareness of his range limitations and Pittsburgh Piper teammate Connie Hawkins, the best passing big man of the 1960s. Hawkins would swoop into the lane, drawing the double-team, and dish the ball to Washington, who would dutifully lay it in.

The secret of his rebounding success against bigger opponents was even easier to see: Washington wanted the ball more than they did.

These two traits made Washington the perfect garbage man and maybe the best ever in the ABA. He never took a bad shot and was always around the basket for rebounds or tip-ins.

In the ABA Finals against New Orleans, Washington was huge. He grabbed 25 rebounds in Game 4 as the Pipers beat New Orleans in The Big Easy, 106–105, in overtime to tie up the series. And in Game 7, Washington ripped down an ABA Finals record 27 boards to help the Pipers capture the first ABA championship with a 122–113 win.

Above: Mississippi State's Bailey Howell snatches the rebound against Tulane.
Left: New York Knicks' Charles Oakley (34) walks all over Chicago Bulls' Dennis Rodman.

rebound totals were the lowest of his career. So at 31, Mikkelsen sat down for good.

The next year, realizing that the team needed someone to help super forward Elgin Baylor on the boards, the Lakers drafted a rawboned, 6' 8" cornerman from Dartmouth named Rudy LaRusso.

LaRusso filled Mikkelsen's shoes perfectly. He was a tough kid almost from day one, not afraid to stick his nose into the melees under the basket. Sportswriters named him "Roughhouse Rudy" for his pugnaciousness. LaRusso set good picks and he knew that when the acrobatic Baylor drove the lane, he would often be double-teamed. LaRusso would cut to the basket,

Above: Oakley strips Vince Carter—and draws the foul.
Left: Howell muscles through for a shot.

and Baylor would inevitably dump the ball down to him for an easy basket.

The best garbage man ever was drafted by the Detroit Pistons the same year as LaRusso. Bailey Howell was a muscular 6' 7" forward who had been All-Southeastern Conference at Mississippi State.

Like Mikkelsen and LaRusso, Howell could battle under the boards with the best of them. Unlike Mikkelsen or LaRusso, Howell could also shoot and he could score consistently. There aren't any specific moves associated with being a good garbage man except a willingness to take a lot of punishment for the good of the team. Howell was a scorer with a high threshold for pain.

He was actually the best player the Pistons had in the mid-1960s and led Detroit to three playoff berths in five years. He was traded to Baltimore before the start of the 1964–65 season, and he starred in that city for two years. The next year, he was acquired by the Boston Celtics, and there, Howell shined.

His scoring average dipped under 20 points with Boston, but Howell quickly became a fan favorite. He was clearly the team's third offensive option behind Sam Jones and John Havlicek, but he was adept at grabbing big rebounds and was unafraid to take big shots.

And he had a little bit of nastiness in him, too. In a 1965 playoff game against the Lakers, Los Angeles guard Jerry West was tearing up the Bullets. Howell broke West's nose during a game. Unfortunately, that didn't work. West still managed to light up the Bullets for a 46-point average in the series, but Howell had tried.

A Printing Error?

Another time, according to New York Knick Dave DeBusschere, Howell was sitting on

the bench and called out to DeBusschere to ask if he was still having problems with a back injury. DeBusschere, a relatively nice guy, responded in the affirmative.

Whereupon Howell called out to Celtics rookie Steve Kuberski to crack DeBusschere in the back if DeBusschere gave Kuberski any trouble.

"Bailey," retorted DeBusschere, "I know you're listed in the program as a human

being, but sometimes I think it's a printing error." Even the Celtics' bench thought that was pretty funny.

Howell played for four years with Boston, and another year in Philadelphia before retiring.

The 1960s and early 1970s were sort of the Golden Age of garbage men. In addition to Howell, 6' 11" forward Clyde Lee toiled for San Francisco and, later, the Golden

The Best Tough Guys

These guys were tough players who were also good players

Bob Brannum (1948–55)

Forward Bob Brannum is best known for his years as the "enforcer" for the Boston Celtics throughout the 1950s. Before he went to Boston at the start of the 1950–51 season, Brannum was the best player on the Sheboygan Redskins. That doesn't sound like much, because no one remembers Sheboygan, but the Redskins had a decent team that finished fourth in the NBA's western division. Led by Brannum, they took the Indianapolis Olympians to three games in the opening round of the playoffs.

Brannum was the team's second-leading scorer with 12.1 points per game, its best passer with 205 assists and, in a foreshadowing of what was to come in Boston, the team's most physical player with 279 personal fouls.

In fact, Brannum had a high of 41 points that season on March 20 against the Denver Nuggets. It was the sixth-best scoring night of the year by an NBA player.

When Red Auerbach picked up Brannum from the Redskins, purchasing his contract for $1,000, it was, to be sure, because Brannum was 6' 5", 220 pounds, and a guy who would ensure that the rough stuff would be kept to a minimum. But Brannum could also put the ball in the hoop, and Red knew it.

Jim Loscutoff (1955–1964)

Loscutoff, or "Lusky," as coach Red Auerbach called him, or "husky Lusky," as some of the newspapers called him, looked like he was made of sculpted marble. The Celtics used him primarily as a garbage man and enforcer, but Loscutoff was an excellent trailer on the fast break and, according to Celtics guard Bob Cousy, had among the best hands on the team.

Jeff Ruland (1981–87, 1991–93)

Ruland was a 6' 10", 280-pound center from Iona College who came into the NBA with a chip on his shoulder about a

foot wide. He set great picks, was an excellent rebounder and possessed a soft, accurate jumper from mid-range. His first five years in the league, he was a solid player for the Washington Bullets, but a series of leg and knee injuries curtailed his career.

Maurice Lucas (1974–88)

In Portland, when Maurice Lucas would rip down a tough rebound, or set one of his trademark teeth-rattling picks, Trail Blazers fans would shout, "Luke, Luke, Luke,' and the chant would eventually morph into one long "Luuuuuuuuuuke." There are many observers who believe that Lucas, not center Bill Walton, was the key player in the Blazers' 1977 championship. Maybe so. It would be hard to imagine Portland winning it all that year without him.

Calvin Murphy (1970–83)

Wait a minute. Calvin Murphy? Little 5' 9", 165-pound Calvin Murphy? You bet. Murphy once grabbed Sidney Wicks by the hair, pulled himself up to the 6' 9" Wicks's face and pummeled him unmercifully. For most of his 13-year tenure with the Houston Rockets, Calvin Murphy was the toughest guy on the team and one of the toughest guys in the NBA. How do we know he was tough? Because the other thing Murphy was great at was twirling a baton, which he sometimes did during halftime of Rockets games. And friend, no one ever made fun of him for that.

Karl Malone (1985–present)

Malone is one of those players who seems to sharpen his elbows on a lathe before he goes out to play. Sooner or later, when the Jazz are playing, during a scrum under the basket, some opponent will come reeling out of the crowd, holding some portion of his anatomy. When that happens, no one ever wants to retaliate against Malone, because at 6' 9" and 255 pounds, he's just too big and nasty.

Above: Keith Van Horn gets the double-whammy from Detroit Pistons' Ben Wallace (3) and Clifford Robinson (30).

State Warriors. 6' 7" Tom Washington set picks and rebounded for several teams in the ABA, as did 6' 9" Gerald Govan (1967–76) and 6' 5" Wendell Ladner (1970–75).

As the NBA evolved into the 1980s and 1990s, these kinds of players were not called garbage men. Rather, they were euphemistically called "role" players. No matter. The job was the same.

Ladner was the best in the ABA. Many garbage men also accepted that they would have to take a role as the team enforcer. Ladner took that to almost a ridiculous extreme. When he played for Kentucky, he watched out for center Dan Issel. When he was traded to the New York Nets, he was the guardian of Nets forward Julius Erving. Interestingly, he came from the same college as Howell, Mississippi State.

Ladner fought at the drop of a hat, once drilling an opponent before the opening tap. He also dove for loose balls with an abandon that was scary. In one playoff game, he dove after a loose ball and crashed into a water cooler. Teammates recall that Ladner seemed to actually like diving over the scorers table to corral a loose ball.

He was also a handsome son-of-a-gun. Former Kentucky Colonels general manager Dave Vance recalled that, as a promotion, the Colonels posed Ladner for a poster wearing nothing but shorts. The poster sold out in a day.

Ladner played in the ABA for five years. During the 1974–75 season, he was killed in a plane crash. Erving was one of his pallbearers at his funeral.

As salaries began to escalate in the 1980s and 1990s, many NBA general managers were unwilling to kick in money for players who didn't put up big numbers. The best teams in the league, however, were still the

ones who could incorporate good garbage men into their rosters, such as the Lakers' Kurt Rambis (1981–95), the Bulls' and Knicks' Charles Oakley (1985–present) and the Celtics' Cedric Maxwell (1977–88).

In the modern playground-style NBA, players who are willing to subjugate their games and simply try to outwork their opponents are rare indeed. The irony is, they are so scarce they are extremely valuable.

Ben Wallace, a superb rebounder and defender, has been raising his stock enormously the past two seasons, despite modest scoring and rebounding totals, but his success may spur the realization that a good garbage man is as valuable as a top scorer in today's NBA.

PLAYERS TO WATCH

Shareef Abdur-Rahim of the Hawks is the Bailey Howell of the 21st century. He battles and battles underneath until he either gets fouled or scores. Or has his shot blocked, which happens a lot. The Spurs' Malik Rose is another player adept at getting position under the basket and putting back an errant shot. Ben Wallace is also in the upper echelon of putback players.

Above: Wallace blocks the shot by Miami Heat's Sean Marks.

The Rebound

The Guys Who Get the Ball for You

THE ORIGIN: The first game

THE FIRST: Joe Lapchick, of the Trinity Midgets, was one of the earliest rebounders

THE ALL-TIMERS:
Dolph Schayes (1948–64),
Harry "the Horse" Gallatin (1948–58)
Bill Russell (1956–69)
Wilt Chamberlain (1959–73)
Wes Unseld (1968–81)
Artis Gilmore (1971–88)
Dennis Rodman (1986–2000)
All but Rodman and Gilmore are in the Hall of Fame.

THE TECHNIQUE:
First, assume the shot will be missed. Then, block out your man by stepping in front of him and making contact with him. If he is much bigger, lean on him to keep him away from the basket.

Keep yourself balanced and your feet wide apart. When you set yourself in position, reach for the ball with both hands. Jump strongly at the ball. You don't have to jump high, just jump high enough to get the ball.

As soon as your fingertips touch the ball, grasp it hard. Keep the ball up, out, and away from your body. Keep your elbows bent and step away from your opponent.

Never stab at the ball with one hand, unless you are Connie Hawkins. If you must reach with only one hand (because you're holding off your opponent with your other hand), try to pull the ball into your body.

Inset: Rodman wanted every ball that caromed off the glass.
Left: Dolph Schayes turned the rebound into an art form.

In professional basketball, possession is ten-tenths of the law.

The earliest rebounders weren't specialists. For the first few decades in which basketball was played, the sport was deemed to be a lot like soccer: a fluid game in which everyone touched the ball, everyone could shoot it and everyone played defense against his opponent.

Thus, the concept of a player whose principal job was to rebound the basketball, or play defense, or just feed other players, was not really a part of the game. (Note: the concession to this concept was that, for the first 30 years basketball was in existence, one player on each team shot foul shots. But even that had soccer roots; in soccer, one man is usually designated by the coach to shoot a penalty kick.)

But coaches and team managers soon realized that a taller man, placed under the basket, had a better chance to retrieve rebounds than a shorter teammate. The irony was that initially, the tallest players' main job was to win the opening tap. As there was a jump ball after every basket until the 1930s, the team that could consistently control the tap would be in control of a game from the get-go. Positioning a taller player under the basket was almost a strategic afterthought in the early days of the game.

But that strategy ensured that a 6' 5" kid from Yonkers would become one of the early stars of the pro ranks.

Just a Guy Named Joe

Joe Lapchick was born in Yonkers, New York, in 1900. As a kid growing up, he had little to no interest in basketball. He liked to play baseball and was caddying at a local golf course when he was nine years old.

But as the saying goes, when you're tall, you don't choose basketball, basketball chooses you. In 1912, the 6' 5" Lapchick was recruited for a team called the Trinity Midgets. His two principal jobs were to win the center jump and collar rebounds off the defensive glass.

The young Joe Lapchick was tall, but ungainly. Yet that soon changed. Lapchick, eager to improve himself, began a self-imposed regimen of skipping rope, exercising and running. It clearly paid off. By 1917, Lapchick was playing for several semi-pro teams and earning $7–10 per game. Playing

April 18, 1962, NBA Finals, Game 7, Los Angeles vs. Boston

The 1962 NBA Finals between the Celtics and Lakers was a war. And with eight seconds left in regulation, this is what it had come down to: the Lakers had the ball, and a chance to win the game, which was tied at 100–100. Lakers forward Rod Hundley threw the ball in from midcourt to teammate Frank Selvy. The 6' 2" Selvy, who had once scored 100 points in a college game while playing for Furman, didn't hesitate. He threw up a jumper from the right side. Selvy's shot skidded over the top of the basket and rolled out. Celtics center Bill Russell ripped the ball down and held it until time ran out. It was the most well known rebound in NBA history. Saved from elimination, the Celtics went on to win the game in overtime, 110–107. Russell? He ended up with 40 rebounds that night.

Above: Illinois' Robert Archibald (bottom) and Lucas Johnson battle Ohio States' Velimir Radinovic for the rebound.

five or six games a week, Lapchick was earning some princely sums.

By the time he was 19, Lapchick was regularly playing for four or five professional teams. Each team usually played two games a week. Since Lapchick usually couldn't make every game, he played each team manager against the other, negotiating to play for the highest bidder.

The standard rate of pay for a good player in those days was a dollar a minute. The games were usually 48-minute games, so Lapchick was looking at about $50 per game. But he was so good, he began getting $1.50 to $2 per minute. One hundred dollars per game for "big" games was not unusual.

In 1923, Lapchick was signed by the Original Celtics, and began a barnstorming

The Triple-Double

The first recorded triple-double in NBA history was on February 8, 1951, by Dolph Schayes of Syracuse in a 96–83 win over the New York Knicks. Dolph had 18 points, 22 rebounds and 13 assists in the game. The latter figure was also an assist record for the Syracuse Arena. This was, of course, long before anyone had come up with the concept of the triple-double, so nothing was really made of it at the time, except to note that Schayes had set the assist mark.

In the 1960s, a number of players regularly made it into the triple-double pantheon. Cincinnati guard Oscar Robertson, in the 1961–62 season, averaged 30.8 points, 12.5 rebounds and 11.4 assists per game. He is the only player to ever average a triple-double, officially. His triple-doubles per game were not measured, but a quick scan of the box scores from the NBA for one season reveals that Robertson appeared to have had about 60 games in which he hit double figures in all three categories. Had the statistic been regularly tabulated in those days, Robertson would be the runaway career leader.

The triple-double stat began being tabulated in Earvin "Magic" Johnson's rookie year, 1979–80, as the official scorer in Los Angeles began to notice that Johnson would regularly accumulate double figures in points, rebounds and assists. Bird, for his part, dismissed the stat as meaningless.

"I could get those [triple-doubles] all the time if I wanted to," he said. "But it wouldn't always help the team."

career that brought him into the Hall of Fame. He played for the Celtics for 13 years, and later became a famous college and pro coach.

Lapchick's style around the basket was pretty basic: he was there to take down rebounds, and if an opponent attempted to contest him, that fellow was usually on the receiving end of a well-placed elbow, hip or knee. That was basically the way the game was played in the first half of the 20th century.

At 6' 5", Lapchick was tall, but by no means the tallest pro player out there in the 1920s and 1930s. And for a long time, the art of rebounding wasn't much of an art; the biggest guy, or the best jumper, usually latched onto the rebounds.

This trend began to alter in the late 1940s and early 1950s. Frontcourt players were now working more on blocking out and getting good position before going after rebounds. While blocking one's man off the boards was always a skill, players like Adolph "Dolph" Schayes turned it into an art form.

Dolph's Game

Schayes (1948–64) was a 6' 8" forward-center from New York University who wasn't a very good jumper. Nor was he very quick, but he could outwork almost everyone on the court. He averaged double figures in rebounds for 11 consecutive years, and it would surely have been 13 straight years had the old Basketball Association of America kept track of rebounds his first two years.

When the league finally did start keeping track of rebounding, Schayes owned the glass. In 1950–51, of the 14 top rebounding games in the league, Schayes had 10 of them, including the league-high (and NBA then-record) 35 boards against Philadelphia on December 28, 1950.

Schayes was living proof of the adage that 90 percent of all rebounds are taken below the rim. In his case, though, it was closer to 100 percent. No one remembers Dolph

Above: Chamberlain with the rebound against the Knicks' Walt Bellamy.
Above center: Harry Gallatin steals the rebound from Hal Tidrick (4) of the Baltimore Bullets.

Above: Boston Celtic's Bill Russell, a rookie here, snatches the rebound.

The Smallest Rebounders

These men were the best rebounders for their size in the pro ranks

Elgin Baylor, 6' 5", Los Angeles, (1958–72)

Baylor, in the 1960–61 season, was 13 rebounds away from averaging 20 rebounds per game that season, taking down 1,447 boards in 73 games for a 19.8 average. The next year, he averaged 18.6. Bill Russell, Wilt Chamberlain, Bob Pettit and Nate Thurmond have all had at least one season averaging 20 or more boards per game. All stood 6' 9" or more. Elgin really was amazing.

Bill Bridges, 6' 6", St. Louis, Atlanta, Philadelphia, Los Angeles, Golden State (1962–75)

Bridges averaged double figures in rebounds for 10 consecutive years and his career average was 11.9 per game. Twice, in 1966–67 and 1970–71, his average topped 15 boards per game.

Paul Silas, 6' 6", St. Louis, Atlanta, Phoenix, Boston, Denver, Seattle (1964–80)

Silas averaged double figures in rebounds in eight of his 16 NBA seasons, including a high of 13 rebounds per game his first year with the Boston Celtics, 1972–73. Silas also averaged more rebounds than points in 11 of his 16 years.

Jerry Sloan, 6' 5", Baltimore, Chicago (1965–76)

For nine of his 11 years, Sloan averaged seven rebounds a game or more. He was the Bulls' second-leading rebounder from 1970 to 1975.

Walt "Clyde" Frazier, 6' 4", New York, Cleveland (1967–80)

Clyde's biggest strength off the boards was slipping in among the big guys and picking off an offensive rebound. Frazier was the number-three rebounder on the Knicks throughout the early 1970s, behind Willis Reed and Dave DeBusschere. He averaged better than six rebounds per game for eight straight years, from 1968 to 1977.

"skying" for a stray carom. Mostly, he muscled his way under the hoop, laid an arm on an opponent's shoulder for leverage, and came away with the ball.

Schayes and fellow widebodies Larry Foust (1950–62), who was 6' 9", 250 pounds, and Harry "the Horse" Gallatin (1948–58), who was 6' 6", 220 pounds, represented the rebounders who just outworked opponents.

Gallatin, at 6' 6", never should have played anywhere but forward. But he was, for most of his career, in the pivot. Like Schayes, he was a lousy jumper and not very fast, although he was quick. But, more than even Schayes, he outtricked a lot of opponents. Gallatin by no means invented standing on a player's foot to prevent him from jumping, or waiting until a player was in the air, and then shoving them out of the way to snare rebounds. But he perfected those moves, and many others. And it worked for Harry; he was elected into the Hall of Fame in 1990.

This is not to say that the taller centers, like George Mikan (1946–56), Arnie Risen (1945–58) and "Easy Ed" Macauley (1949–59), Hall of Famers all, were not excellent rebounders. These men, however, relied more on finesse, height and quickness to get the job done. There was certainly room in the NBA for both.

The advent of the 24-second clock prior to the 1954–55 season did two things: it eliminated stalling, since teams had to shoot at least every 24 seconds, and it speeded the game up considerably.

A faster game meant more shots, which in turn meant more misses and more rebounds. This is why most individual rebound records were set in the late 1950s and 1960s, when the pro game's pace was at its most frenetic. Even the Showtime Lakers of the 1980s didn't put up as many shots as the Boston Celtics of the 1960s or their own predecessors, the Baylor-West Lakers. And they certainly didn't miss as many.

Still, only the exceptional rebounders, like Boston's Bill Russell (1956–69) and Philadelphia and San Francisco's Wilt Chamberlain (1959–73) had the stamina and will to put up the overwhelming numbers seen in that era.

Above: Wilt (13) emerges victorious from the crowd.

Off the Charts?

Russell and Chamberlain are, statistically, off the charts when it comes to rebounding. These two men own 19 of the top 20 rebounding evenings in NBA history. Wilt, with an NBA-high 55 rebounds against the Celtics in a game in 1960, has 12 of them. Russell, who had 51 boards in a game against Syracuse, also in 1960, has the other seven. Only San Francisco center Nate Thurmond, with a 42-rebound game against Detroit in 1965, cracks the list.

Their secret was blending exceptional athleticism with desire and durability. Both Russell, at 6' 9", and Chamberlain, at 7' 2", could outjump every other big man in the league, and by a wide margin. Their advantage was that they didn't rely on sheer leap-

ing ability. Russell was a master at gaining position for a rebound, while Chamberlain could outmuscle anyone in the league.

In the American Basketball Associa-tion, 7' 2" center Artis Gilmore (1971–88) used a similar combination of skills to dominate the boards in that league and later in the NBA. Gilmore had upper thighs that were bigger

Top: Shaq and Greg Ostertag jockey for the rebound.
Above: Cincinnati's Oscar Robertson flies up, spread-eagle, to catch the ball coming down during an NCAA regional elimination game against Kansas State.

BIG NIGHTS ON THE BOARDS
The top rebounding games in NBA history:

55—Wilt Chamberlain,
Philadelphia vs. Boston, 11-24-60

51—Bill Russell,
Boston vs. Syracuse, 2-5-60

49—Bill Russell,
Boston vs. Philadelphia, 11-16-57

49—Bill Russell,
Boston vs. Detroit at Providence,
3-11-65

45—Wilt Chamberlain,
Philadelphia vs. Syracuse, 2-6-60

45—Wilt Chamberlain,
Philadelphia vs. Los Angeles,
1-21-61

43—Wilt Chamberlain,
Philadelphia vs. New York,
11-10-59

43—Wilt Chamberlain,
Philadelphia vs. Los Angeles,
12-8-61 (3OT)

43—Bill Russell,
Boston vs. Los Angeles, 1-20-63

43—Wilt Chamberlain,
Philadelphia vs. Boston, 3-6-65

around than the torsos of some of his teammates. He was an explosive leaper.

So how to explain Wes Unseld (1968–81)? Here was a player who was listed at 6' 7" and was probably no more than a Gallatinish 6' 6". Yet as a rookie for the Baltimore Bullets, Unseld was second only to Chamberlain in rebounds that year and actually finished ahead of Russell with 1,491 recoveries. He became the first player since Chamberlain to win the Rookie of the Year award and Most Valuable Player award in the same season.

Unseld, at 250 pounds, was no leaper. At 6' 7" (or 6' 6"), he was the shortest center, by many inches, in the league. His secret was enormous upper-body strength, coupled with his beer-barrel legs, that enabled him to overpower much bigger opponents while holding his ground. In addition, he possessed the greatest outlet pass in the history of the game.

The outlet pass was not a new thing. Fast breaks from the 1930s were often triggered by a big player recovering a missed shot and pitching it out to a ballhandler. No big deal there. But Unseld would take a rebound off

CAREER TRIPLE-DOUBLES, 1979–2001
Magic Johnson: 138
Larry Bird: 59
Fat Lever: 42
Jason Kidd: 38
Grant Hill: 29
Michael Jordan: 28
Michael Ray Richardson: 21
Clyde Drexler: 21
Charles Barkley: 20
Scottie Pippin: 17
Mark Jackson: 17
Source: Harvey Pollock

the defensive glass and whip the ball with two hands over his head to a waiting guard 40 or 50 feet downcourt. That was a big deal.

Unseld's outlet passes were the deepest, most accurate in the league. The Bullets of the 1970s had the luxury of beginning their offense at the half-court stripe instead of the backcourt line. Unseld's outlet pass prowess became so intimidating for teams that many of Baltimore's playoff opponents assigned a forward, not to rebound, but to stay back and contest the Unseld outlet pass.

The throwback to the Gallatin-Schayes

days is 6' 8" forward Dennis Rodman (1986–2000). Rodman isn't as physically imposing as those two, but he is as sly. Rodman won seven consecutive NBA rebounding titles, from 1990–91 to 1997–98, and his teams won five World Championships in that span. He is the only player in the history of the league to win seven such crowns.

Rodman, like his 1950s forebears, had desire and aggressiveness on his side. He wanted every ball that caromed off the glass. He twice averaged more than 18 rebounds per game, both times more than four rebounds a contest better than the runner-up in the league, an amazing margin. Dennis Rodman was, by far, the best of the modern rebounders.

PLAYERS TO WATCH

When it comes to sheer desire, the player everyone thinks of immediately is the Piston's Ben Wallace. He has earned the ultimate compliment among rebounders: people say he reminds them of Paul Silas. But please, don't dismiss either the Spurs' Tim Duncan or the Timberwolves' Kevin Garnett.

Duncan is one of those guys who seems to have arms longer than his body. Garnett is one of those players with the footwork of a Moses Malone: he is very difficult to box out and he can jump better than Moses ever thought of jumping. Finally, after all is said and done, don't dismiss the efforts of "The Big Aristotle", Shaquille O'Neal. When he does not want to be moved out, he will not be moved out. That alone is worth six or seven rebounds a game.

Below: Rebecca Lobo of the New York Liberty pulls one down agains the Los Angeles Sparks.

22 The Little Big Men's Moves

Players Who Play with Heart

ORIGIN: The 1940s

THE FIRST: Harry "the Horse" Gallatin (1948-58)

THE ALL-TIMERS:
Gallatin, Nat Clifton (1950-58)
Jerry Lucas (1963-74)
Wes Unseld (1968-81)
Dave Cowens (1970-83)
Dan Issel (1970-85)
Alonzo Mourning (1992-present)
Gallatin, Unseld, Cowens, Lucas and Issel are Hall of Famers.

Above: Alonzo Mourning. The best little big man of the NBA. Right: Jerry Lucas was a force as a height-challenged center.

TECHNIQUE:

It helps to be quicker. It helps to be faster. It helps to be able to jump higher. The secret to being an undersized center in an oversized league, however, is to have the heart of a lion and the work ethic of a plowhorse. It is a trait all the great "little big men" share.

If you are playing a bigger opponent, try to beat him down the floor. When you get a rebound, release it quickly or, if you are under your basket, put it back up quickly. When you are shorter than the man guarding you, you have to be everywhere before he gets there.

The Big Man in professional basketball wasn't actually a "big" man until the early to mid-1940s. That's when players like 6' 10" George Mikan, of Depaul University and the Minneapolis Lakers (1946–56), 7' Bob Kurland, of Oklahoma A&M and the Phillips 66ers (1946–52), 7' Don Otten of several NBL and NBA teams (1947–53), and 6' 10" Harry Boykoff of St. John's and several NBL and NBA teams from 1947 to 1951 arrived on the scene.

Those were big guys. Prior to that, except for the odd gangly 6' 10" stringbean, there weren't a lot of overly tall men playing basketball. Very quickly, professional teams realized that to compete with a Mikan or an Otten, they needed to find players of comparable size.

In 1948, the New York Knickerbockers were in the market for a big man. Ned Irish, the president of the Knicks, had his eye on an All-American center from Northeast Missouri State, Harry Gallatin.

The game was changing even as Gallatin was drafted. He was a 6' 6" center at Northeast Missouri and by Gallatin's rookie year in the professional ranks, he was already the shortest center in the league.

Gallatin, nicknamed "the Horse" for his work ethic (not his girth, as many sportswriters imagined), was also one of the toughest centers in the pros. He was not a great jumper, but he had an excellent hook shot that he could get off over just about everybody in the league. His best move was just lowering his shoulder and banging around under the basket. Eight of the 12 years Gallatin played, he scored more free throws than field goals. In the 1953–54 season, Gallatin hit 258 field goals, and 443 free throws.

It was about the most inelegant way to score one could imagine, but it was tremendously effective.

What also helped was that Gallatin also had a terrific nose for the ball. Although rebounds were not recorded in the NBA in Gallatin's first two seasons, the Horse averaged double figures in rebounds every year of his career they were measured. He grabbed more than 30 rebounds in a game five times, with a career high of 33 in the 1952–53 season.

But he needed help, and Irish obtained it a few years later, outbidding Celtics coach Red Auerbach for the rights to Nathaniel "Sweetwater" Clifton.

Clifton had formerly been playing center with the Harlem Globetrotters. At a reported 6' 8", 235 pounds, Clifton, Knicks officials believed, would be the missing ingredient to the Knicks' playoff hopes.

Except for one small thing: when Clifton reported to the Knicks' training camp in the fall of 1950, he was clearly not 6' 8". In fact, he was barely 6' 6".

Again, for the Knicks, it wasn't the size of the dog in the fight; it was the size of the fight in the dog. Clifton may have been only 6' 6", but he was an immediate contributor, finishing second on the Knicks in rebounds, fourth in assists and fifth in scoring on the team.

The Cagey Vet

And he was a better defensive center than Gallatin, who was moved to forward. Sweetwater (so named because of his affinity for soft drinks) may have been a rookie in the NBA in the 1950–51 season, but he had been a star for years with the Globetrotters. When Lakers center George Mikan was asked that year if he knew of the Knicks new rookie, Mikan snorted.

MAY 12, 1974, NBA FINALS, GAME 7, BOSTON VS. MILWAUKEE

It was one of the most intriguing matchups in NBA history: the Celtics' 6' 8" center, Dave Cowens, against the Milwaukee Bucks' 7' 2" center, Kareem Abdul-Jabbar. For the first six games, there was simply no doubt about it: Abdul-Jabbar had come out on top by a wide margin, outscoring Cowens in five of the first six games of this frenetic seven-game series, and outrebounding him four out of the six games. It was simply a case of a good big man bettering a good little man.

The seventh game, however, was a different story. Cowens, getting help from forwards Paul Silas and Don Nelson, fronted and banged Abdul-Jabbar (much to the displeasure of a partisan Milwaukee crowd, who felt certain that Kareem was getting hammered). From late in the first quarter to the 5:33 mark of the third period, Abdul-Jabbar went scoreless. This allowed the Celtics to stretch their tenuous 22–20 lead to a 63–46 advantage.

The Bucks never led after that, but pulled close several times. With 11:30 to go in the game, a Milwaukee score cut the margin to 71–68. But Cowens took a pass from guard Jo Jo White, whirled and lofted a running hook shot over the outstretched hand of Abdul-Jabbar, beating him by sheer will. Milwaukee never got any closer. The final margin was 102–87. Cowens had outscored Abdul-Jabbar, 28–26, and outrebounded him, 14–13. It was the only time in the series he had achieved a statistical edge in both categories.

Above: Cowens (18) shooting here in a game against the Golden State Warriors in 1975.

Above left: Washington Bullet's Wes Unseld (41), the smallest center in pro basketball, snags one away from the Seattle Supersonics.
Above right: Jerry Lucas (11) going up for the rebound against Northwestern's Charley Brandt.
Below: Lucas, laying in two points in a Los Angeles Basketball Classic game against UCLA.

"Know him?" said Big George, who was 26 at the time. "I've been playing against him since I was 16 years old."

"Sweets" wasn't the scorer or rebounder Gallatin was, but he was one of the best defensive players in the league and one of the smartest. Clifton was one of the strongest men in the NBA during his career and could trick opposing pivotmen all night. Harry the Horse was a straightforward muscleman; Sweets Clifton was a canny veteran before he even pulled on a Knicks uniform.

Clifton and Gallatin moved the Knicks to the next level: three consecutive trips to the NBA Finals, from 1950 to 1953. But there, the twin tanks couldn't push the Knickerbockers over the top. They just weren't big enough down low. In 1950–51, the Rochester Royals, with slick 6' 9" center Arnie Risen, were too much for New York. In 1951–52 and 1952–53, it was Mikan.

Interestingly, the next great small center was also a Knick. Actually, 6' 8" Jerry Lucas began his pro career as a forward for the Cincinnati Royals and later, the San Francisco Warriors, where he did well. But it was as a center that Lucas first made it to the NBA Finals (the 1971–72 season) and then won it (1972–73).

Again, as was the case with Gallatin, necessity was the mother of New York coach Red Holtzman's invention. Lucas was obtained by the Knicks prior to the 1971–72 season for explosive forward Cazzie Russell. In his autobiography, *Maverick*, former Knick forward Phil Jackson conceded that Lucas, at the time, had a reputation for being a stat-obsessed flake who had never really played for a winner. Many Knicks wondered how the little big man would fit in.

As it turned out, perfectly, despite almost everyone's misgivings. When Knickerbocker center Willis Reed went down that year with a leg injury, Holtzman eventually inserted Lucas at center. Far from hurting the Knicks, the canny Lucas turned out to be the reincarnation of Sweetwater Clifton on defense and a force on the high post on offense.

Lucas was an excellent passer, set a bruising pick but, most importantly, could drain set shots from 30 to 35 feet out, taking advantage of his speed and maneuverability to overcome his lack of height. He would heft the ball onto his right shoulder and

Above: Alex Groza with the rebound during the NCAA semi-finals against Columbia in 1948.

release it in almost a shot-putting motion. It was maddening for opposing centers. Behemoths like Wilt Chamberlain and Kareem Abdul-Jabbar had no choice but to follow Lucas to the perimeter. If they did not, he would kill them with wide-open shots.

The Purest Game

His perimeter game also opened up the middle for cutters and drivers, which helped the Knicks get to the NBA Finals that year, and the next year. With a reasonably healthy Willis Reed, they won the whole magilla. During this span, many hoops purists believe that this incarnation of the Knicks, with small Lucas at center, played the "purest" bas-

ketball of this or any era because of the versatility of the players at the pivot position.

Lucas had shown the pro world that a championship center need not be 7' 2". A year later, the Celtics' very active 6' 8" leaper, Dave Cowens, proved it again when he led Boston to the first of two titles over the next three years.

Cowens, like Lucas, had an excellent outside jump shot. But unlike Lucas, he also had a strong low post game. He could shoot running hooks and quick turnarounds and had a nice baseline move. He was the amalgamation of what had come to the small center to date: Gallatin's work ethic, Clifton's sturdy defense and Lucas's perimeter game. And he could run.

ALEX GROZA'S TOP SCORING GAMES, 1950–51
40–Indianapolis vs. Minneapolis, 3-23-51 (playoff game)
38–Indianapolis at Minneapolis, 3-25-51 (playoff game)
37–Indianapolis at Baltimore, 3-17-51
35–Indianapolis at Fort Wayne, 3-14-51
34–Indianapolis vs. Fort Wayne, 12-19-50

Once again, wither Wes Unseld? At 6' 6", Unseld was the smallest center in pro basketball his entire career, from 1968 to 1981. He was not a fast runner, a high jumper, or a great outside shooter. Yet he won a Rookie of the Year Award, an MVP, and his teams were in the NBA Finals four times, winning it all in the 1977–78 season, for which Unseld won the MVP award.

Again, like Gallatin, Cowens, Lucas, and others, it was work ethic that got Unseld through. He was completely unselfish, set a mean pick, could pass well from the high post and, despite his size, was one of the best

HARRY "THE HORSE" GALLATIN'S BEST REBOUNDING GAMES, 1952–53

33–New York at Fort Wayne, 3-15-53 (tops in the NBA)
28–New York vs. Baltimore, 11-1-52
25–New York at Philadelphia, 1-1-53

Note: Gallatin also scored his season-high 30 points in that March 15 game against Fort Wayne, officially becoming the second player in league history to score 30 or more points and grab 30 or more rebounds in the same game. George Mikan was the first, scoring 61 points and grabbing 36 rebounds in a double-overtime game against Rochester on January 20, 1952.

Left: Alonzo Mourning with the slam against the Atlanta Hawks.

defensive rebounders of his generation. He averaged 14 rebounds a game during his career and was even better in the post-season, averaging 14.9 in 119 playoff games. Unseld let others score; he did just about everything else well.

The NBA of the 1990s and 2000s hasn't really featured a small center, although a number of pro teams have forwards playing out of position, such as the Celtics' 6' 9" Vitaly Potapenk. The best "Little Big Man" of the NBA in the 21st century is 6' 9" Alonzo Mourning (1992–present) of the Miami Heat, a solid shot-blocker and rebounder for Pat Riley's team. Sadly, Mourning, as of this writing, is battling a kidney ailment that may force him to retire.

Right: Mourning and New Jersey Nets' Richard Jefferson battle for possession.

Left: Unseld goes up to block a shot by Supersonic Marvin Webster during the 1978 NBA Championship series. Unseld was named MVP of the series.

PLAYERS TO WATCH

The Knicks' Kurt Thomas is 6' 8", 235 pounds. Thomas is a muscular widebody who is basically all the Knicks have for a post player. Popeye Jones, the 6' 7" forward for the Wizards, was another guy who didn't get a lot of help, although Kwame Brown is coming along quickly. The Sonics' 6' 8" Vitaly Potapenko has been a forward playing center for the past six years.

23

The Big Little Men's Moves

ORIGIN: 1955

THE FIRST: **Tom Gola**
(1955–66)

THE ALL-TIMERS:
Gola, Oscar Robertson
(1960–74)
Jerry Sloan (1965–76)
George Gervin (1972–86)
Earvin "Magic" Johnson
(1979–91, 1995–96)
Michael Jordan
(1983–93, 1994–98, 2001–present)
Reggie Miller (1987–present)
Gola, Robertson, Gervin and Johnson are
in the Hall of Fame. Jordan is pending.

How to Be a Big Guard in the Big Leagues

THE TECHNIQUE: A "big guard" is expected to do guard things, like score, pass and handle the ball, and also do big man things, like rebound and block shots. Be strong, be smart and be tough. That's all there is to it. Always post up a smaller opponent. Always try to take him under the basket. You should be the stronger player, nine times out of 10.

Inset: Kobe Bryant
Right: Magic Johnson is both
fast and marvelously coordinated.

In the pantheon of "Big Guards Who Can Do It All," before there was Magic Johnson or Jerry Sloan, there was Tom Gola. Gola was a 6' 6" guard who starred at LaSalle University in college and had a stellar career with the Philadelphia Warriors and New York Knickerbockers from 1955 to 1966.

Gola had been a schoolboy sensation in Philadelphia, and opted to remain in town and play his college ball for LaSalle University. He started as a freshman and was one of only a handful of players in NCAA history to be named to the All-America team four consecutive years.

Gola was a great scorer and, a strong passer and he remains the all-time rebounding leader in NCAA history with 2,201 for his career. He was primarily a guard, because of his skills, but Gola actually played all three positions for the Explorers.

During his collegiate career, Gola was hailed as the greatest all-around basketball player ever. He was the first really tall player to be used in the backcourt. At the same time, he also often played forward and sometimes center.

"He makes plays only a little man could make, but then he turns around and does things only a big man usually does," said Paul

The "Point-Forward"

Milwaukee Bucks coach Don Nelson is credited with creating the concept of the "point-forward" when he turned 6' 6" forward Paul Pressey (1982–93) into the Bucks' principal passer in the 1984–85 season. But the first real point-forward was Oscar Robertson when he played for the University of Cincinnati from 1957 to 1960. Robertson usually played forward, but that was because coach George Smith needed Oscar underneath as well as out on the point. The Bearcats were not a particularly big team, and Smith couldn't afford to play Robertson at guard. Of course, a player like Robertson didn't really have a set position. He played wherever he was needed.

Unruh, an All-American from Bradley in the 1950s.

And Unruh's definition of Gola has been pretty much the definition of a "big" guard since then.

When he graduated to the professional ranks, Gola was used primarily at guard, although he also played some forward. But at 210 pounds, he was simply too small to play a professional pivot.

Interestingly, when Gola first arrived on the collegiate scene, there were a few sportswriters who actually decried his existence. The fear, in their minds at least, was that college and professional basketball were essentially crowding out the little man. Gola, some feared, was the first wave of 6' 6" and 6' 7" guards that would eliminate the clever 5' 10" ballhandler.

As silly as that sounds, it was not entirely unfounded. The 6' 6" Gola paved the way for

Above: Gola lays up a shot against the Celtics.

MAY 16, 1980, NBA FINALS, GAME 6, LOS ANGELES VS. PHILADELPHIA

Two days earlier, Lakers center Kareem Abdul-Jabbar had sprained his ankle late in Game 5, a 108–103 victory over the Philadelphia 76ers. Abdul-Jabbar was questionable for Game 6, and in fact, the Lakers coaching staff planned to keep him out of the game and hopefully have him ready to play in Game 7 in Los Angeles, if necessary.

Incredibly, it wasn't necessary. Lakers coach Paul Westhead decided to throw the curve of curveballs: 6' 9" rookie guard Earvin "Magic" Johnson would start at center in Abdul-Jabbar's place.

"Really?" asked a surprised Caldwell Jones, the Sixers center, when Johnson stepped to midcourt for the opening tap of the game.

Really. And it worked beautifully. Johnson guarded Jones on defense and boxed him off the boards all night. With no Abdul-Jabbar, the Lakers kicked their running game into high gear and blew the Sixers out of the building. Earvin scored 42 points, grabbed 15 rebounds and dished off for seven assists as the Lakers won the title, 123–107.

moving players 6' 5" and over into the backcourt, and ultimately, for a 6' 9" player such as Johnson to play guard, as well.

Even after Gola made the switch, the concept of 6' 5" and 6' 6" guards was not a universal one. Oscar Robertson (1960–74) took the way a "big" guard played the game to the next level, but not too many guards were up there with him.

Like Gola, Robertson played every position available at the University of Cincinnati, although he mostly played forward. But unlike Gola, after he was drafted by the Cincinnati Royals prior to the 1960–61 season, Oscar never played a minute at any other position other than guard.

The reason was that he was just too valuable to move to forward. In addition to being taller than most of the players guarding him, Robertson was usually quicker and invariably

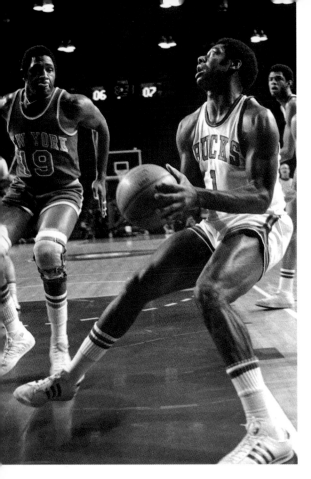

Above: Oscar Robertson perfecting the art of the "big" guard.

George or the Doctor?

For one glorious season, 6'-7" George Gervin and 6'-6" Julius Erving played for the same team, the Virginia Squires (1972–73). Both started at forward, and coach Al Bianchi reported that there was never any difficulty in the two men sharing the basketball.

What there was, was problems on defense and under the boards. The "Iceman" averaged about 8 rebounds per game that year, and Erving averaged 12. That wasn't too bad, but neither was physically big enough to contest the bigger forwards in the ABA on defense. The Squires generally had to outscore the opposition, which, by the way, wasn't necessarily a daunting task, as both Gervin and Doc could put points on the board.

But by the next season, the Squires had sold Gervin off to the San Antonio Spurs and traded Erving to the New York Nets.

stronger. In fact, his determination was legendary.

Give Oscar What He Wants

"Give Oscar a 12-foot shot, know what he wants?" said Knickerbockers forward Rich Barnett in a quote from the 1960s that is now legendary. "A 10-foot shot. Give him 10, he wants eight. Give him eight, he wants six. Give him six, he wants four. Give him four, he wants two. Give him two, you know what he wants? That's right: a layup, baby."

Jerry Sloan (1965–76) was sort of a poor man's Oscar Robertson, which is not meant as a knock on the former Evansville University star. Sloan was not the shooter Robertson was, and he couldn't control a game by controlling the ball. What he did was control a game by rebounding and playing tough defense. Sloan, at 6' 6", would take the opposition's best backcourt player and physically wear him down. In addition, Sloan crashed the boards with centers and forwards with impunity. He was another option for "big" guard: an intimidator who became an added frontcourt player.

The Chicago Bulls had a unique squad when Sloan and backcourt mate Norman Van Lier (1969–79) were on the roster in the early and mid-1970s. Chicago's forwards, Chet "the Jet" Walker (1962–75) and Bob "Butterbean" Love (1966–77) were essentially finesse players who were the Bulls' main scorers. The job of Sloan and Van Lier, on the other hand, was to be the enforcers and rebounders. It worked, to an extent: the Bulls were always in the playoffs, although they never reached the NBA Finals in Sloan's tenure.

If there was one player who virtually forced his coach to play him at guard rather than forward, it was George Gervin

Above: Jerry Sloan muscling past Kareem Abdul-Jabbar.

(1972–86). In his rookie year, Gervin was 6' 7" and weighed 185 pounds. And for a year or so, he did play forward with the Virgina Squires, but when he was traded to the San Antonio Spurs his second year, Gervin moved to guard and became a devastating force.

In fact, the San Antonio backcourt from 1973–76 was easily the best in the ABA and one of the best in the professional basketball world. That's because Gervin's running mate at guard was 6' 2" James Silas (1972–82), who was almost as good a shooter as Gervin.

Guarding either one was a tough assignment. Trying to deal with both of them game after game was a nightmare for ABA coaches.

The 6' 9" Passing Whiz

It would be hard to imagine a bigger player than 6' 9", 220-pound Magic Johnson playing the guard position. As it was, the sight of the Lakers' passing whiz scooting downcourt to lead the break was intimidating for NBA players, because Johnson was both fast and marvelously coordinated.

Johnson played forward on defense and guard on offense while in college at Michigan State. When he came to the Lakers in 1979, there was some talk of keeping him at forward. Los Angeles already had an excellent point guard in Norm Nixon.

But Magic was simply a better one. From his unique vantage, he could see seams in a defense better than any other guard. And his upper body strength enabled him to fire one-handed passes the length of the court, or three-quarter court bounce passes. There is, and really has been, no one else like him, before or since.

Michael Jordan (1984–93, 1994–98, 2001–present) presents a similar, though not identical, problem. His leaping ability and athleticism enable him to get off just about any kind of shot he desires. He and Indiana Pacers 6' 7" shooting star Reggie Miller (1987–present) present unique problems for so-called regular-size guards. Jordan is just too big and strong and quick for anyone. Miller, on the other hand, moves extremely well without the ball, and for a man 6' 7", gets open with maddening regularity.

If there is one position in the NBA that continues to evolve, it is the position of the big guard. In the modern NBA, a large number of teams have a 6' 5", 6' 6" or 6' 7"

GEORGE GERVIN'S SEASON HIGHS DURING HIS NINE YEARS IN THE NBA
1976–77: 42
1977–78: 63
1978–79: 52
1979–80: 55
1980–81: 49
1981–82: 50
1982–83: 47
1983–84: 44
1984–85: 47
1985–86: 45

The "Power" Guard

In the 1972–73 NBA playoffs, Bulls guard Jerry Sloan led his team in rebounding with 59 in seven games, a series the Bulls lost to the Lakers. In fact, the 6' 5" Sloan was the second-best rebounder in the series behind Los Angeles center Wilt Chamberlain.

Below: Magic Johnson soaring past Kevin McHale.

EARVIN "MAGIC" JOHNSON'S SEASON HIGHS IN THE NBA:	
1979–80:	42
1980–81:	41
1981–82:	40
1982–83:	36
1983–84:	33
1984–85:	39
1985–86:	34
1986–87:	46
1987–88:	39
1988–89:	40
1989–90:	38
1990–91:	34
1995–96:	30

player in the backcourt. This is a sort of basketball version of the arms race of the 1950s and 1960s between the United States and the Soviet Union. If Team A has a 6' 6" guy that can play the backcourt, then Team B starts looking around for a similar player to

Left: Kobe Bryant. The guard who's a nightmare to guard. Right: 76er's Allen Iverson attempts to guard shooting start Reggie Miller.

PLAYERS TO WATCH

The Lakers' Kobe Bryant is a 6' 7" guard who can drive to the basket, pull up for the jump shot or even post up. He is a nightmare to guard. Bryant would be averaging Michael Jordan numbers if he played for a team without a center. The Bucks' Ray Allen is not as dominating, but at 6' 6", he can shoot over just about anyone. And with his superb touch, he can be nearly unstoppable. Celtic Paul Pierce, at 6'-7", poses similar problems as Bryant. Pierce is a better shooter than Kobe, but not as explosive a driver.

1960–61:	716 (10.1)
1961–62:	985 (12.5)
1962–63:	835 (10.4)
1963–64:	783 (9.9)
1964–65:	674 (9.0)
1965–66:	586 (7.7)
1966–67:	486 (6.2)
1967–68:	391 (6.0)
1968–69:	502 (6.4)
1969–70:	422 (6.1)
1970–71:	462 (5.7)
1971–72:	323 (5.0)
1972–73:	360 (4.9)
1973–74:	279 (4.0)

Note: Robertson led team in 1961–62 and was eighth overall in the NBA, the only time a guard has finished in the top 10 in rebounding.

ensure that the team has a player to match up with the Team A big guard.

Some players make the transition better than others. The Boston Celtics drafted 6' 7" forward Paul Pierce (1998–present) out of the University of Kansas in 1998 with the full intention of keeping him at forward, which is where Pierce began his pro career. But his range, quickness and work ethic made it easy for Celtics coach Jim O'Brien to move Pierce to the guard spot for a majority of the 2001–02 season. As a result, Pierce led the Celtics' resurgence and figures to be one of the NBA's brightest stars in the coming decade.

Right: Michael Jordan. Big, strong, quick.

24 The Big Big Men's Moves

The Biggest Players of All

ORIGIN: 1924

THE FIRST: Clyde Shoun, billed as the "World's Tallest Man," at 7' 1"

THE ALL-TIMERS:
Don Otten (1946–53)
Wade "Swede" Halbrook (1960–62)
Tom Burleson (1974–81)
Ralph Sampson (1983–92)
Manute Bol (1985-95)
Arvydas Sabonis (1995-present)
None is in the Hall of Fame.

THE TECHNIQUE:
Always remember: when everyone is tired, you're still tall. Stay close to the basket. Keep your hands up. Don't jump out, jump up when you want to block or deflect a shot. Practice your foul shots, because smaller players will often foul you. Remember that God made you big for a reason: to get rebounds.

Stay in shape because shorter players will try to beat you down the court. Even if your man is not as big as you, box him out on rebounds. Learn a hook shot.

Above: Yao Ming.
Probably the best player
over 7' 3", ever.
Left: Don Otten.

It was probably in 1924 when George Halas, owner of the Chicago franchise of the old American Basketball League, realized that if he could get the biggest player in the league, he would have an advantage over everyone else when it came to jump balls.

Hence, after an extended search, Halas found and signed 7' 1" Clyde Shoun, billed as the "World's Tallest Man."

Halas then realized, as many coaches would over the years, that size wasn't everything. Shoun, for example, was not a good jumper. When the Chicago team came to Brooklyn to play the Original Celtics, 6' 5" Joe Lapchick of the Celtics was clearly a better, more coordinated leaper than Shoun. Lapchick not only won the tap several times that day in the Celtics' win, but he threw head-and-shoulder fakes at Shoun all game, and the giant Chicagoan got sucked in every time.

At the very beginning era of pro basketball, in fact, tall players weren't necessarily considered an asset. The game was slow, and post play up until the 1940s or so wasn't considered a major facet of an offense. Even the players who were in the pivot were expected to go outside and shoot set shots, or set screens or hit cutting passers. The "all-around" player was emphasized, and tall players were not necessarily considered an asset.

There was one exception. Tall players who were somewhat coordinated and could jump fairly well might be used to win jump balls. Until 1937, there was a jump ball after every made basket or free throw so an extra tall player might be an advantage if he could consistently tap the ball to a teammate. Unfortunately, Shoun couldn't do that every time.

MAY 21, 1986, GAME 5, NBA WESTERN CONFERENCE FINALS, HOUSTON VS. LOS ANGELES

It was already the most improbable of scenarios: the Houston Rockets, who had finished 11 games behind the Los Angeles Lakers in the Western Conference standings, had, amazingly, beaten L.A. in three of the first four games of the West Finals. In Game 5, it looked as though the Lakers were poised to narrow the gap, leading the contest for most of the way.

The Rockets hung tough and even managed to tie the game with time running down. With a second left, Houston had the ball at midcourt. Rocket forward Rodney McCray would inbound. There was little time for anything but a quick shot. McRay lobbed the ball into Houston's 7' 4" power forward, Ralph Sampson.

Sampson caught the ball, turned halfway in the air and lofted the sphere toward the basket, barely even looking at it. The ball bounced on the rim and, just as the buzzer went off, fell through the hoop for a 114–112 stunning Rockets win. As the amazed Houston players celebrated and cheered themselves, the Lakers players could only look up at the scoreboard in stunned silence.

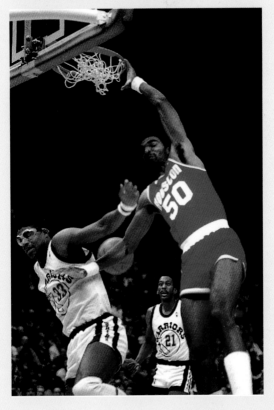

Above: Sampson slams one in, over Golden State Warrior Jerome Whitehead.

Changes

Uncoordinated or poorly coordinated big men were the rule rather than the exception in the first part of the 20th century, even with the arrival of DePaul's 6' 10" George Mikan and 7' Bob Kurland in the mid-1940s.

Don Otten (1946–53) was a classic example. Otten, the former Bowling Green star, made it to the NBA in 1949–50, after three solid but unspectacular years in the old NBL. Otten was 7' and 250 pounds. He was one of the few players who could guard George Mikan straight up. He rebounded pretty well, shot well from the foul line and averaged 12 points per game in the NBA and NBL.

Like a lot of big men down the years, from game to game Otten sometimes simply didn't play up to his potential. He was sort of the Benoit Benjamin of the 1950s. Or the Darryl Dawkins.

Manute's Game

The story of Manute Bol is legendary. He was a Dinka tribesman who ended up playing at Division II Bridgeport College in Connecticut for a year before being drafted by the Washington Bullets prior to the 1985–86 season. In his first few years in the United States, Bol's adventures in Africa were constantly highlighted by sportswriters. He was asked if he was afraid of lions. "No," said Bol, "but a gorilla, on the other hand, will kick your ass."

Bol was very clearly drafted by the Bullets to block shots, something he did better than almost any player in the history of the league. Bol's first game was in the Worcester Centrum in Massachusetts, an exhibition game against the Boston Celtics.

Before the game, Celtics forward Larry Bird warned his teammates not to allow their shots to be blocked by Bol, because it would be on every late-night sports show in the country.

Sure enough, Bol's first block came when he rejected center Bill Walton's hook shot. And, sure enough, it was on every late-night sports show in the country.

Above: Ralph Sampson, again, making a statement in a game against the Chicago Bulls.

Coaches still wanted the big men and were willing to trade for them. In his seven years in the NBL and then the NBA, Otten played for Tri-Cities, Baltimore, Washington and Fort Wayne before returning to the Hawks for his final seasons.

This excitement about big men was not confined to the United States. When the Olympics were held in Melbourne, Australia, in 1956, the Soviet Union unveiled 7' 4" center Jan Kruminsh, a towering player who had "slingshots for arms," according to his coach.

What the heck that meant was left to the imagination, because the center for the United States was 6' 9" Bill Russell, who was faster, quicker, more coordinated, more skilled, smarter and a much, much better jumper than Kruminsh. It didn't help that Kruminsh's Soviet companions, along with everybody else in the arena, clapped and cheered when Russell put on a spectacular dunking exhibition prior to the game, which the U.S. won, 89–55. Kruminsh didn't score.

You Can't Teach Height

By now, it was clear that while a coach certainly couldn't teach height, as the saying went, he also couldn't teach aggressiveness or desire. And it seemed that, except for a few super-big men like Kurland, many seven-foot-plus players simply lacked all the tools to play the game well.

That, of course, didn't preclude coaches from drafting them. Wade "Swede" Halbrook (1960–62) was a highly touted big man from Oregon State who was signed by the Syracuse Nationals after playing five years of minor-league basketball. Like Shoun, he was billed as "the World's Tallest Man"

Above: Portland Trail Blazers Arvydas Sabonis shoots over Greg Ostertag.

(obviously, whoever did the billing had never heard of Kruminsh).

The Swede (who was actually Dutch) was an affable fellow who, believe it or not, enjoyed knitting while on the road. This was not exactly what his teammates were hoping to see. Halbrook was the backup center for the Nationals for two years. He averaged about six rebounds and five points a game during his two-year career.

He drove his coach, Alex Hannum, nuts. Halbrook was probably better coordinated than Otten, could shoot with both hands and jumped fairly well. But, like Otten, there were games when Swede played well, and there were games when he didn't play well.

Unlike the animosity that would be directed at Chamberlain and Bill Russell a

few years later, many fans, both in Syracuse and on enemy courts, cheered Halbrook, apparently sensing his reluctance to be a star.

As seven-foot players became more common, coaches were still on the lookout for the really, really big guys. In 1976, the Seattle Supersonics drafted 7' 4" Tommy Burleson out of North Carolina State. Burleson (1974–81), like many of his ultra-tall peers, was a hard worker who eventually became a decent player, but he never really lived up to the expectations set for him.

Big Ralph

The most ballyhooed supergiant was 7' 4" Ralph Sampson (1983–92), who was Rookie of the Year in the 1983–84 season and helped lead the Houston Rockets to the NBA Finals in 1985–86.

Sampson, for whatever reason, didn't fully exploit his strengths, which is ironic because he was one of the few big, big men who had developed coordination. He once complained that his coach at the time, Bill Fitch, wanted him to develop one unstoppable shot, like Kareem Abdul-Jabbar's hook, that he could use on a regular basis. Sampson thought that concept absurd. He replied to Fitch that he would rather have a repertoire of shots, so that his opponent would be harder pressed to stop him.

What Fitch saw, and what Ralph didn't, was that players developed a repertoire of shots because they had to. There was always a bigger player out there who could block a jump shot, or a turnaround hook, or whatever. Developing more than one shot was the only way to keep bigger players off balance.

Sampson was a bigger player already. A dead-accurate jumper or hook shot would have made him a devastating force. But he

Already, the Rockets' 7' 5" Yao Ming is becoming the best player over 7' 3" ever. Ming can post up and shoot a little turn-around, he can handle the ball and he can block shots. He is very well coordinated for such a big guy. The Mavs' 7' 6" Shawn Bradley is the other extra-big guy who has some coordination. But Bradley isn't as aggressive as Ming. He is, in fact, too nice a guy. Shaquille O'Neal wrote in his autobiography that Bradley once hit Shaq in the face with an elbow and spent the next five minutes apologizing.

PLAYERS TO WATCH

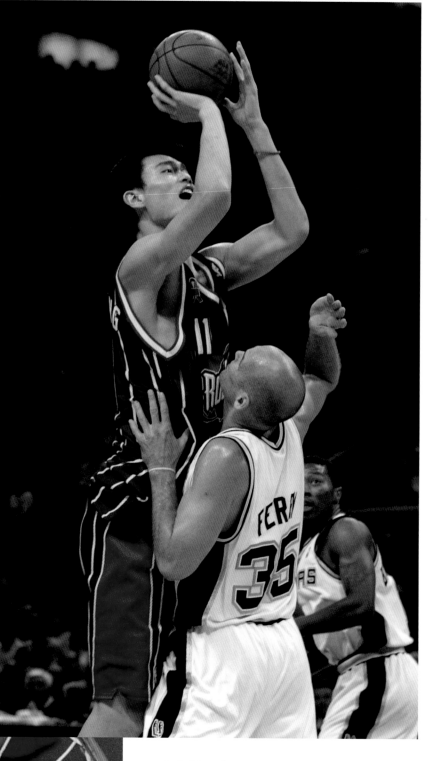

Right: Yao Ming going up and over San Antonio Spurs' Danny Ferry.

Left: Ming drains one.

never developed one. He retired at the much too young age of 32.

We talked about 7' 7" Manute Bol (1985–95) and 7' 5" Mark Eaton (1982–93) in a previous chapter. These were among the best shot-blockers in the history of the league. The decision to make them shot-blocking specialists was their coaches' way of conceding that they could not really be well-rounded players.

Eaton, for example, was a decent rebounder and set a better than average pick, but was limited offensively and wasn't much of a passer.

Bol couldn't really set a pick, was a fair to poor passer and, although he blocked lots of shots, had difficulty picking his man up on switches.

Interestingly, when Bol was traded to the Golden State Warriors prior to the 1988–89 season, Warrior coach Don Nelson tried to expand Bol's two-dimensional game by having him shoot three-point shots. It would have been a brilliant move had Bol hit a modest percentage. He didn't, draining about 21 percent of the shots.

Chuck Nevitt (1982–94) played for the 1984–85 World Champion Los Angeles Lakers. The 7' 5" center, called "the Human Victory Cigar" was so two-dimensional that when he turned sideways you almost couldn't see him.

He almost never played except when Los Angeles was way ahead or way behind because he couldn't do much of anything except be tall. He did win a ring with Los Angeles that year. He was also briefly on the roster of the 1991–92 World Champion Chicago Bulls.

Arvydas Sabonis (1994–2001) is, so far, the best of the giant big men. The 7' 3" for-

MANUTE BOL'S THREE-POINT SHOOTING STATISTICS	
1985–86: 0-1	
1986–87: 0-1	
1987–88: 0-1	
1988–89: 20-91	
1989–90: 9-48	
1990–91: 1-14	
1991–92: 0-9	
1992–93: 10-32	
1993–94: 0-3	
1994–95: 3-5	

ARVYDAS SABONIS'S THREE-POINT SHOOTING STATISTICS	
1995–96: 39-104	
1996–97: 48-132	
1997–98: 30-115	
1998–99: 7-24	
1999–2000: 7-19	

mer star of the Soviet National team was probably one of the best centers in the world in the 1980s and 1990s, before he sustained Achilles tendon injuries to both ankles. Even now, Sabonis, who is contemplating a comeback with the Portland Trail Blazers, is an excellent passer, a strong rebounder and the best seven-foot three-point shooter in the history of the game, with a career percentage of 34 percent.

Right: The legendary Manute Bol in his first game against San Antonio.

25 The Little Little Men's Moves

Getting By in a Big Man's World

THE FIRST: **Barney Sedran**

THE ALL-TIMERS:
Barney Sedran (1911–26, various leagues)
Buddy Jeannette (1938–50)
Slater Martin (1949–60)
Nate Archibald (1970–84)
Calvin Murphy (1970–83)
Muggsy Bogues (1987–present)
All except Muggsy are in the Hall of Fame.

THE TECHNIQUE:
You'd better be quicker and faster than 99 percent of the people you face, because that's about all you have going for you. Don't let anyone post you up. Treat free throws with reverence, because it's the only time in a game you know you won't have to shoot over someone a foot or so taller.

Make friends with your big man, because you'll be relying on him to bail you out with putbacks and defensive muscle. Also, make friends with your coach, because everyone else will be telling him not to play you.

Above: Calvin Murphy making a move.
Right: Muggsy Bogues

It's not about being the shortest guy on the court; if you're a guard, that's the way it is. This chapter is about guys who were shorter than short, and how they worked around that considerable handicap.

The first, and one of the best, little men ever to play the game was Barney Sedran, at 5' 4", the smallest man ever elected to the Hall of Fame.

Sedran played at the turn of the 20th century and was short even for those times. A 1907 graduate of DeWitt Clinton High School in New York City, and a 1911 graduate of the City College of New York, Sedran was considered too small to play for his high school team. That didn't discourage him. He played Amateur Athletic Union (AAU) ball and was part of two metropolitan championship teams in New York City in his three years.

Thus, by the time Sedran graduated from high school, he was more of a known quantity, and he ended up playing four years at CCNY. Sedran was the team's top scorer his last three years there.

He turned pro the next year, and was a key player in leading the Newburgh Tenths to the Hudson River League championship in 1912.

Sedran was a quick player with great anticipation on both offense and defense. He didn't have to worry about being posted up, since no one in those early days did that. Pro teams in those years played straight up, man-to-man defense, and Sedran was a burr to opposing dribblers and shooters. With his speed, he could anticipate passes and pick them off.

On offense, he and his teammate Max Friedman (1909–27) played in various Eastern leagues for years and worked out a great two-man game. Nat Holman of the Original Celtics believed Friedman and Sedran were

the best practitioners of the two-man game, or "buddy system," of that early era.

Sedran was a good driver and a great shooter. He played for the Utica Utes of the New York State League from 1912 to 1915, and helped the team win three consecutive NYSL titles. In 1914, Utica won the unofficial World Championship.

The New York State League, like many Eastern leagues in the 1910s, didn't believe in backboards. Their baskets were suspended 10 feet off the ground and attached to long poles. In one game in 1914, Sedran hit 17 shots, many of them long sets, to score 34 points in a Utica win. And with no backboard, he had to swish them all.

Above: Jack Driscoll, only 5'6", with his teammate Mike Novak, 6'9".
Right: Calvin Murphy, of the Houston Rockets, driving airborn against San Anotnio's Johnny Moore (00).

DECEMBER 15, 1972, DETROIT VS. KANSAS CITY–OMAHA (AKA TINY'S BIG NIGHT)

Nate "Tiny" Archibald, at 6', was the most explosive little man in the history of the NBA. In 1972–73, he averaged 34 points per game as well as better than 11 assists per contest for the Kansas City–Omaha Kings. On December 15, in a home game against the Detroit Pistons, he had his best game of the year. A year, we might add, in which he had an awful lot of very big games.

That night, Tiny scored 41 points and had 21 assists in a 141-132 overtime win over the Pistons. That means he accounted for 83 points that game. The 21 assists were the high for the year that season (Tiny had eight of the top 10 assist games in 1972–73). The 41 points was the 45th best scoring night in the league that year. Archibald had 15 games of 40-plus points and three more games of 50-plus points that season. In fact, the Detroit game was the third consecutive game that Archibald scored 41 points that season. No little man has ever dominated the NBA as completely as Tiny did that year.

Nate the Skate, Nate the Great

Nate "Tiny" Archibald, as we mentioned, was the greatest little man in the history of the game, statistically. His 1972–73 season was one of the most unique seasons in basketball history.

The 6' guard was a New York City playground legend before he moved on to the University of Texas at El Paso. Upon his graduation, Archibald was drafted by the Kansas City–Omaha Kings. The coach of the Kings was former Boston Celtics legend Bob Cousy, who was also a playground star in New York City in high school, albeit 20 years before Archibald.

At the beginning of the 1972–73 season, Cousy gave Archibald the ball. Literally. Tiny, for the first and last time in the history of the NBA, led the league in scoring with a 34.0 average, and in assists with an 11.4 mark.

So let's take a longer look at this season. Archibald scored 2,712 points, or 426 more points than runner-up Kareem Abdul-Jabbar of Milwaukee.

He passed for 910 assists, a ridiculous 273 more than Pistons guard David Bing, who was number two in the league that season. Wilt Chamberlain's feat of averaging 50.4 points per game in the 1961–62 season was probably a more physically dominating feat. Chamberlain averaged 2.4 assists per game, so he was "responsible," if you will, for about 55 of the 125.6 points the Philadelphia Warriors averaged that year. Amazing! Meanwhile, Archibald was "responsible" for a hair under 57 of his team's 107.6 points per game. Where does that kind of season fit in among the all-time great years? Some would put that ahead of Wilt's big year. Some might not, but it's arguably one of the more amazing feats in the history of the league.

Tiny got worn down that year. He played 3,681 minutes, averaging 46 minutes per contest. In 48 of the 80 games Archibald played, he never came out. It was too much. The next year, he struggled all season, battling injuries and playing in only 35 games. Worse, the Kings weren't winning. Instead of trying to surround Archibald with better players, management first blamed him, then got rid of him.

Eventually, Archibald was traded to Boston prior to the 1978–79 season, and two years later, he helped the Celtics to a World Championship. He proved that with better teammates, he could be a winner. Archibald was elected to the Hall of Fame in 1990.

Sedran was a maverick, of sorts, although that wasn't really that strange in the early days of professional basketball. He played for anyone and everyone in his 20-year career. From 1915, to about 1924, he usually played for as many as three teams during the same year. Of course, in that era of no contracts and cash on the barrel after a game, if he had to deal with a scheduling conflict, Sedran often played one team against the other and would play for the highest bidder.

His teams won nine league championships and one world title. He scored a rare double one year. During the 1920–21 season, Sedran led Albany of the New York State League to its championship and also was the best player for Easthampton, Massachusetts, when that team won the Interstate League title that same year, 5-4.

Sedran set the standard for all small men to come: quickness and smarts enabled him to hold his own in the land of the giants.

Above: Muggsy Bouges and teammate Alek Radojuevic.

Sedran was small, but he actually played a forward at times because he was an excellent block-out man on rebounds and tough as a nickel steak. No way did anyone smaller than Sedran ever play up front in a pro league.

The Backcourt Stars

As the pro leagues proliferated into the 1930s and 1940s, the small man was often the playmaker and the team leader. Buddy Jeannette (1938–50) was the best of these. In fact, he might have been one of the smartest players ever.

He had to be, because he didn't have a lot of physical weapons. By his own admission, the 5' 11" Jeannette was not particularly fast and not much of a leaper. But he was a fearsome clutch player who always seemed to make the right plays.

Jeannette was a graduate of Washington and Jefferson College and matriculated to Cleveland of the old National Basketball League at the start of the 1938–39 season.

Right: Bogues dives to make a save.

He won the NBL's Rookie of the Year Award along with Lou Boudreau of the Hammond (Illinois) All-Americans. Boudreau would go on to a Hall of Fame career in baseball.

Jeannette was sort of a one-man dynasty. In 1943–44 and then again in 1944–45, he led the Fort Wayne Pistons to back-to-back NBL titles. He jumped to the Baltimore Bullets of the old American Basketball League before the 1946–47 season and, as a player-coach, led that team to the championship. He became the first player-coach to win a pro title.

When the Basketball Association of America (the forerunner of the NBA) was founded, the Bullets were invited to "jump" to that league. Jeannette, the spark for the Bullets that year, directed them to the BAA title in 1947–48, his fourth in five years—in three separate leagues.

THE SHORTEST TEAMS IN THE LEAGUE

These were the teams whose cumulative height was the lowest in the league in 2000–01

Vancouver, average height
6 feet, 6.2 inches
Orlando, average height
6 feet, 6.4 inches
Minnesota, average height
6 feet, 6.5 inches
Detroit, average height
6 feet, 6.5 inches
Boston, average height
6 feet, 6.6 inches

Source: Harvey Pollock

Jeannette's game was nothing like Sedran's. He was a more conventional back-court man: a smart defender and a clutch shooter. And, of course, a winner. He won five league MVP awards from 1941 to 1947.

In the latter part of the 1940s, Jeannette teamed up in the backcourt with 5' 11" Bobby McDermott, a high school dropout who had been playing professionally since the early 1930s. While Jeannette made his mark as a passer, defender and dribbler, McDermott made his as a scorer. He was one of the best long-range shooters in the game at the time. The two men were among the smallest backcourt combinations in the NBL, but they were still an unbeatable tandem for a few years.

McDermott was the beginning of a trend that saw smaller men use quickness and speed against larger opponents. He was recognized as being a smart player as well, but McDermott brought more physical ability to the table than many of his contemporaries and predecessors.

There were also small men who made their mark in the league as relentless defenders. Men such as Slater Martin (1949–60) and Al Cervi (1937–53), both 5' 11", used their quickness to harass larger players. Both were also smart playmakers.

The Scoring Machines

Calvin Murphy (1970–83) and Nate "Tiny" Archibald (1970–84) came into the NBA in the same year. Murphy was 5' 9", Archibald was 6'. The perception at the time was that if these two made an impact, it would be along the lines of previous smallish guards: they would be playmakers with some scoring ability. Murphy, it was predicted, would not be able to generate the 38 points per game he had in college.

The 12-Foot Basket, Not

In the 1953–54 season, concerned about the dominance of the big man in the league, the NBA scheduled a regular season game between the Lakers and the Milwaukee Hawks featuring a 12-foot basket. The idea was that the higher basket would somehow help the little man because, ah, well, actually, no one really knew how it would help the little man.

Thus it was that on March 7, the Lakers and Hawks met in Minneapolis and played with a 12-foot basket. Shooting 28 percent and outrebounding the Hawks by a wide margin, the Lakers still barely won, 65–63.

No one was impressed.

"It was a strange game," recalled Kundla.

"It seems to me that the little guys were at an even greater disadvantage," said Minneapolis center George Mikan after the game. "I don't think it helped them at all."

"It screwed up everybody's shot for days after," grumbled Lakers forward Jim Pollard, years later.

That was, needless to say, the end of the 12-foot experiment.

And he didn't, but Murphy, at 5' 9", became the shortest NBA player to ever lead his team in scoring in 1975–76 and again in 1977–78. In fact, in 1977–78, Murphy was the smallest man to ever finish in the top five in scoring in the NBA when he hit for 25.3 points per game, fourth best in the league.

His basic weapon? Sheer speed. Watching old films of players trying to guard Murphy one sees, inevitably, the same thing over and over: whichever guard tries to take Murphy invariably will backpedal like crazy as he comes down the court, forced to respect his speed. That meant lots of open jumpers for Murphy, which he was happy to drain.

Murphy averaged 20 or more points per game five times in his 13-year NBA career, and hit double figures every season he played in the pros.

Archibald had a more up-and-down career, due to injuries, but in 1972–73 he had the greatest season a guard of any size ever had, averaging 34.0 points and 11.4 assists per game, both league-leading totals.

As with Murphy, Archibald was simply too fast for the opposition. Both men, who are now Hall of Famers, expanded on McDermott's foundation. Their physical gifts not only leveled the playing field between them and bigger opponents, but gave them a clear advantage.

"I told Tiny that he should be able to get any shot he wants in a game," said Archibald's former coach, Bob Cousy. "Because of his speed, he should never have to settle for a shot he didn't want."

He usually didn't.

The Most Unique of All

The success of Archibald and Murphy belied the myth that in the "modern" NBA, the little man could not succeed. In subsequent years, small players were regularly on many NBA rosters. Still, no one could have possibly foreseen Muggsy.

There is, and will probably never again be, anyone like Tyrone "Muggsy" Bogues (1987–01), the 5' 3" backcourt star who simply upended all preconceptions about backcourt play.

Bogues was a star in high school, playing the point for DeMatha High of Washington, D.C. When he graduated, he had a number of offers, but the word was, the kid was too small for college.

Except he wasn't. Bogues was like a jet-fired bowling ball. He was 5' 3", but he could dunk a tennis ball, dribble a basketball so close to the ground that he dragged his other hand along the floor, and so quick he could pester opponents all the way up the floor, if he had to.

When Bogues graduated from Wake Forest, there was great interest in which team

would take a chance on him. Again, the scuttlebutt was that the kid was too small for the pros. Then he was drafted by the Bullets and became one of the league's better guards.

Why did Muggsy make it everywhere he played? Did NBA GMs keep him around as a kind of Eddie Gaedel in short pants to entertain the crowds? Did they admire his courage, his pluck, his sand? Well, if you have any sense of how the NBA operates, you know that all that is baloney.

The one thing about Bogues was that he almost never lost the ball. His career assist to turnover ratio was four to one, which is tremendous. In the 1994–95 season with the Charlotte Hornets, that ratio was a difficult-to-believe six to one.

Super Stats

LITTLE MAN STATS, 2000–01

Damon Stoudamire (5' 9") and Travis Best (5' 10") both had two tip-ins.

Khalid El-Amin (5' 10") had one tip-in.

Almost half (15 of 35) of Tyus Edney's (5' 7") shots were layups.

Almost half of (12 of 25) of Earl Boykin's (5' 9") shots were 12- 15- foot jumpers.

No player under six feet dunked the ball in a game in 2000–01.

Source: Harvey Pollock

For comparison, a two-to-one assist to turnover ratio is very good for an NBA player. Magic Johnson's assist-to-turnover ratio, for example, is about three to one for his career. John Stockton, the best ballhandler of this era and maybe the best ever, has a four-to-one career ratio.

That stat alone was what made Bogues a great player. Think about it: your point guard, the guy who handles the ball maybe 70 times a game, loses it maybe once or twice a game. How valuable is that? How many points is that worth? How many wins? Obviously, there's no real way to calculate that, but clearly, it was a huge plus for any team.

Plus, Bogues could drive to the basket and draw fouls, hit his free throws pretty well, could usually be counted on to pick up a steal or two, and actually grabbed over two rebounds per game.

If there was a knock on Muggsy, it was that he was always a defensive liability. Regardless, he led the Charlotte Hornets to their best season (54–28) in 1996–97, and to their second-best year (50–32) in 1994–95. He probably should have made the All-Star team that year. Even at the beginning of the 2002–03 season, there were more than a few general managers who were considering re-signing him to an NBA contract. You can never have too many guys as careful as Bogues is with the basketball.

Realistically, though, we should not expect to see the likes of Muggsy Bogues anytime soon: a singular package of determination and ability that defied both logic and the odds to become a player with an exceptional career. And if ever we see a smaller player than this guy make the NBA, I would pay to see him.

Still, the NBA of the 21st century reveals a large number of smaller players on NBA rosters: a total of 44 players 6' 1" or shorter. That is only three fewer than the 47 seven-foot players on rosters. It is still, clearly, a big man's game. Just as clearly, teams find ways to use smaller players effectively.

Above: Damor Stoudamire tries for the deuce against Kobe.
Right: Travis Best driving to the hoop.

PLAYERS TO WATCH

Mini-mite Terrell Brandon, if healthy, is one of the best point guards in the league, even at 5' 11". The problem is staying healthy. Brandon, who plays for Minnesota, likes to drive, and the big people on the other team don't like him to do that. Hence, he gets blasted when he ventures into the paint, which translates into a lot of punishment. In 2001–02, he missed the last half of the season with a leg injury. The Bulls' Travis Best is 5' 10" but is built a little more solidly than Brandon. Plus, Best doesn't drive as much. The Lakers' 5' 11" Robert Fisher doesn't drive at all. That's because his job is to shoot threes to take the pressure off Shaq, and to stick like glue to other fast guards. It's a nice job, as long as your shots go in.

26 The In-Betweener's Moves
The Truly Unclassifiable Players

ORIGIN: 1950

THE FIRST: Paul Arizin (1950-62)

THE ALL-TIMERS:
Arizin, Cliff Hagan (1956-70)
John Havlicek (1962-78)
Bill Bradley (1966-76)
Adrian Dantley (1976-91)
Charles Barkley (1984-01)
Larry Johnson (1992-present)
Everybody but Dantley, Barkley and Johnson are in the Hall of Fame, and Charles is a lock.

THE TECHNIQUE:
Make sure you can get your shot off quickly, or it could easily be blocked. Go to the hoop and expect to be fouled. Make your free throws. When rebounding on the offensive glass, and you get the ball, try to put it back up in one jump. If you come down, it gives the big guys a chance to set themselves and block your shot. If you have to come down with the rebound and go back up with the shot, protect the ball with either your off-hand or your body, by turning away from your opponent.

Above: Jerry Stackhouse goes from forward to guard, and back again.
Right: "Dollar Bill" Bradley

Tracing the moves of in-betweeners, or "'tweeners" for short, is tough. All the guys we refer to at the beginning of the chapter had to pretty much make their own way in the world of professional basketball. They had to make their own rules, because the rules they were playing by didn't really fit them.

Cliff Hagan, for example, was the same height, 6' 4", and played the same position, forward, as his spiritual forefather, Paul Arizin, yet Cliff Hagan played the game in a completely different manner. Both were very successful, both won World Championships and both are in the Hall of Fame, and deservedly so. So if this seems a little more biographical, that's because it is. Most of these guys were one-of-a-kind players.

The term in-betweener has been, for many years, a sort of politely pejorative way of defining a player who didn't have the size to play up front, but who also didn't really have the quickness or ballhandling skills to play in the backcourt.

Though it was coined after Paul Arizin's career (1950–62), Arizin was the first of the in-betweeners. And his career did not follow the typical routes. For one thing, he didn't play basketball in high school, and he almost didn't play in college.

Arizin, in fact, didn't touch a basketball until he was in eighth grade, and his lack of skill caused him to be cut from his high school team as a freshman the next year. Arizin enjoyed basketball, though, and played in local leagues and on playgrounds.

After graduating high school, he attended Villanova University as a chemistry major and didn't even go out for the team as a freshman. Instead, Arizin played a lot of

basketball in a Philadelphia recreational league. In one of the city tournaments, his team won the championship, defeating a team of players from Villanova. Arizin was named MVP of the tournament.

The Villanova athletic department heard about him and offered him a scholarship. Arizin was on the team for his last three years at Villanova, becoming one of the best players in the country in his senior year, once scoring an unbelievable 85 points in a game. (Arizin waves off that game, noting that the competition, a team from a local Navy base, "was terrible." Still, 85 points is 85 points.)

Arizin was only 6' 4" but was an exceptional jumper. He was also an exceptional shooter. He was what is known now as a "quick jumper," that is, he didn't need to set himself much to jump. He could stop and jump high in the air quickly to release his shot before the defender had a chance to set up. It was a tough combination to stop.

As a rookie in the NBA, he played some guard, but was more comfortable at forward.

Above: Philadelphia Warrior, Paul Arizin, leaps out of a crowd of Baltimore Bullets to sink one in.

Above: New York Knicks' Bill Bradley goes up for the shot.

A. D., The Greatest 'Tweener Scorer

Adrian "A. D." Dantley won his first NBA scoring title in 1980–81, totaling 2,452 points for a 30.7 average. It was the first of four consecutive years Dantley would average 30 or more points in a season, although he would win only one more scoring title. Dantley scored a league-high 55 points in one game and scored 40 or more points eight other times.

Dantley, a former Notre Dame All-American and a member of the 1976 Olympic team, was a sort of Cliff Hagan of the 1980s (Red Auerbach, in fact, once called Hagan the "Adrian Dantley of the 1950s"). The two men had a similar style of play. Both could hit from the outside, but both preferred to drive to the basket and use their superior strength to either get a shot off, get fouled, or both.

Dantley was not a great shooter in the style of Reggie Miller, though he almost never took a bad shot, and as a result his career field goal percentage is .543. In fact, he hit better than 51 percent of his shots for 12 consecutive years, with a high of .576 in 1979–80.

He was also an excellent free-throw shooter, topping 80 percent from the line in 12 of his 14 years, and finishing his career with an .819 percentage. In fact, in two seasons, 1983–84 and 1987–88, Dantley connected on more free throws than field goals.

Above:Charles Barkley puts one up from under the basket.

And after that first year, Arizin remained one of the smallest forwards in the NBA. He was also one of the best.

"I used my quickness to drive around players and make them back off me," recalled Arizin. "I could usually jump high enough to release my shot over the man guarding me."

Arizin also burst one of the myths about his health. The story goes that he played his whole career with asthma, or some bronchial ailment. Not true, according to him.

"That was misreported," said Arizin. "I never had asthma when I played. I don't know how that got started."

Another Path for Hagan

Cliff Hagan, of the St. Louis Hawks, was the same size as Arizin, but his career took an opposite path. Hagan (1956–70) was a graduate of the University of Kentucky, where he had been a 6' 4" forward-center who, at 220 pounds, was a tremendous physical specimen. He eventually joined the St. Louis Hawks, and coach Red Holzman figured Hagan would be better suited in the backcourt.

It was a mistake, because Hagan wasn't a perimeter shooter. He was a driver who also loved to mix it up under the boards. The Hawks struggled early in the year, and coach Holzman was fired and eventually replaced by Alex Hannum.

Still, Hagan's big break didn't come until Hawks star Bob Pettit broke his wrist in a game against the Celtics later in the year. Hannum, needing firepower, moved Hagan from guard to forward. Hagan found he could maneuver better against bigger opponents and still get off his running hook shot. After his first year with the Hawks, Hagan played forward for most of the rest of his career.

"It was a bad break for me, but a great opportunity for Cliff," said Pettit in his autobiography. "He stepped into that starting

Above: New York Knicks' Larry Johnson going up for the shot.

lineup that year and played very well."

Hagan was not a great shooter or leaper, but he had the strength and smarts to find ways to score against bigger players. In other words, he was the athletic opposite of Arizin, yet he still got the job done.

Basically, 'tweeners have fallen into one of those two categories down the years: the athletic tweener, like Arizin, or the low-post 'tweener, like Hagan.

The Celtics' John Havlicek (1962–78) was a variation on the Paul Arizin theme, as was the New York Knickerbockers' Bill Bradley (1967–77). Some players played more guard than forward, some more forward than guard. Havlicek was the one player who could—and did—play both point guard and shooting guard for the Celtics, as well as small forward. Over his career, Havlicek filled a variety of roles for Boston, including coming off the bench, or starting. He did, essentially, whatever it took to enable his team to win.

Incredibly, it always seemed to be such a seamless transition from position to position! In the 1977–78 season, when everything was falling apart for the Celtics (who would end up with a 32–50 record), and with Havlicek planning to retire, he ended up playing point guard for most of the season because the Celtics had no one better (his running mate was former Pistons and Washington Bullets guard Dave Bing, also in his last year). Name another player in the history of the game who began his career as a forward and ended it as a point guard. I can't.

There are an awful lot of people who believe that "Hondo," as he was nicknamed, was the best all-around player ever. (*Hondo* was a movie starring John Wayne, and Havlicek was a big John Wayne fan.)

Bradley, by contrast, played just one position, small forward, almost all his career. Like

Hagan, he was a terrific flop as a guard early in his career with the Knicks. It was only when newly hired Knicks coach Red Holzman moved Bradley to forward in the 1968–69 season that "Dollar Bill" really flourished.

Bradley was, by NBA standards, not particularly athletic. And he was a lousy rebounder, usually fifth or sixth best on the team.

His strengths were being able to move without the ball endlessly, an excellent passing eye and a fearless jump shot. He was called "Dollar Bill" because of his penchant for taking and making clutch shots late in a game.

On defense, Dollar Bill was one slick dude. His relationship with the referees was extremely low-key; he never argued a call. At the same time, Phil Jackson recalled in his autobiography, *Maverick*, "If you watched Bill, he was grabbing, clutching and holding his man the whole game. But the refs never seemed to see it."

Bradley realized that the best way to get the job done on defense was to play as physically as he could and keep the complaining to a minimum. He needed the refs more than they needed him.

The careers of Adrian Dantley (1976–91) and Charles Barkley (1984–01) opened up a different type of era: that of the "power 'tweener." Barkley, listed at 6' 6" but closer to 6' 4", was an amazing leaper with terrific upper-body strength. He was a powerful driver, rebounder and dunker. In fact, Barkley is easily the greatest rebounder, inch for inch, in the history of the league. Barkley averaged double figures in rebounds for 15 consecutive years, more than any other player in NBA history. That's any player, folks, not just forwards.

Dantley, at 6' 4", 210 pounds, was not the dunker Barkley was, but he was just as fearless going to the basket. In fact, he was one of those players who relied on getting fouled to score a lot of his points.

Larry Johnson, at 6' 6", 230 pounds,

The Big 'Tweeners

In addition to guys the size of guards who played forward, there is another sort of subgenre that is worth mentioning: guys the size of forwards playing center. The NBA of the 21st century is full of them, since there are only, in a given decade, about five to six players who can be legitimately called centers. Here are the five best big 'tweeners ever.

Bob Pettit (1954–65), St. Louis Hawks

The 6' 9" Pettit was a center in college at LSU, and was drafted by the Hawks to play that position. But Pettit was mobile and a good enough outside shooter to move the Hawks to pick up seven-foot Charlie Share to play the post. Pettit, who was also an outstanding passer and rebounder, became the prototype for the NBA power forward. He was also a tremendous clutch player. Pettit scored 19 of the Hawks' last 21 points (and 50 points in all) in Game 6 of the 1958 playoffs to preserve a 110–109 win for St. Louis, the only time the Hawks franchise has ever won a World Championship. This also prompted one of the best lines of the 1950s, when, after the game, Celtics coach Red Auerbach admonished forward Tommy Heinsohn, who had been guarding Pettit, "Tommy, if you'd have held Pettit to 48, we'd have won the game!"

Maurice Stokes (1955–58), Rochester Royals

Stokes played center for the Royals two of his three full years in the league, although he was only 6' 7". He was extremely mobile and quick, a dominating rebounder, a solid scorer and a very good passer. Stokes was the 1955–56 Rookie of the Year and was second in the league in rebounds. In his second year, he was the top rebounder in the league and, incredibly, third in the league in assists, an amazing feat for a center. But Stokes was, long before anyone had ever heard of Wilt Chamberlain or, later, Bill Walton, one of the great passing big men in the history of the pro game. He could also handle the ball like a guard. He was an amazing athlete who was a near-certain Hall of Famer.

But at the end of his third season, Stokes contracted encephalitis. Reportedly, Stokes fell on the court in the Royals' final game against the Minneapolis Lakers and struck his head, which eventually caused the illness. The encephalitis paralyzed Stokes from the neck down. For the next 12 years, until his death in 1970, Stokes could barely speak. Royals forward Jack Twyman, a former teammate of Stokes, spent those 12 years raising money to pay for Stokes's medical bills and supporting him.

Elvin Hayes (1968–84), Houston Rockets, Washington Bullets

The "Big E," as he was known, spent his first four years in the league as a center with the San Diego and then Houston Rockets. But just prior to the 1972–73 season, Hayes was traded to the Capitol (later Washington) Bullets. With wide Wes Unseld manning the center post, the Big E played power forward. He was perfect for it. At 6' 9", Hayes was among the stronger players in the league, and one of the most agile for his size. His bread-and-butter move was a devastating turnaround jump shot, and he could usually twist his body in midair to draw a foul from opponents who played too close to him.

Moses Malone (1974–95), Nine Different Teams

Malone actually grew into the center position. He was the first player in modern pro basketball history to be drafted as a high school player (by the Utah Stars of the ABA). At that point, he was a skinny, awkward 6' 9" forward. After his stint in the ABA, he played forward for several NBA teams, most notably the Houston Rockets.

Malone was such a devastating offensive rebounder that he was eventually moved to center. He was a well-conditioned athlete who had a knack for retrieving basketballs off the offensive glass. His other secret was amazing footwork. Malone could insinuate himself under the offensive glass before his defender could find him. He led the NBA in rebounding six times.

Kevin Garnett (1995–present), Minnesota Timberwolves

The whipsaw-thin, 6' 11" Garnett, like Malone, was drafted out of high school. Garnett is a solid all-around player who performs better when he plays forward. He has three-point range, is a very good ballhandler and has been a franchise player for the Timberwolves in his eight years there.

PLAYERS TO WATCH

The Mavs 6' 7" Michael Finley is the best of the 'tweeners, a good ballhandler, scorer, rebounder and defender in the John Havlicek mold. (He's not as good, but he works as hard, which is saying something.) The Spurs have two good 'tweeners, 6' 8" Steve Smith and 6' 7" Bruce Bowen. Both guys come off the bench. Smith is the scorer, Bowen the defender and rebounder.

Below: Minnesota Timberwolves' Kevin Garnett shoots over Charles Outlaw.

Left: Stackhouse (42) goes under the basekt.

(1991–2001), is of a similar style. Johnson seems to be almost as wide as he is tall, which has helped him. He is one of the more physical players in the league, which has hurt him to an extent, as all the banging around under the basket seems to have worn him down physically over the years.

Except for Johnson, most of the players in the league who move back and forth from guard to forward, guys like 6' 6" Jerry Stackhouse (1996–present), 6' 7" Kobe Bryant (1996–present), 6' 5" Vince Carter (1998–present) and 6' 7" Paul Pierce (1998–present), generally stay in the backcourt. Pierce, of this crew, is more of a swingman than the others, but the Celtics used him at guard a lot in 2001–02.

This is because the level of ballhandling skill in the NBA has gone up exponentially in the past 20 years. Bryant and the others play guard because they can handle the ball and pass as well as guys six inches shorter. Thus, they are usually more valuable at guard than at forward.

27 The Playground Moves

How Stylin' Began

ORIGIN: **May 1894**

THE FIRST: **Several members of various YMCAs in New York City**

THE ALL-TIMERS:
Johnny Beckman (1913-40)
Bob Cousy (1950-63, 1969-70)
Dick McGuire (1949-60)
Connie Hawkins (1967-76)
Earl Manigault, Raymond Lewis,
Julius Erving (1971-87)
Allen Iverson (1996-present).
All but Lewis, Manigault and Iverson are in the
Hall of Fame.

THE TECHNIQUE:
Playground basketball puts a premium on style, creativity, athleticism and one-upmanship. So, don't take a layup; throw down a dunk. Don't fire a chest pass if you can whip a ball between your legs to a teammate. Don't grab a rebound, rip it down with one hand.

On defense, since no one calls offensive fouls in a play-ground game, it's better to try to block your man's shot if you can. If not, hit his elbow when he's shooting and be prepared to argue that you never touched him when he calls the foul.

Also, if you get to be the captain in a pickup game, and a guy nicknamed "Helicopter" is on the court, pick him first. Same goes for anybody whose nickname is "Jumpin'"-anything.

Above: Jonathan O'Neill on Goat Courts in New York City.
Right: Michael Trujillo in Mosquero, New Mexico.

Basketball is the only team sport that can, and is, played just about anywhere. It can be played indoors or outdoors on virtually any kind of surface. The Buffalo Germans played outdoors on grass in a 1901 tournament wearing cleats. The first Olympic tournament in Berlin in 1936 was played outdoors in a dirt arena that became a sea of mud when the final between the United States and Canada was rained on. Joe Lapchick recalled playing on slippery tile floors as a barnstormer with the Original Celtics in the 1920s and 1930s.

The venue flexibility has fostered this unique genre of basketball, the playground game that has no equal in any other sport. Certainly, there is sandlot baseball and touch football and six-to-a-side soccer, but all those games still incorporate the basic rules of those respective games. Playground basketball takes the essential rules of basketball and pushes the athletic and creative envelope of the sport in a way seen by no other athletic activity.

Playground basketball has been around almost as long as the game itself. In May of 1894, more than 500 people watched and

1946, THE RUCKER TOURNAMENT IS ESTABLISHED

In the summer of 1946, Holcombe Rucker began a league to try to keep inner-city youngsters off the street. (He called it the Rucker Tournament, but it actually was a weekend summer league.) The initial site was on Seventh Avenue near 130th Street in Harlem. Rucker was a junior high school teacher who had modest goals: he was just trying to find a way to keep the local youth occupied. Kids in Harlem were already playing basketball, but Rucker's vision was to lend the schoolyard game a little more dignity by providing referees, trophies and publicity.

It started modestly, with four teams, and exploded in popularity a few years later. Rucker had established leagues and tournaments in four divisions: junior high, high school, college and pro. It was the pro division that sparked everyone's imagination. NBA stars came to test their mettle (and reputations) against the best playground players New York City had to offer. Wilt Chamberlain, Walt Frazier, Nate "Tiny" Archibald, Stephon Marbury, Allen Iverson and others all brought their sneakers to the Rucker. While the pros usually prevailed, there was more than one instance where they did not. Before Connie Hawkins matriculated to the ABA, and later to the NBA, his exploits against future pros like Chamberlain and Willis Reed were legendary and remain so.

The Rucker still exists today. It is located at Rucker Park on 155th Street and Frederick Douglass Boulevard and is run by Holcombe Rucker's grandson, Christopher. Holcombe Rucker died of cancer in 1965. NBA players still come by to test themselves. Last year, Marbury and the Toronto Raptors' Vince Carter were two of the more prominent pro stars that participated in the league.

Left: Gonzalo and Joe Ortiz of Brooklyn, New York, shoot hoops in Vermont.

Left: Jump shots at Cameron Park Recreation Center in Brownsville, Texas.

applauded as members of several YMCAs from the area played in an exhibition basketball game on the first "open air" court in New York City. It was built by the YMCA in the Mott Haven section of the Bronx on 150th Street near the Harlem River. At the time, there was only one other outdoor court, located in Springfield, Massachusetts.

"An outdoor basketball court is a decided novelty in this city," noted an unknown correspondent for the *New York Times*. "A crowd of more than 500 witnessed the exhibition, three-quarters of which had never seen a game."

The game's popularity almost literally exploded in New York. Players, young and old, took it up. And if they couldn't find one of the courts that were springing up almost overnight in which to play, kids were throwing various objects into various types of containers of various configurations.

In Yonkers, New York, in 1910, for example, a young Joe Lapchick and his friends stuffed an old soccer ball with socks and tossed it at a "goal" drawn onto the roof of a house. Was the goal 10 feet high? Probably

not, but that's how Lapchick got his start.

In Brooklyn about 10 years later, future NBA star Sonny Hertzberg (1946–51) stuffed an old stocking cap with paper and shot it through the rungs of the ladder on his fire escape. In 1930, 10-year-old Bob Davies (1949–59) tacked a paint can up on a telephone pole and played by using a tennis ball as a basketball.

Since the inventor of the game, Dr. James Naismith, worked for the YMCA, the game spread quickly throughout the country as local YMCAs picked it up. In many metropolitan and rural areas, baskets were put up in community centers and gyms. It was also being introduced in other places. In more rural towns and villages, baskets were nailed to balconies, or to the sides of barns, or even to telephone poles. In metropolitan areas, local parks departments began laying out basketball courts outdoors.

The game's popularity was part of the reason. The other part was cost. The price of putting up one basketball goal, or, if space allowed, two, and buying a basketball or two was negligible compared to outfitting a foot-

The First "Playground" Pro

Again, when we think of modern playground players, we think of pioneers like Connie Hawkins, Julius Erving and Wilt Chamberlain. However, the first man to play what we would call "playground" basketball was not a black man but a white player, "Jumpin' Jim" Pollard in the 1940s.

Pollard was almost certainly the first man to dunk behind his head, mostly because he was almost certainly the only guy who could do it. Pollard was 6' 5" or so, and he had a vertical leap that was reportedly once measured at 45 inches. David Thompson's vertical leap was 44 inches. Michael Jordan's was 43.

Pollard never did fancy dunks in a game, because to do that would be "showing up" an opponent, and players just didn't do that. Mikan, coach Johnny Kundla and other former Lakers swore that Pollard did all kinds of tricky slams in practice, including jumping with his back to the basket and slamming the ball home.

But he was not above a little flash. He (not Connie Hawkins) was, according to those who were there, the first player to palm the ball in one hand, sweep it around his head and drive to the goal. Nobody called it "playground" basketball then. That's because nobody had ever seen a lot of the things Pollard did.

"He was a beautiful, graceful player," recalled Hall of Famer Bob Kurland, who played against Pollard when the two men played AAU ball. "A great jump shooter, but a great driver, too. He'd hold the ball over his head with one hand, and the next thing you knew, he'd go right by you. You know who reminds me a lot of Pollard? That kid (Paul) Pierce for the Celtics. Same kind of player."

"When Pollard used to block shots," recalled Lakers coach John Kundla, "he would sometimes pin the ball against the backboard. I had never seen anyone do that before Jim. He was an amazing jumper."

Pollard was the greatest leaper of the 1940s. In Mikan's first year with Minneapolis, Pollard played center. And even after big Vern Mikkelsen came along, Pollard was a terrific rebounder on the both the offensive and defensive glass. He was also a low-post threat: he often posted up much bigger men on the blocks and just shot over them.

Pollard was probably one of the fastest, if not the fastest, player in the league. Bob Pettit recalled that as a rookie, he tried to pick up Pollard at the head of the key as Pollard was driving. Pollard didn't even slow down: he drove around Pettit like he was standing still.

In fact, such was Pollard's ability that in 1954 coaches and writers voted him as the best player in NBA history up to that point, beating out Mikan.

ball or hockey team. While baseball required just a ball, a bat and gloves, the playing area required a certain degree of diamond-shaped space. Basketball? You could put a basket up in a driveway, or on the side of a building. Its very flexibility contributed mightily to its rapid expansion.

Thus it was that while the game was being taught in a more formal manner in YMCA and community center gyms, another, less formal and more expressive style of the game was also flourishing.

The Stars of New York

The first playground star is difficult to pinpoint. The first Mecca, if you will, of playground basketball was clearly New York City. The game had taken hold of the sporting populace there by the mid-1890s. The city's early playground stars were young Irish and Jewish players, some of whom would later matriculate to many of the city's larger universities, like St. John's, City College of New York and New York University, and turn the city into a hotbed of college basketball.

Others, like the legendary Johnny Beckman, didn't play high school or college basketball. Beckman, born in 1895, began playing professionally in 1913 in his teens in a variety of leagues (my favorite: the New York Treat 'Em Roughs of the Interstate League in 1919–20). Beckman, in his youth, also played in community centers and on street corners wherever and whenever he could.

Other early New York schoolboy stars included future Celtics coach Arnold "Red" Auerbach, a 5' 10" guard who haunted Brooklyn community centers while starring at Eastern District High School from 1932 to 1935.

"My players used to kid me when I told them I was second-team all-city," recalled Auerbach years later. "But there were more good ballplayers in Brooklyn than anywhere

Above: Children playing in Guinea-Bissau, West Africa.

else in the country in those days."

Future Knickerbockers coach William "Red" Holzman was a slick 5' 9" guard at Franklin J. Lane High School in Jamaica, New York, where he was all-city in 1938 and was eventually inducted into the New York Public School Athletic League Hall of Fame. Future NBL and NBA star Bobby Wanzer (1947–57) was a playground legend while he played at Ben Franklin High School from 1938 to 1941. All three men are now in the Basketball Hall of Fame.

The most well known early playground star was Richard McGuire, better known to old-time basketball fans as "Tricky Dick" McGuire.

McGuire was a star at LaSalle Academy in New York City from 1939 to 1943. He attended St. John's University for one year before leaving to serve in the armed forces. McGuire returned to St. John's for his final three years from 1946 to 1949. He was drafted by the New York Knickerbockers and played in the NBA for 11 years, from 1949 to 1960.

McGuire was a sensational ballhandler, known for his no-look passes and behind-the-back dribbling, particularly in the pros. There were clearly players before McGuire around the country who were stars on city playgrounds, but most old-timers remember Tricky Dick as one of the first all-time greats.

His brother, Al McGuire, a strong player at St. John's Prep in the late 1940s, who also ended up at St. John's and also played briefly for the Knicks, tells an interesting story in Pete Axthelm's fine book about playground basketball, *The City Game*.

Al noted that in the 1940s, the best city players played on the New York City playgrounds on the weekends. Many were Irish and many were Catholic. On Sunday, as Al McGuire relates it, the younger players had to get up and attend 7 A.M. Mass to ensure they got to the courts at 8 A.M. to get into a game.

"As the day went on, more and more players would be lining the fences of the playground, waiting to challenge the winner or to be asked to join a team. The good high

WILT'S SCORING

Super Stats

Wilt Chamberlain had 122 games in which he scored 50 points or more, easily the highest number of all time. The rest of the top 10 are Michael Jordan, 36; Elgin Baylor, 18; Rick Barry, 15; Kareem Abdul-Jabbar, 10; Bernard King, 8; Dominique Wilkins, 7; Jerry West, 7; Bob Pettit, 7; Allen Iverson, 7. If you do the math, you realize that Wilt had more 50-point games than the rest of the next nine players combined (122–115). One more stat: in 1961–62, the year he averaged 50.4 points per game, Wilt had 46 50-plus games, or more in one season than runner-up Michael Jordan had in his career.

Below: Dr. J. Moves the ball past Larry Bird.

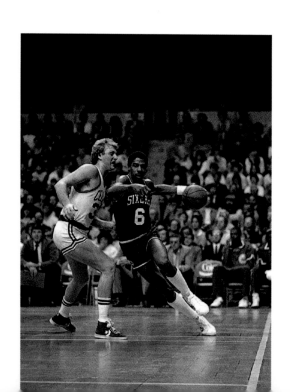

school players could sleep in a little bit," McGuire recalled, "and attend 10 A.M. Mass, knowing they would be asked to play in a game when they got to the courts. College players could afford to sleep in a little later and go to 11 A.M. Mass, and if you became a pro star like my brother Dick, you could go to 12:30 Mass, come out and stand in the back of the crowd—and you'd still be invited to play right away."

That pecking order hasn't changed terribly much 60 years later.

Another trick that works even now is to buy an expensive leather ball. Sooner or later, a player would notice the ball and ask the owner to join the game—with his ball. Of course, the owner of the ball had to have some ability, or he wouldn't be on a team for very long.

The playground style of the 1930s, 1940s and 1950s was a lot like the play on regulation courts in those days. Players, for the most part, eschewed the "hot dog" pass and the crazy shot unless unable to make the play any other way. Still, there is no doubt that great players like Dick McGuire and Bob Cousy, a star at Andrew Jackson High in Queens from 1942 to 1946, weren't afraid to put a little "mustard" on those hot dog passes when performing on the playgrounds of the city.

And, as Holcombe Rucker's tournament grew in popularity and reputation, the 1950s began to see the first great black playground players, like Ed Warner, a 6' 9" center who would go to play at City College in the late 1940s, and Lenny Wilkins, a 6' 1" guard who didn't make his high school varsity team until his senior year (1955–56) at Boys High. Wilkins honed his game on the playgrounds and in various local Catholic Youth Organization leagues.

The Hawk and the Goat

The two most legendary playground performers, both from New York City, are relative contemporaries, yet the lives of Connie "the Hawk" Hawkins and Earl "the Goat" Manigault took very diverse paths since their beginnings in New York 40 years ago.

Hawkins, a 6' 8" forward, began as a star player for Boys High in the Bedford-Stuyvesant section of New York from 1957 to 1960. He led the school to back-to-back unbeaten seasons in 1958–60. The Boys High team of Hawkins's junior year was, along with Lew Alcindor's Power Memorial teams a few years later, considered among the greatest schoolboy basketball teams in the history of the city.

Hawkins (1969–76) was a star as a sophomore at Boys, and his playground rep grew in the late 1950s. He outperformed college players and even professionals as a high schooler and was seemingly fated for stardom in the professional ranks after his college career.

Then Hawkins, unfairly as it turned out, was kicked out of college and banned from the NBA for allegedly participating in a gambling scheme in 1959. He played in the old American Basketball League, later with the Harlem Globetrotters and then the American Basketball Association until his innocence was proven. He was finally allowed to play in the NBA in 1969.

In the 1960s, Hawkins was basketball's forgotten man, at least nationally. In the playgrounds of New York City, he was still well known and admired.

Hawkins's huge hands enabled him to cup a basketball like a softball. He had an explosive leaping ability that made him nearly impossible to guard. He could hold off an opponent with one hand while shooting with the other. His amazing one-handed layups, push shots and dunks were electrifying. He was a great scorer but an even better passer.

His exploits were legendary. His best shot was a "hook-dunk" whereby he would elevate over a player and turn his body as if to shoot a jump hook. Instead of releasing the ball, Hawkins would twist his body in the air and slam it through the net. One year, in the Rucker Tournament, Hawkins didn't play in a single game but was still voted to the All-Star team. Hawkins showed up for that tilt and was named MVP of the game.

After a prolonged legal battle with the NBA, Hawkins eventually played in the league, from 1969 to 1976, playing in four All-Star games. In 1996, Hawkins was named to the Hall of Fame.

Manigault's story is less glamorous, although in the end, he managed to right himself and turn a difficult life around.

"The Goat," as he was called, was a star player at Ben Franklin High School in 1962 and 1963. (His nickname is a shortened version of his last name.) Manigault was expelled from the team for his use of marijuana, so he transferred to Laurinburg Institute in North Carolina for his senior year. Upon graduation, Manigault matriculated at Johnson C. Smith College, also in North Carolina.

He quarreled openly with his coach about playing time, and spent only one semester at Johnson C. Smith before returning to Harlem.

At 6' 2", Manigault played forward. He was an extraordinary athlete, one of the greatest leapers in New York playground history. He was able to maneuver his body over and around opponents and his "hang time" was legendary. He had a number of colorful dunks, including one where he dunked a basketball, caught it as it was going through the basket and dunked it again. Another move featured Manigault jumping from near the foul line, bringing the basketball over his head and down to his waist—twice—before dunking. His vertical jump was said to be 53 inches, an extraordinary figure, though it was never officially documented.

His dunks and overall offensive skills were considerable. At a time when a teenaged, 7' 2" Lewis Alcindor also prowled the playgrounds, Manigault was considered as dangerous a scorer, despite being a foot shorter.

Then Manigault's drug use progressed to heroin, and he spent two stints in jail for

drug possession. He was contacted by the Utah Stars of the ABA in 1971 for a tryout, but drug use had eroded his skills to the point where he could not make the team.

Manigault's story brightened in the 1980s. He kicked his drug habit and became a drug counselor and basketball coach. At the time of his death in 1998, at 53, he was a respected member of the Harlem community for his efforts with local youth. In 2002, the park where Manigault played on 98th Street

Above: Minneapolis Lakers' Jim Pollard sinks a layup against the Knicks.

was renamed "Goat Park" in his honor.

These men were among the first who developed the notion of "playground basketball" into a more self-expressive art form. The idea was still to score more baskets than one's opponent. Beyond that, the idea of playground basketball was to do it all with more élan than the next guy.

The Los Angeles Legend

These players were not limited to New York City. In Los Angeles, city playground players still speak with reverence about Raymond Lewis. Many fans living on the east coast have never heard of him. But if you lived in Los Angeles, and basketball was your game, the name Raymond Lewis was a household term.

Lewis was an incredible shooter with great range and quickness. His moves were not nearly as colorful, perhaps, as those of Hawkins or Manigault. Rather, Lewis just shot the bejeesus out of the hoop, sometimes from near half-court.

Lewis was a streetball legend who had actually been playing for money since his career began in junior high in the late 1960s. Lewis led his high school, Verbum Dei, to three California state championships (1969–71). Heavily recruited, he signed with Los Angeles State in 1971 and scored 73 points in one game as a freshman. After his sophomore year, he entered the NBA draft.

But Raymond's pro career didn't pan out. He was drafted by Philadelphia in 1973 and signed a contract with the Sixers, but, frustrated by what he thought was misrepresentation by Philadelphia, he never played a regular season game in two years. In subsequent tryouts with the Knicks, Clippers and the ABA, Lewis played well but could never come to terms with management. A player who many Los Angeles players believe was

PLAYERS TO WATCH

Certainly, Jason Williams of the Grizzlies is the flashiest player in the league. Problem is, sometimes the behind-the-back, no-look pass works and sometimes it doesn't. The Raptors' Vince Carter is a playground player because of his prodigious dunks. Otherwise, he is pretty fundamentally conservative, believe it or not.

the best ever to come out of that city never made it into the NBA Encyclopedia.

Hawkins and Manigault, and others, like playground legend Herman "Helicopter" Knowings, so named for his fantastic leaping ability, began to steer the game in a direction away from fundamental basketball. To some, it has made the game more balletic and more pleasing to watch. To others, it is a bastardization of the original tenets of founder James Naismith.

Hawkins was the first, but by no means the last, ultra-athlete to make the transition from the playground to the pros. Others, like Earl Monroe of Philadelphia, who played for the Washington Bullets and the New York Knickerbockers in his 12-year career, and New York's Nate Archibald, also came aboard the NBA. These men and others managed to retrofit their respective games for the professional ranks with little trouble.

Then there was Julius Erving. Erving (1971–87) was acrobatic, explosive, high-scoring and undeniably great. His game flourished in the American Basketball Association, but when the ABA and NBA merged before the 1976–77 season, Erving made a seamless transition to the older, more

traditional NBA. Erving had no interest in "toning his game down" and he didn't have to. He was good.

Players, fans and coaches who had expressed doubts about Hawkins and his playground contemporaries had no choice but to accept Erving, because he was clearly one of the best two or three forwards in the league: he was a strong defender, an excellent passer and rebounder and an explosive scorer. It was undeniable that he accomplished these goals in a manner more flamboyant than his roundball predecessors. Equally undeniable was that Erving's arrival pushed the league as a whole in a more athletic direction.

Thus, the door to the playground swung wide open and has stayed that way. The NBA is now much faster, much more athletic and much more colorful than it has ever been. The dunks of Vince Carter, of the Toronto Raptors, Paul Pierce, of the Boston Celtics, Kobe Bryant, of the Los Angeles Lakers, are greeted with gasps of delight by audiences throughout the league.

But we may have seen the first momentum shift in this colorful style with the ignominious defeat of the U.S. NBA All-Star team at the World Championships in Indianapolis in the summer of 2002. The United States team finished a stunning sixth in the tournament, and U.S. players, flashier and more athletic, were consistently beaten by teams of skilled, fundamentally solid ballplayers.

During his induction speech at the Basketball Hall of Fame later that year, former Lakers guard Magic Johnson warned the NBA intelligentsia that this defeat at the hands of foreign teams would not abate until the United States players "got back to basics." His statement was greeted by thunderous applause from the audience.

28 The One-on-One Moves

The Gunslingers
of the 20th Century

THE ORIGIN: The 1960s

THE FIRST: Roger Brown (1967–75)

THE ALL-TIMERS:
Brown, Jerry West (1960–74)
Earl Monroe (1967–80)
Julius Erving (1971–87)
Vinnie Johnson (1979–92)
Michael Jordan (1984–93, 1994–98, 2001–present)
West, Monroe and Erving are Hall of Famers.

THE TECHNIQUE:
Look your man in the eye. Then, while he's looking into your eyes, pull up for a jumper, or blow past him on a drive. Good ballhandling skills are a must, because you have to be able to maneuver to be in position to get your shot. Always remember, you have the advantage of knowing what you're going to do. Make your move with confidence. And keep making that move until your opponent can prove that he can stop it.

Above: Kobe Bryant
Right: Earl "The Pearl" Monroe thrived on the drive

If one wants to be technical about it, the first one-on-one professional player was probably someone like Leroy "Cowboy" Edwards (1935–42) or Edward "Big Ed" Sadowski (1940–50), muscular centers from the early days who posted up and were fed the basketball. Both Edwards and Sadowski had pretty good post moves, and could take opponents into the low block and usually do considerable damage.

But we're talking here about guys who didn't really need anybody to get them the ball. They could do it all themselves.

One of the pioneers of this genre was 6' 5" forward Roger Brown (1967–75). Brown was a legendary one-on-one player when he was a star at Wingate High in New York City in the 1950s. Brown had two basic moves: a 25- to 30-foot jumper and a devastating drive to the hoop with either hand. But the key to his success was that he started both moves from the same position on the court: about 30 feet from the basket. Opponents never knew whether he would pull up for a shot or drive.

At Wingate, Brown was All-City with another schoolboy legend, Connie Hawkins of Boys High School. There, he was considered the best one-on-one player in the city. And, like Hawkins, Brown was eventually ensnared in the betting scandals of 1960 and banned from the NBA for life.

Also like Hawkins, Brown searched for an outlet for his talent. He eventually played AAU ball for several years, but when he was signed by the Indiana Pacers in 1967, he was working at a car dealership as a salesman.

Brown was an immediate star in the ABA, averaging almost 20 points per game his first year. And the ABA was tailor-made for his skills. Brown, whose specialty in high school had been the long-range shot, could drain three-point baskets with ease. He holds the record for most threes in an ABA championship game, when he drilled seven in a game in the 1970 Finals against the Los Angeles Stars.

But if his opponent moved in too tightly to try to cut off the three, Roger would take one huge step and drive to the hoop. Brown led the Pacers to three ABA titles, and is the all-time leading playoff scorer for the ABA.

Along with Brown, the 1970s saw the explosion of the one-on-one player in the professional ranks. Pacers coach Bob "Slick" Leonard was one of the first coaches to realize that Brown could overmatch just about anyone who guarded him. Thus, Leonard would order one side of the court cleared of all players but Brown and his defender, and allow Brown to work his man.

MAY 22, 1988, THE NBA EASTERN CONFERENCE FINALS, GAME 7, ATLANTA VS. BOSTON

Moments after the Boston Celtics had defeated the Atlanta Hawks in Atlanta in Game 6 of the Eastern Conference Finals, Boston forward Larry Bird told the Hawks what to expect in Game 7, which would be played in Boston.

"They might as well forget it," said Bird of the Hawks' Game 7 prospects. "They've got no chance. They had a chance to beat us and we all knew that if we lost, it meant vacation tomorrow."

Bird's prediction came true, but not before the Hawks gave the Celtics a heck of a battle. In the final minutes of the fourth quarter of that game, won by Boston 118–116, Bird and Atlanta forward Dominique Wilkins had perhaps the most electrifying man-to-man shootout ever seen in the seventh game of a playoff.

Wilkins started the shootout with a 20-footer with 5:55 left to tie the contest at 99–99. From there, it went like this:

Boston: Bird, lefty push shot off a drive, 5:36 (101–99).
Atlanta: Wilkins, 25-footer, 5:28 (101–101).
Boston: Bird, 20-footer, 5:10 (103–101).
Atlanta: Wilkins, high-arching bank shot, 4:32 (103–103).
Boston: Kevin McHale, two free throws, 4:23 (105–103).
Atlanta: Randy Wittman, 20-footer, 3:48 (105–105).
Boston: Bird, short-drive, double-teamed, 3:29 (107–105).
Boston: McHale, two free throws, 2:10 (109–105).
Boston: Bird, three-point basket, right in front of the Hawks' bench, 1:43 (112–105).
Atlanta: Wilkins drive, 1:26 (112–107).
Atlanta: Wilkins, two free throws, 0:58 (112–109).
Boston: Bird, lefty drive, 0:26 (114–109).
Atlanta: Wilkins, tips in own miss, 0:20 (114–111).
Boston: Danny Ainge, layup, full-court pass from Bird, 0:17 (116–111).

Dennis Johnson hit two free throws and the Hawks added a couple of free throws and a hoop from Rollins to create the final. But that full-court pass from Bird to Ainge was the greatest play in a game that saw about a dozen in the last six minutes.

One final note: After Bird drilled that three-pointer, he trotted back down the court. As he turned to play defense, he caught Hawk forward Cliff Levingston shaking his head and muttering to himself. Bird caught Levingston's eye and grinned.

Left: 76er's Fred Carter marks Jerry West stride for stride.

The Best Game 7 Ever?

Possibly because teams from either Boston or Los Angeles were not involved, the 1978 NBA Final has been overlooked as one of the most exciting in league history. The series had everything: close games, great comebacks, and the winning team, Washington, taking the title on the home court of the loser, Seattle, in the seventh game. That, folks, has only happened three times in league history, and the Bullets are the only non-Celtics team to do it.

Anyway, Game 7 of this two-week war was, as one would expect, close and hard-fought. The Bullets, trailing three games to two in the series, had won Game 6 in Washington, 117–82. Both teams flew back to Seattle for the finale.

The seventh game featured a pair of unlikely heroes: reserve guards Charles Johnson for Washington and Freddie Brown for Seattle, dueling in the latter stages of the game. In fact, Bullets center Wes Unseld was named the MVP of the 1978 NBA playoffs, and there is no doubt he had a fine series. He was the Bullets' leading rebounder and he did everything coach Dick Motta asked of him. But the guy that pulled his teammates' collective cojones out

of the fire in Game 7 of the Finals was Charles Johnson.

Johnson, a sixth-year pro out of the University of California, had been released by Golden State in mid-season. He had been a huge part of the Warriors' 1974–75 World Championship team, but in 1977–78, with Phil Smith, Charles Dudley, Ricky Green and swingman Nate Williams, the Warriors figured they were set at guard.

Johnson was signed by the Bullets in mid-season after injuries had depleted their roster to only eight players. When the team got healthy, Johnson spent a lot of time on the bench.

By the time of the Finals, Johnson had worked his way up as the team's third guard. Johnson averaged 8.2 points per game in the regular season and 8.5 in the playoffs. In Game 7, Bullets starter Kevin Grevey, banged up with leg and arm injuries, played only 10 minutes. Johnson came in and hit nine of 21 shots and a free throw for 19 points. Late in the fourth quarter, with Elvin Hayes fouled out, Johnson drilled four 20-footers with Seattle guard Dennis Johnson draped all over him. On one shot, with about three minutes left, he had to jump backwards because D. J. was almost wearing Johnson's pants, he was so close to him.

The shot fell, and Charles Johnson got fouled. He made that shot, too.

As good as Charles Johnson was for the winners, "Downtown" Freddie Brown of Seattle actually played better. Over the course of the fourth quarter, Brown hit, in order: (1) a soft leaner in the lane over Johnson; (2) a scoop shot in which he ducked under Bullets forward Mitch Kupchak's arm and laid the ball in; (3) a double-pump floater in which he split forwards Bob Dandridge and Kupchak and shot the ball under Kupchak's outstretched arm again; (4) a shot over Dandridge from the deep left corner during which he had to jump sideways and land out of bounds; (5) one of three free throws and (6) another scoop shot in the lane while sandwiched between Charles Johnson and Dandridge.

"It's obvious," said commentator John Havlicek during the game (yeah, that John Havlicek), "that Freddie Brown is really the only Seattle player who's confident enough to take the ball to the basket for Seattle. If he keeps doing that, the Sonics have a chance to win."

Brown ended up with 11 points in the quarter and 21 for the game, but the Bullets won the title with a 105–99 victory.

The NBA Catches On

Brown's success did not go unnoticed. During the 1969–70 season, the Los Angeles Lakers saw a similar strategy as the answer to a problem. Early in the season their center, Wilt Chamberlain, had injured his Achilles tendon, a debilitating wound from which many believed he would never recover. Also early in the year, the Lakers' All-Star forward, Elgin Baylor, suffered another painful leg injury and was out for long stretches that season. That left Lakers guard Jerry West as the team's principal scoring threat.

Lakers coach Joe Mullaney, believing he had little choice, opted for a very basic strategy: he would line up the other four players on one side of the court, and West on the other side. West would simply take his man one-on-one virtually every time down the court.

Right: Ron Williams of the San Francisco Warriors guards West.

West was not as explosive a driver as Brown, although Jerry could go to the hoop in a pinch. West's weapon was a stop-and-pop jumper that he could launch in the blink of an eye. Even when players were aware that he was preparing to shoot it, they could do little about it. If they tried to anticipate it, West drove around them. If they waited for it, West drained the shot before the defender knew what happened.

Above: Earl Monroe drives against Jeff Judkins of the Celtics.

Right: Dr. J. demonstrates the one-hand dunk.

The strategy often worked. West led the league in scoring that year with a 31.2 average, and was also fourth in assists with a 7.5 mark. It also wore West out, and at his request, Mullaney eventually scrapped the one-on-one offense later in the season.

"Thomas Edison" and the Invention of the Spin Dribble

While West relied on his stop and pop, Earl "the Pearl" Monroe thrived on the drive. Monroe (1967–80) honed his game on the playgrounds of Philadelphia. His high school teammates called him "Thomas Edison" after

the inventive ways he would drive to the basket. Monroe is almost surely the inventor of the "spin dribble," whereby he would back into an opponent, lean into the man, cup the ball in his hand and spin around him to the basket.

Before Monroe, there were players who could reverse their dribble and spin off in another direction. Monroe accomplished this in one smooth motion by cupping the ball in one hand. Not surprisingly, the move was picked up by everybody after he began dazzling professional players with it beginning in 1967.

"Every day after school," recalled Magic Johnson, "my older brother would make me practice the Earl Monroe spin dribble before we could play a game. And he would make me practice it until I did it right."

Monroe was a decent outside shooter, but unlike West or Brown, his principal strength was going to the hoop. Although big guards like Oscar Robertson (1960–74) would turn their back on a defender and just muscle him toward the basket, Monroe's moves were more delicate. He would also back his man in, but Monroe would be facing away from his man and bringing the ball up to his chest on the dribble. (He called it "yo-yoing.")

Then, suddenly, Monroe would spin one way or the other, completely losing his man, and drive to the hoop. If a defender was particularly tenacious, Monroe would sometimes feint a half-spin in one direction to fake his defender into thinking he was going that way, then cup the ball and spin back the other way. In fact, in a variation on that move, the Pearl would fake a spin left, fake one right, and spin back left again. That maneuver usually left his defender trying to find his own shorts.

As he exploded toward the hoop, Monroe's humiliation of his opponents was often not over. Sometimes, he would shoot what he and others called a "facial"; that is, Monroe would stop quickly and release a jump shot right in the poor guy's face. In the 1971 NBA Finals against the Milwaukee Bucks and their center Kareem Abdul-Jabbar, Monroe drove on Kareem in one game. As Abdul-Jabbar leapt to block his shot, Monroe adjusted his arms and shot the ball between Abdul-Jabbar's outstretched arms. The ball banked in.

Back in the ABA, New York Nets coach Kevin Loughery was faced with the same situation as his Los Angeles counterpart Joe Mullany: how to get the most mileage out of a great player. In Loughery's case, it was 6' 6" forward Julius Erving. Erving in his ABA days was such an amazing leaper with such extraordinary body control that he was nearly impossible to stop, so Loughery ran a lot of plays through him.

Unlike the Lakers or Bullets with Monroe, though, the Nets spread out on either side of the lane and let Erving have the middle of the court. This was because Erving could drive to the basket with either hand. And when he pulled up to shoot a

Left: San Antonio Spurs' Gene Banks tries to guard rookie Michael Jordan.

jumper, he was often so high in the air that his defender could only watch as Erving released the shot.

Nets fans knew they were in for a treat, usually near the end of the game, when Loughery pulled his other four players to either side of the court and let "Doctor J" operate on his defender. Thus, the court became a very, very lonely place for that defender.

New York actually had two one-on-one stars in the mid-1970s. In addition to Erving, the Nets had John Williamson (1973–81). Williamson was built like a linebacker and called "Super John" for his amazing scoring runs.

In the ABA's final game in 1976, in which the Nets played the Denver Nuggets

for the last championship of the league, Williamson scored 24 of his 28 points in the second half to win the contest nearly single-handedly. Several times, he brought the ball up against the Nuggets and waved off Erving before driving to the hoop. Erving had no problem with that: "Supe," as he called Williamson, was on fire that night.

The Isolation Play

Teams began using one-on-one, or "isolation," plays more and more as the 1970s progressed. In the 1980s, Philadelphia 76ers coach Bill Cunningham took that a step further: he put his explosive guard, Andrew Toney (1980–88) on the right side of the court along with his equally explosive center, Moses Malone (1974–95) in a two-on-two situation. If Toney's man sagged to help defend Malone, Andrew shot the ball. If Toney's man stayed tight on him, Toney would dump the ball into Malone and let him work on his man.

The 1980s and 1990s saw more teams isolating their best player on an individual defender. The Detroit Pistons, for example, had a very good starting unit, but when coach Chuck Daly needed points, he would look down his bench and call for Vincent "the Microwave" Johnson (1979–92).

Johnson got his nickname from former Boston Celtics guard Danny Ainge, a frequent victim of Johnson's offensive incursions.

"That guy," said Ainge after one such individual assault, "is like a microwave, he heats up so fast."

Thus was a nickname, and legend, born.

Johnson helped the Pistons to a pair of NBA titles in 1988–89 and 1989–90. Like Williamson, Johnson was powerfully built at 6' 2", 200 pounds. His forte was muscling as close to the basket as he could and shooting the lights out. He only started about 11 percent of the games in which he played, but still averaged 12 points per game for his career.

Michael Jordan (1984–93, 1994–98, 2001–present) is the latest and one of the best of the great one-on-one players. Like West, he can start out on one side of the court or the other and either drive or pull up. Like Erving and Williamson, Jordan can also start his moves at the head of the key. He won the 1998 NBA championship against the Utah Jazz by beating Byron Russell, a solid defender, off the dribble and pulling up for a 15-footer.

The player that has really been wearing the one-on-one champion crown is Paul Pierce of the Celtics. Pierce faces his man and just goes up for the shot. He is a great leaper and deadly accurate. He has already had a couple of 16- and 18-point fourth quarters in his short career.

Most, if not all, NBA teams use some variation of the one-on-one offense. It makes sense from a technical standpoint: most clubs have at least one dominant scorer they believe they can go to in a pinch. The problem might be that the overall concept tends to slow the game down, a trend that has been ongoing for the past decade or so.

Left: John Stockton goes up against a more seasoned Jordan.

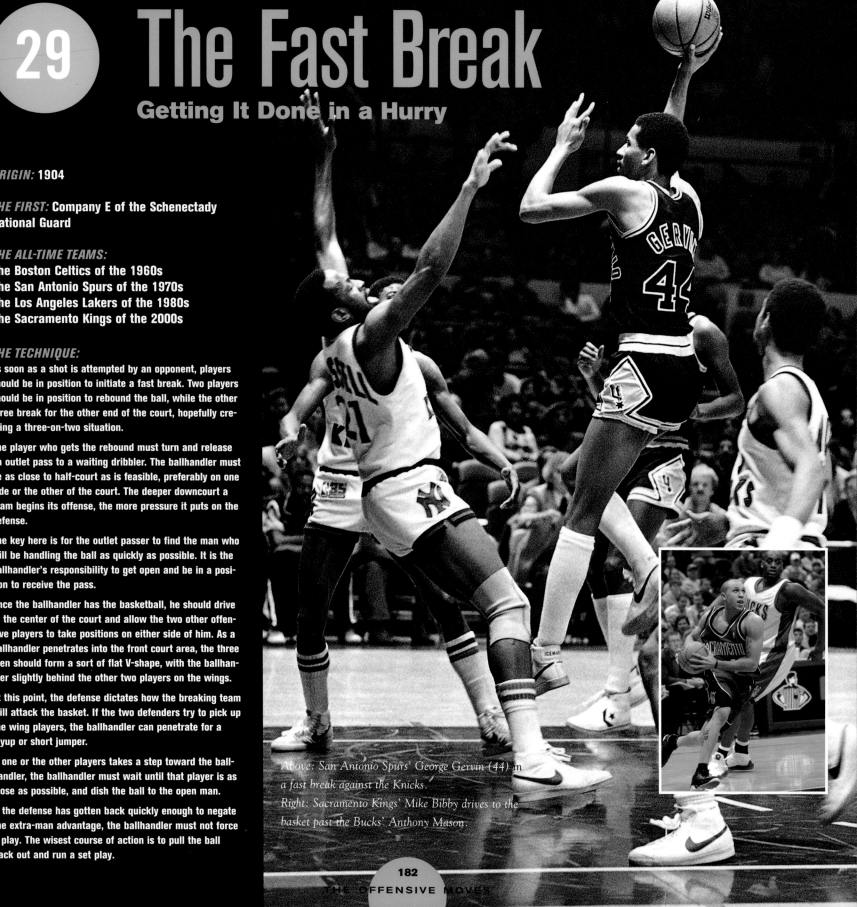

29 The Fast Break

Getting It Done in a Hurry

ORIGIN: 1904

THE FIRST: Company E of the Schenectady National Guard

THE ALL-TIME TEAMS:
The Boston Celtics of the 1960s
The San Antonio Spurs of the 1970s
The Los Angeles Lakers of the 1980s
The Sacramento Kings of the 2000s

THE TECHNIQUE:
As soon as a shot is attempted by an opponent, players should be in position to initiate a fast break. Two players should be in position to rebound the ball, while the other three break for the other end of the court, hopefully creating a three-on-two situation.

The player who gets the rebound must turn and release an outlet pass to a waiting dribbler. The ballhandler must be as close to half-court as is feasible, preferably on one side or the other of the court. The deeper downcourt a team begins its offense, the more pressure it puts on the defense.

The key here is for the outlet passer to find the man who will be handling the ball as quickly as possible. It is the ballhandler's responsibility to get open and be in a position to receive the pass.

Once the ballhandler has the basketball, he should drive to the center of the court and allow the two other offensive players to take positions on either side of him. As a ballhandler penetrates into the front court area, the three men should form a sort of flat V-shape, with the ballhandler slightly behind the other two players on the wings.

At this point, the defense dictates how the breaking team will attack the basket. If the two defenders try to pick up the wing players, the ballhandler can penetrate for a layup or short jumper.

If one or the other players takes a step toward the ballhandler, the ballhandler must wait until that player is as close as possible, and dish the ball to the open man.

If the defense has gotten back quickly enough to negate the extra-man advantage, the ballhandler must not force a play. The wisest course of action is to pull the ball back out and run a set play.

Above: San Antonio Spurs' George Gervin (44) in a fast break against the Knicks.
Right: Sacramento Kings' Mike Bibby drives to the basket past the Bucks' Anthony Mason.

Contrary to common belief, the fast break did not begin with the invention of the 24-second clock in the NBA in 1954. Rather, it began at least 50 years before that when one of the best players in the country realized that beating the other team down the court was the easiest way to score baskets.

Ed Wachter, the 6' 1" center who toiled for a number of teams in the northeast in the early part of the 20th century, was the author of a number of innovations, including the bounce pass. At some point early in his career, Wachter, along with his brother, Lew, figured out easier ways to score baskets.

The basic rules of basketball were drawn, in part, from the game of soccer. Unlike baseball or football, both soccer and basketball allowed their participants virtually free reign in the playing area. Both featured putting a ball in a goal as a way of tallying points.

There was also an interesting difference between soccer and basketball: unlike soccer, there was no offsides in basketball. Teams did not have to wait for defensive players to get into position before they could begin their own offense.

It isn't clear whether the Wachter brothers actually figured this all out in a linear way. They certainly didn't write it down anywhere. But that's the way the fast break developed. And the brothers Wachter may have begun fast-breaking before they worked it all out with Company E of the Schenectady, New York, National Guard in the 1904–05 season. That year was the first year the two brothers were together all season, and it was also the year that writers began noticing the accelerated style of play.

Not Much Different

And it's not terribly different from what's done now. The Wachters positioned players on either side of the court, and when Ed cleared a rebound, he would toss it to a waiting ballhandler. Then everybody would hustle down the court.

In fact, Company E undoubtedly also had what is now called a "secondary break," although that technical term didn't come along for decades. When Big Ed took down the rebound, he didn't just stand there. He'd bust down court, too, and sometimes get there in time to tip in a miss or take a pass for a driving layup.

Company E was the class of the East that season, dominating most of the teams on their schedule. At the end of the 1904–05 season, they challenged the Kansas City Blue Diamonds, the best AAU team in the Midwest, in a three-game series that was billed as "The World's Championship of Basketball."

Company E won all three games, although Game 2 was called prematurely after a huge fistfight broke out on the court. By that time, Company E was ahead of the Diamonds, 37–11, with four minutes left, so no one griped when the game was called. The New Yorkers had won the first game, 34–26, and the third contest, 35–28. Make no mistake, the fast break was only part of the reason why Company E was so good. The squad was also a fine defensive team for that era, and all the players could pass well.

In this running style, the Wachters clearly were onto something, and it's no secret that a lot of other teams picked it up pretty quickly. The fast break became a regular weapon of college, professional and high school teams by the 1930s.

FEBRUARY 27, 1959, BOSTON 173, MINNEAPOLIS 139

Even before the invention of the 24-second clock, the Boston Celtics could get up and down the floor. With all-time All-Star Bob Cousy orchestrating the fast break, Boston could put up points in a hurry.

On the night of February 27, 1959, the Lakers, another run-and-gun team, came to town. And it was a game no one would ever forget.

The two teams set seven league records that night, as the Celtics cruised to a 173–139 victory. Boston guard Bob Cousy shattered the assist record of 21 by making 28 feeds.

Ironically, the Celtics did all this without center Bill Russell, who was nursing a sore foot. Cousy added 31 points and forward Tommy Heinsohn poured in 43 points and Russell was never missed. In fact, the score of the game was so outrageous that then-Commissioner Maurice Podoloff ordered an investigation.

"One hundred seventy-three to 139!" said Podoloff after being informed of it by a reporter. "That's beyond belief!"

Podoloff questioned the officials to determine if the two teams were deliberately ignoring their defensive assignments or "just goofing off." The reality was that both teams employed the fast break so much during the game that making a basket took almost no time off the clock. There was plenty of time to score.

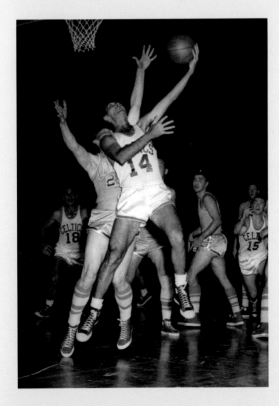

Above: Bob Cousey over the shoulder.

Left: Allan Iverson drives to the basket.

The 1971-72 Los Angeles Lakers

This edition of the Los Angeles Lakers was an interesting squad. It was an odd amalgamation of Lakers players in the 1970s toiling under the Celtics' system of the 1960s.

While that may seem to be an odd match, the combination worked so well that the Lakers captured the NBA championship that year. In addition, Los Angeles won an amazing 33 games in a row, a record for professional sports teams that has never been threatened.

At the end of the 1970-71 season, the Los Angeles franchise seemed to be stumbling toward mediocrity. Its three stars—center Wilt Chamberlain, forward Elgin Baylor and guard Jerry West—were all on the wrong side of 30. And all had been struggling with injuries over the previous few years.

Los Angeles owner Jack Kent Cooke believed his stars could shine. He fired Lakers coach Joe Mullaney and hired former Celtic Bill Sharman prior to the season. Sharman in turn hired another former Bostonian, K. C. Jones, to be his assistant.

Sharman was a soft-spoken gentleman, but he was also a shrewd coach. At the beginning of the 1971-72 season, he wanted the Lakers to run like his old Celtic teams had run. Sharman believed he had a player, in Chamberlain, who could rebound and block shots to trigger the break, as former Celtics great Bill Russell did for those Celtics squads.

There was just one problem, though, and it was a big one: while Sharman saw that Baylor, at 37, could still score, he clearly could not run as well as second-year pro Jim McMillian. Baylor was offered the chance to come off the bench. He declined and retired eight games into the season.

The speedy McMillian teamed with guards West and Gail Goodrich to lead the break. Chamberlain and rugged forward Harold 'Happy' Hairston were the rebounders. On the bench were guard Flynn Robinson, center Leroy Ellis and forwards John Q. Trapp and Pat Riley.

It was a strange combination of senior citizen players (West, Chamberlain) and frisky youngsters (McMillian, Hairston, Goodrich). But it worked beautifully, in part because Chamberlain completely subjugated his game and became a rebounder and shot blocker.

After a 5-3 start, Los Angeles won the aforementioned 33 consecutive games. Few of those contests were even close. The team went 69-13, the best record in league history until the Chicago Bulls of 72-10 came along in 1995-96.

The Lakers swept the Chicago Bulls in the 1972 playoff quarterfinals, struggled to knock out the defending champion Milwaukee Bucks in the semis and dominated the New York Knickerbockers in the Finals in five games. It was an amazing run, but it didn't last. The next year, Los Angeles won 60 games and again reached the Finals, but were beaten by the Knicks.

THE TOP FIVE TEAMS TO BREAK 100 POINTS IN 2000-01:

Sacramento:	50
Milwaukee:	49
Dallas:	46
Lakers:	45
Orlando:	38

Teams that scored fewer than 80 points in 2000-01:

New York:	20
Vancouver:	15
Miami:	15
Clippers:	13
Atlanta, Charlotte, Chicago, Golden State, New Jersey:	12

Source: Harvey Pollock

As the NBA began play in the 1940s, the principal devotee of the fast break in the pros was the 28-year-old coach of the Washington Capitols, Red Auerbach. Auerbach had played at George Washington and learned the game at the feet of GW's legendary coach, Bill Reinhart.

Reinhart is credited, by Auerbach among others, with breaking down the elements of the fast break and refining it by teaching the outlet pass, the "trailer" (in which a center "trails" his fast-breaking teammates and becomes another option as he runs down the lane) and the system of rapid-fire passes downcourt.

Auerbach took these elements with him when he began coaching, and forged a strong professional team in Washington from 1947 to 1950, a team that was well conditioned and used the fast break. But Washington never managed to win a pro title under Auerbach. Auerbach, after three years there, literally was off to greener pastures, to Boston.

It is a mistake to assume that no one but Auerbach's Caps, as they were called, used the fast break. Most teams in the BAA/NBA ran fast breaks, particularly the Rochester Royals and the Philadelphia Warriors. The problem was that without the 24-second clock the game would inevitably slow down in its latter stages. It simply didn't make sense to run-and-gun when the team with the lead could stop-and-hold.

Auerbach brought his fast-breaking concept to Boston in the early 1950s. This is where the concept was honed to perhaps its finest incarnation. Even before future Hall of Famer Bill Russell made his debut in Boston, the Celtics were a running crew.

The Boston Celtics were the first team in the NBA to average better than 90 points per game (91.4 in the 1951-52 season) and the first to average more than 100 points per game (101.4 in 1954-55). Both of those teams featured Russell's predecessor, Easy Ed Macauley, in the pivot. After Russell arrived, the Celtics then became the first team to top 115 points per game (116.4 in 1958-59) and the first to crack the 120-point barrier (124.5 in 1959-60).

The 1959-60 team was one of the most explosive in the history of the game. That lineup of Boston Celtics averaged the aforementioned 124.5 points per contest, a whopping 5.6 points per game better than runner-up Syracuse, who averaged 118.9 points per game.

It was a team with seven future Hall of Famers on the roster: Bill Russell, Bob Cousy, Bill Sharman, Tommy Heinsohn, Frank Ramsey, Sam Jones and K. C. Jones; a future Hall of Fame coach in Auerbach; and a future Hall of Fame owner in Walter Brown. For crying out loud, the Celtics team statistician and director of promotions that year was a guy named Billy Mokray, and he even made it into the Hall of Fame (admittedly for other accomplishments, such as

Only two. Okay, two and a half. The Sacramento Kings, when Mike Bibby is healthy, are a joy to watch. Every starter is an excellent passer and their spacing on the court is usually impeccable. Someone is always open on the Kings' break. The other running team is the Mavericks. Dallas has two great passers, Steve Nash and Michael Finley, and a bunch of great shooters. As long as Nash or Finley have the rock, things are good. It's when Nowitzki envisions himself as the Teutonic Bob Cousy that things go awry. The other team that does a little running is the Lakers. Sometimes. Most times, it's hard not to want to throw it into Shaq and watch the carnage. But Kobe is hell in the open court.

PLAYERS TO WATCH

compiling the first basketball encyclopedia and promoting the game internationally).

There have been teams that scored more per game following that 1959–60 year, including the 1961–62 Philadelphia Warriors, who averaged 125.4 points per game, and the 1966–67 Philadelphia 76ers, who averaged 125.2 points per tilt, but neither squad combined offense and defense as successfully as the 1958–60 Bostonians.

Setting the Bar

The Celtics teams of the late 1950s to the mid-1960s set the bar for all the fast-breaking teams to come after them. With center Russell and forward Heinsohn taking care of the defensive boards, and guards Cousy, Sharman and later Sam Jones, forwards Ramsey, Jim Loscutoff, and later Tom "Satch" Sanders and John Havlicek, getting

out on the break, Boston dominated the NBA. When Cousy retired, guard K. C. Jones took over the playmaking chores, and the Celtics didn't seem to lose a step until center Bill Russell retired in 1969.

The great fast-breaking team of the next decade didn't play in the NBA. The explosive San Antonio Spurs of the American

Above: Magic Johnson lays one up near the top of the key.

Basketball Association were one of the most exciting teams in league history. Led by guards George "the Iceman" Gervin and James "Captain Late" Silas, San Antonio had the most explosive offense in the ABA in the last five years of that league's existence, even though the Spurs never won a title.

When the Spurs were admitted into the NBA prior to the 1976–77 season, George Gervin and Co. didn't lose a step, leading the league in scoring three of their first four years in the league.

The Celtics of the mid-1970s, led by guard Jo Jo White, Havlicek and center David Cowens, brought the glory days back to Boston from 1974 to 1977, but it wasn't until the Los Angeles Lakers drafted 6' 9" guard Earvin "Magic" Johnson that the league saw a fast break to rival the Celtics run-run-run style of two decades earlier.

Showtime

The Lakers break was not unlike Boston's. Lakers center Kareem Abdul-Jabbar and a host of physical rebounders controlled the boards for Johnson and his cadre of fast-moving teammates.

Johnson was always trying to push the ball up the court after missed shots, missed foul shots and even after a made basket by Lakers opponents. What made the Lakers the most efficient offensive team throughout most of the 1980s was the break in combination with the team's exceptional half-court game. In Abdul-Jabbar, the Lakers had the best post-up center in the league. When Los Angeles added forward James Worthy in 1982, they then had one of the best post-up forwards in the NBA.

As the 1980s melted into the 1990s, the fast break began to melt. Coaches infatuated with the bruising half-court defense of the

CHAMPIONSHIP TEAMS' SCORING AVERAGES (1984–2002)
2001–02: Lakers, 101.3
2000–01: Lakers, 100.6
1999–00: Lakers, 100.8
1998–99: Spurs, 92.8
1997–98: Bulls, 96.7
1996–97: Bulls, 103.1
1995–96: Bulls, 105.2
1994–95: Houston, 103.5
1993–94: Houston, 101.1
1992–93: Bulls, 105.2
1991–92: Bulls, 109.9
1990–91: Bulls, 110.0
1989–90: Pistons, 104.3
1988–89: Pistons, 106.6
1987–88: Lakers, 112.8
1986–87: Lakers, 117.8
1985–86: Celtics, 114.1
1984–85: Lakers, 118.2

Detroit Pistons of the early 1990s (which brought the Pistons a pair of NBA titles) began emulating that style of ball. The Pistons controlled the tempo of games and forced teams to play their half-court style. It was clearly the best way for that team to play. The Pistons were a deep and physically imposing unit, and the half-court game usually simply wore teams down at the end of games.

Detroit was regularly in the middle of the offensive pack in scoring average, even as they led the league in defense, but the Pistons' success curbed the fast break. Their physical, grind-it-out game was soon being emulated around the league, whether teams had the athletes to play it or not.

It was successfully imitated by Chicago and Houston, the two teams who split the rest of the NBA titles of the 1990s, although the Bulls ran a little in the early 1990s, when Michael Jordan was younger.

In 1997–98, though, the Chicago Bulls, averaging 96.7 points per game, became the first team since the 1954–55 Syracuse Nationals, who averaged 91.1 points per game, to win the NBA championship while averaging fewer than 100 points per contest. That Syracuse team was the first team to win a championship following the introduction of the 24-second clock.

It was, for those who enjoyed watching the game played at a more lively pace, a daunting trend. The San Antonio Spurs continued it the following season, managing 92.8 points per game en route to the championship.

Over the past three years, the Los Angeles Lakers championship fives of Kobe Bryant and Shaquille O'Neal have at least cracked the 100-point barrier. Not by much, though: the three championship Lakers teams have averaged a hair over 100 points per game through 2002–03. Showtime in L.A. has become Slowtime. And why not? The Lakers of Shaquille have come full circle from their days in Minneapolis and George Mikan. Like those Lakers of yore, it makes little sense to outrun the best player in the league. Los Angeles will continue to pound the ball in low until someone beats them.

The trend is beginning to reverse itself ever so slightly, at least in Sacramento. The Kings, with point guard Mike Bibby dishing to Chris Webber, Vlade Divac and Predrag Stojakovic, have brought a little of that Showtime magic back to the league. But don't kid yourself. Sacramento may be filling it up for a team playing in the NBA of the 21st century, but they still only averaged 104.6 points per game in 2001–02. In 1961–62, that average would have put them dead last, a full six points per game less than the next worst team.

Part 5

The Rest of the Moves

30 The Trash-Talking Moves
When Not to Keep Your Mouth Shut

ORIGIN: The late 1940s

THE FIRST: Arnold "Red" Auerbach

THE ALL-TIMERS:
Auerbach, Sam Jones (1957-69)
M. L. Carr (1975-85)
Larry Bird (1979-92)
Charles Barkley (1984-00)
Michael Jordan (1984-93, 1994-98, 2000-present)
Auerbach, Jones and Bird are in the Hall of Fame. Jordan is pending. Did you notice how many of these guys are Celtics?

Right: Reggie Miller
Left: Larry Bird

THE TECHNIQUE:
The key to good trash-talking is making a statement you can back up, otherwise, it's all just hot air. Case in point: Celtics forward Cedric Maxwell boasted prior to the 1984 NBA East semifinals that "no way will that bitch get 40 on me." The gentleman to whom Maxwell was referring was Knicks forward Bernard King. Not only did King resent being called a "bitch," but he was eminently capable of dropping 40 points on just about anyone. The Celtics won the series in seven games, but King scored more than 40 points twice. Not trash talk, just dumb talk. On the other hand, prior to the seventh game between the Celtics and the Atlanta Hawks in 1987, Boston forward Larry Bird assured fans that the Hawks should have won Game 6, because he would ensure they would not win Game 7. He did, by hitting nine of 10 shots in the last quarter. Great trash talk.

The fact is, there has always been trash-talking to some degree in professional sports of all kinds. Professionals have always used any kind of perceived slight to motivate them. In 1954, during a very physical NBA Finals series, Minneapolis Lakers center George Mikan, who was usually careful not to say too much to rile the opposing team, was pretty confident after Minneapolis had won Game 3 over the Syracuse Nationals, which gave the Lakers a two-games-to-one advantage in the best-of-seven series. After the Lakers' 81–67 win, Mikan admitted to several newsmen, "I think we can win on Thursday and then wrap it up on Saturday so that I can play some golf on Sunday."

That was locker room bulletin board material, and the inspired Nationals carved out a win in Game 4, 80–69. Right after the game, Nationals guard Paul Seymour reflected on Mikan's comment.

"Well," said Seymour, "I guess George won't be golfing on Sunday after all."

Mikan didn't get to golf until after Game 7, an 87–80 win by the Lakers, but the point is, Mikan wasn't necessarily trying to be disrespectful of the Nationals. Rather, he was trying to be glib for a sportswriter. Of course, the Syracuse players chose to look at the comment differently.

Red Auerbach, who coached in the NBA from 1947 to 1965, took this discourse to another level. In addition to being an excellent coach, Auerbach was, to the rest of the league, a major-league pain in the butt. He was very blunt and very outspoken. He often didn't wait for reporters' questions to announce what he might have thought of a particular opponent. And he always looked for an edge.

Auerbach's strategy was transparent: verbally abused opponents, fans and referees would focus on him, and not his players. It worked. He was regularly the league leader in technical fouls and ejections, particularly when he was coaching the Celtics. He also seemed to regularly get into fights with fans. In fact, Celtics haters often remarked in the Auerbach era that he did not acquire policemen, such as 6' 6" Bob Brannum and, later, 6' 5" "Jungle Jim" Loscutoff to protect his players; he needed those guys to protect him.

It is nearly impossible to argue with the results Red got: nine championships in a 10-year span as coach of the Boston Celtics. He also remains the only coach who ever punched an owner out on national television, which he did just prior to Game 3 of the

PRIOR TO THE 1965–66 SEASON, BOSTON

It was at a press conference just prior to the 1965–66 season. Longtime Celtics coach Red Auerbach made no secret of the fact that he was leaving the bench (although he continued as the team's general manager), but he couldn't do it humbly.

"If I had quit after last year's playoffs, everyone would say I got out just in time," he said. "I didn't want that. So I'm announcing my retirement now, ahead of time, to let the whole league know they had one last crack at Auerbach."

How about that? Auerbach had coached his Celtics to seven consecutive World Championships, and eight in nine years. By his own admission, he was burning out, but the feisty redhead had no intention of ducking out the side door. He put it on the line: You guys have one chance left to knock me off. Let's see if you can do it.

Of course, they couldn't. The Celtics defeated the Los Angeles Lakers for the 1966 World Championship, their eighth in a row, and Red walked out of Boston Garden a winner.

Above: Red Auerbach celebrates with Boston Celtics' Bill Russell.

PLAYERS TO WATCH

Left: Reggie Miller working the room.

In 1960–61, his first season in the NBA, Robertson was third in the league in scoring with an average of 30.4 points per game, first in assists with a 9.7 average and 10th in rebounding with a 10.1 average, but believe it or not, there were initial doubts in some corners. The first time Robertson faced the Philadelphia Warriors he scored only 14 points. Philadelphia guard Tom Gola told a sportswriter that Robertson wasn't a bad player, "but not as good as I expected."

Oh baby, was that a huge mistake. The next time the two teams met, Robertson scored 45 points and talked to Gola all night, asking him if he had improved any over the last game.

New York Knickerbockers guard Dick Barnett inherited the King of the Trash-Talkers" mantle from Robertson in the 1970s. Barnett had an unusual jumper that he launched while kicking his legs up. As he let the ball fly, Barnett would announce, "Fall back, baby!" That meant, in essence, forget about it, I've already launched the shot.

Barnett was also known for announcing, during a blowout, that the game was over. "This m-----f----r is in the book, baby," he'd say, meaning the scorebook. Few could argue, even though he was putting the screws to them.

Prior to the 1979 season, the Celtics drafted forward Larry Bird and traded for guard-forward M. L. Carr. Those two men, with teammate Cedric Maxwell, launched what might be called the "Golden Age" of trash-talking. Those guys elevated the whole thing to an art form.

Maxwell was a good player and a better talker. An exceptional post player, he would remind opponents just prior to the game that he would be taking them into the "torture chamber," which was Maxwell's term for the

1957 Finals when he socked St. Louis owner Ben Kerner.

Oscar and Sam

Although the term "trash–talking" didn't come into vogue until the late 1970s, the concept was around for years. In his second (and best) book, *Memoirs of an Opinionated Man*, Celtics legend Bill Russell recounted, in very funny detail, how Celtics guard Sam Jones, who appeared to be pretty reserved in front of newsmen, used to taunt former Philadelphia Warrior center Wilt Chamberlain during games. Jones, in a high falsetto voice, used to remind Chamberlain, who was usually parked under the basket, guarding Russell, that he would never be able to get out to Jones, usually stationed near the head of the key, to block Sam's jumper.

"Wilt, of course, knew he couldn't, which didn't improve his disposition much," Russell admitted.

Russell also noted in the book that one of the great trash-talkers of the 1960s was Cincinnati guard Oscar Robertson. Robertson would drive on Russell, maneuver his body between Russell and the basketball and then let the ball fly. "You're not going to get this one, big fella," Oscar would say. And, Russell admitted, he often didn't.

This isn't really trash-talking, but it is the origin of a phrase that is, these days, just about beaten to death. In 1978, after the Bullets fell behind in the NBA Finals, three games to two, coach Dick Motta was asked by a reporter if Seattle had won the series.

"I don't know about you," said Motta, "but as far as I'm concerned, the opera isn't over until the fat lady sings."

That quote remains the most ubiquitous sentence in NBA history, a phrase still bandied about today. By the way, after the Bullets easily won Game 6 in Washington, a Seattle fan held up a sign before Game 7 with the answer to Motta's quote: "The Fat Lady Sings Tonight." And she did, but not for the SuperSonics. The Bullets won Game 7, 105–99.

low post area in which he excelled. Carr loved to whip Celtics home crowds into a frenzy while on the bench, whirling a white towel around his head to incite the home crowd. He would also turn around when the Celtics were on the road and, if Boston was well ahead, advise fans to leave and beat the traffic, as the game was over. (Maxwell, of course, often said that Carr, as a substitute, had more time to think up these lines because he was on the bench so much.)

Number 33, William Shakespeare?

Bird was the William Shakespeare of trash-speech. How do we know? Because even the guys he talked smack to loved to tell Larry Bird stories.

There was the time in Portland in 1984 when Bird drained shot after shot with his left hand (Bird was right-handed), all the while announcing to the Blazer players ("left hand, left hand") that he would be doing it.

There was the time, in 1985, when Bird missed a playoff game against the Cleveland Cavaliers, a game the Celtics lost. Late in the game, Cav fans chanted, "We want Larry! We want Larry!"

"They want me?" said Bird after the game. "They got me. I'll be their worst nightmare."

Bird played the next game and was a key performer as Boston beat Cleveland, 117–115, eliminating the Cavaliers from the playoffs.

Bird was also the master of the delayed trash-talk comment. In 1981, after the fourth game of the NBA Finals, Houston center Moses Malone was convinced that he was playing for the better team.

"I could take four guys from [his hometown of] Petersburg [Virginia] and beat this team," Malone said of the soon-to-be NBA champions. "I just don't think the Celtics are that good. I don't think they can stop us from doing what we want to do."

Regardless of what that comment said about his Rockets teammates, Malone was adamant about the "four guys off the streets" statement, even after the Celtics eliminated the Rockets following the sixth game of the series.

As usual, Bird had the last word. Following their annexation of the championship, the City of Boston held a parade and a rally at City Hall a few days later. Virtually every Celtic got a chance to speak his peace. As the rally went on, one onlooker held up a sign that said, "Moses Malone Eats Poop." Except that the sign didn't say "poop."

Bird, spotting the sign, pointed to it and said, "I agree with that guy. Moses Malone does eat poop." Except that Larry didn't say "poop," either.

So clearly, Bird was the master. The problem is, most of the guys that are in the league now can't hold a candle to him. No one seems to understand that a good trash-talker picks his spots and backs up his boasts. Charles Barkley (1984–2000) is the best of the later era. He's actually a better trash-talker as a television analyst than he was as a player.

Michael Jordan is the best of the post-Bird talkers, but now that he's trying to play as a 40-year-old man, he's getting a lot of his stuff thrown back into his face. There really hasn't been anyone as good as Bird in this category, and if you think otherwise, you don't know what you're talking about. Fool.

That's right. In 1953, Celtics coach Red Auerbach published *Basketball for the Player, the Fan and the Coach*.

It is an excellent book that, 50 years later, still stands the test of time. (Well, there are some outdated chapters, like the one on successfully freezing the ball.) Red's explanations of teamwork, fundamentals, coaching, setting good screens, using time-outs and dealing with players from the high school to the professional level still ring very true.

So do his thoughts on "strategy." Here are a few suggestions, straight from the book.

–If the opposing team has a high scorer, keep reminding the other players [on the team] of their uselessness.

–When your opponent makes a good play, don't congratulate him, tell him that he was merely lucky.

–When your opponent needs one more foul to be disqualified or has a slight injury, keep reminding him about it.

–Players may agitate opponents by incessant chatter, even ridicule, or by not talking at all.

–It is up to the player himself to decide what is "dirty" and what is "tricky."

It should be said that the book is filled with far more helpful hints on a variety of hoop-related subjects, such as good conditioning, making good passes, being a good teammate, being a good coach and even making sure the team cheerleaders get to the game. But for anyone who thinks trash-talking began in the last two decades or so, you're wrong. Here it is, in black and white.

31 The Innovative Moves

The All-Stars and Other Innovations

ORIGIN OF INTEGRATION:
1950 in the NBA

THE FIRST BLACK PLAYER: Earl Lloyd of the Washington Caps was the first to actually step onto the court, by a fluke of scheduling.

THE ALL-TIME INNOVATORS:
Walter Brown, Chuck Cooper (1950–56)
Earl Lloyd (1950–60)
Nat "Sweetwater" Clifton (1950–58)
Brown is in the Hall of Fame.

Above: Don Chaney
Right: Earl Lloyd

The Story of Integration

The 1950–51 season was the year the NBA integrated. This was a significant step, but not as unexpected as the integration of baseball a few years before.

For one thing, black players had already been participating in professional basketball leagues and tournaments for more than a decade. There had been several black players in the old NBL, and the World Professional Basketball Tournament in Chicago had been won by the New York Rens in 1939 and the Harlem Globetrotters in 1940, both all-black contingents.

Unlike the exhibition games played by major-league baseball teams against Negro League nines or touring black teams, black teams' participation in the pro basketball tournament was not mere exhibitions in those early days; it was participation at the highest level of the game. Both teams wanted to beat the other.

Still, black players' appearance in the newly constituted NBA was relevant because this was the first truly "national" association of basketball teams, playing in major cities. But there was also no doubt in anyone's mind that it would happen sooner or later. A number of teams were already scouting blacks.

Most of the team owners were a little

THE DEFINING MOMENT FOR INTEGRATION

The 1963–64 season. The Celtics have five black players on the floor.

In a league where the mantra about black ballplayers was, "Play one at home, two on the road and three when you're behind," the Boston Celtics were so far ahead of everyone it wasn't funny. They were the first team in NBA history to draft a black player, the first team in league history to hire a black coach (Bill Russell, 1966–67), the first team to start a majority of black players (1961–62, Russell, Sam Jones, Tom Sanders) and the first team to play five black players on a regular basis (1963–64, Russell, Sanders, Willie Naulls, Sam Jones, K. C. Jones, although John Havlicek usually started in place of Naulls). That was simply unheard-of in the early 1960s, in part because the other popular saying in those days was, "It's a white dollar," meaning that a vast majority of fans in the NBA were still white people, and, presumably, they would not pay to see black men play basketball.

The Celtics danced all over that concept, particularly in the playoffs. And, of course, it didn't hurt that they won and won and won with black ballplayers.

Above: Bill Russell signs with the NBA in 1956.
Left: Wilt Chamberlain playing with the Globetrotters in 1959.

The Story of the 24-Second Clock

File this under "Greatest Moments Ever." When Syracuse owner Danny Biasone came up with the 24-second clock, it created the NBA we know today.

And like almost anything that is perfect, the way Biasone came up with the 24-second clock was simplicity itself. Biasone took the number of average possessions by both teams in a regulation NBA game and divided that by the number of seconds in the game. The answer he came up with was 24. That's it.

Rarely has a rule change solved a problem so completely as Biasone's shot clock. Teams were forced to play an uptempo game the entire 48 minutes. There could be no dribbling out the clock. And teams no longer had to foul to get the ball back. They simply had to play good defense for 24 seconds. Biasone eliminated a host of bad things about pro ball with one stunning idea.

The league still uses 24 seconds today, and will probably be using it as long as the league is in business.

Above: Danny Biasone

gun-shy about drafting blacks. Why? Because the unofficial deal at the time was that black players were the purview of Harlem Globetrotters owner Abe Saperstein. Saperstein was so far ahead of the NBA/BAA in terms of promotion that it was embarrassing. For one thing, his team never played in Harlem; Saperstein needed to let folks know his teams were made up of black players. For another, they didn't "Globe Trot" until 1952; Saperstein just wanted people to think they were international stars.

The Harlem Globetrotters, because of their tireless barnstorming, were the number-one attraction in the league by far. A doubleheader that featured a Globetrotters game in the opener guaranteed a full house in any arena.

Thus, the other owners believed that drafting black players would (1) draw Saperstein's ire and cause him to boycott their arenas and (2) destroy the Globetrotters, who regularly filled those arenas.

They weren't thinking. Saperstein needed

the NBA's arenas to make money as much as the NBA's arenas needed him.

And it certainly didn't destroy the Globetrotters. Despite integration, the Harlem Globetrotters are still, in 2003, one of the top attractions in basketball 75 years after their inception in 1927. They were inducted as a team into the Hall of Fame in 2002.

Back to the NBA. On April 25, 1950, the Boston Celtics drafted a 6' 6" forward from Duquesne named Chuck Cooper. The popular story goes that Celtics owner Walter Brown was asked if he knew that Cooper was black. Brown reportedly asserted that he didn't care if Cooper was black, brown or polka-dotted as long as he could play.

The real story of that day is in former Celtics coach Red Auerbach's book, *Winning The Hard Way*. According to Red, no one asked Brown anything. Rather, "There were quite a few raised eyebrows," as Red noted. Probably because the league owners realized that the pressure was off. They figured that if they drafted a black player and Saperstein

exploded, they could then point to Brown and say, "Abe, it was Walter! Blame him!"

So, a few hours after the Celtics drafted Cooper, the Washington Capitols drafted Earl Lloyd of West Virginia State in the ninth round. Once it was clear that Saperstein didn't have much of a say in the matter, Knicks signed former Globetrotter Nat "Sweetwater" Clifton to a pro contract (beating the Celtics to it, as Auerbach admitted in one of his books).

So Cooper was the first to be drafted, Clifton the first to sign, and because the Caps opened their season a day before the Celtics and Knicks, Lloyd was the first to actually play in a regular NBA game. Congratulations to all of them and cheers to Walter Brown. He started it.

The Story of the NBA All-Star Game

Brown was also the catalyst for another innovation, one that, like integrated teams, is taken for granted in the NBA these days: the All-Star game.

Haskell Cohen, the NBA publicist at the time, thought it up, basing the idea on baseball's All-Star game. Commissioner Maurice Podoloff supported it, but while the owners liked the idea of an All-Star game, and the players were very excited about it, no one knew if the fans would like it. The popular thinking at the time was that fans would not be interested in rooting for a team of players with which they were mostly unfamiliar.

Obviously, unlike Cohen, the owners were unaware of the popularity of the baseball version of the contest. Brown clearly wasn't.

"I'd enjoy seeing all these great players on one floor," he said in an interview that year. His fellow owners said, "Fine, Walter. Then YOU host it."

So Brown did. In fact, he was so sure the game would be a success, he agreed to allow the NBA to use the Boston Garden free of charge.

He was right, of course. On March 2, 1951, the first game drew more than 10,000 fans, who saw the East, led by Celtics center "Easy Ed" Macauley, whip the West 111–94. Macauley won the game's first Most Valuable Player Award.

196

THE REST OF THE MOVES

The Indianapolis Olympians, the Strangest Team Ever

The old Indianapolis Olympians were the first, and only, socialist team in the history of pro sports.

The squad was made up primarily of alumni from the University of Kentucky's NCAA champions of 1949. Four of the starting five were Kentucky grads: 6' 7" center Alex Groza, 6' 2" guard Ralph Beard, 6' 4" swingman Wallace "Wah Wah" Jones and 6' 2" guard Cliff Barker. Those four had also made up a portion of the 1948 U.S. Olympic team, hence the name. The squad had a total of eight Kentuckians on the roster. (By the way, Jones's nickname was acquired because his younger sister couldn't pronounce Wallace when the two were growing up. But Beard and the rest of the Cats didn't call him "Wah Wah." They just called him "Wah.")

Even odder than that, the players actually owned part of the team. Kentucky sportswriter J. R. Kimbrough, who thought up the idea, was president. Beard, Barker and Groza were vice presidents, while Jones was the secretary.

Each player on the roster got a salary, a bonus and stock income. Barker, a rookie, was also the player-coach, the only time in the history of pro sports such a thing has happened. Barker was a World War II veteran and was 26 years old when he got out of Kentucky, so he was a natural for the job. But really, the whole thing was utterly unheard-of in professional sports. It was never done before, and it has never been done since. Initially, it was very successful.

"After we won the 1949 championship, our eligibility was up, so the whole team barnstormed around the state of Kentucky for about a month," recalled Beard. "And we each made $3,000, which was a nice sum of money in those days. And so we figured we'd try to go to the NBA as a unit. So the long and short of it is, we hired a lawyer, and he petitioned the NBA. And they said we could come into the league as a team, and that we could choose one of three cities: Louisville, Indianapolis or Cincinnati.

"We chose Indianapolis because the city was a great basketball city, and because of Butler Field House," said Beard. "It was a beautiful gym. Real big. Seated 17,000. And well-lit, with a nice floor. The whole thing was a very unique situation."

That is certainly correct, but the fact is, the NBA/BAA in 1949 was still in competition with the NBL. Getting the 1949 National Collegiate Champions who were also Olympic heroes to play in the league was somewhat unorthodox, to be sure, but also a sure draw. This was, remember, long before televised sports. Ned Irish, president of the Knicks, recalled that the Olympians were the second-best draw in the league, after Mikan and the Lakers. And the first two years of their existence, when Beard and Groza played, the team was solidly in the black.

Groza was a terrific pro. And Beard was classed with Bob Davies and Bob Cousy as a ballhandler and passer. Fred Scolari recalled that Beard was tougher to guard than

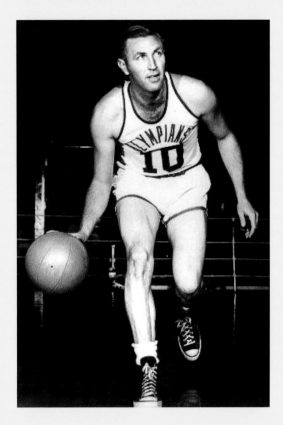

either, because of his tremendous foot speed. Beard, too, may have had a Hall of Fame career.

"My first year, I was second-team all-pro," said Beard. "And the next year, Groza and I were both first team. We had a very strong team. I think if we had both stayed in the league, we'd have won a championship."

They didn't. Beard and Groza were indicted in 1952 for taking money from gamblers while playing at Kentucky. Although they were never convicted of anything, they, along with Barker, were banned from the NBA. Without them, the team struggled the next two years, and eventually closed up shop.

Both Beard and Groza denied the allegations over the years, noting, ironically, that when they played at Kentucky, there were a large number of guys around the team that handed them money after games. They were called alumni.

Neither player ever thought any of them were gamblers, and both players deny ever throwing games. Groza, who got back into pro basketball when he worked in the ABA, died a few years ago. Beard admitted recently that it changed his life.

'It ruined me," he said. "My career as a pro athlete was over. I had signed a baseball contract, and I was banned from baseball, too."

Beard admits he has little use for the NBA, but he still loves the game.

"Goodness, I love to watch that Jason Kidd move the ball," he said. "Isn't he something?"

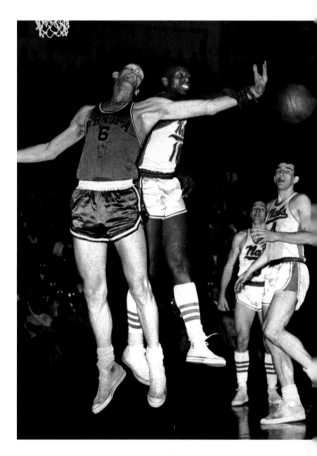

Left: Cliff Barker
Below: Syracuse's Earl Lloyd blocks a shot by Philadelphia Warriors' Neil Johnson (6).

The Coaching Moves

Where Bench Jockeys Came From

ORIGIN: **1896**

THE FIRST: **Fred Burkhardt, Buffalo Germans** (1896-1929)

THE ALL-TIMERS:
Bobby Douglas (1922-49)
Red Auerbach (1946-66)
Johnny Kundla (1947-59)
Lenny Wilkins (1969-present)
Bill Sharman (1961-76)
Pat Riley (1981-present)
Phil Jackson (1990-present)
All but Riley and Jackson are Hall of Famers.

Above: Phil Jackson
Right: Red Auerbach

TECHNIQUE:
There are as many ways to coach as there are coaches, practically, but there is one secret, according to Arnold "Red" Auerbach.

"Somebody has to be in charge. This isn't a democracy. It's a dictatorship."

There was a time in basketball's beginnings when there were no coaches. In fact, the inventor of the game, Dr. James Naismith, was firmly against the concept of coaching basketball players. Just before Hall of Fame coach Forrest "Phog" Allen embarked on his legendary coaching career at the University of Kansas, he mentioned to Naismith that he was taking the job. Naismith was amused. "Why, Forrest," he said. "Basketball is just a game to play. You can't coach it." Allen replied that one could certainly teach players to pass and shoot, and that he planned to do so.

In fact, in 1910, Naismith was one of the principal sponsors of a rule that prohibited coaches from, well, coaching.

According to the rule, teams were still allowed to have a coach sitting on the sidelines, but those coaches could not actually coach the players on the floor. Frankly, it was a rule referees didn't enforce, and it was taken off the books a few years later.

In the game's early days, some teams had coaches, some had managers, some had both and some had neither. The first actual coach of a team that played professionally was probably Fred Burkhardt, the coach of the Buffalo Germans. Burkhardt organized the Germans in 1896 while he was working as physical education director for the German YMCA in Buffalo, New York.

The six players at the time—Al Heerdt, George Redlein, William Rohde, Henry Faust, Ed Miller and John Maier—were all 14 years old or under, but they fell in love with the game and played games endlessly at the YMCA. By 1900, the teenaged Germans, still intact, were claiming the Eastern championship.

Burkhardt learned the game under

APRIL 23, 1950, NBA FINALS. MINNEAPOLIS 110, SYRACUSE 95. JOHNNY KUNDLA'S THREE-PEAT

Okay, no one, but no one called this a "three-peat," but it was the first one in NBA history, and it was the fourth World Championship in four years (one in the NBL, three in the NBA/BAA) for the George Mikan Lakers. Coach John Kundla won five NBA titles and one NBL championship in a seven-year span, from 1948 to 1954. He is almost forgotten by the casual fan, which is a shame, because this guy was one of the all-time greats.

Only Red Auerbach and Phil Jackson have won more in the history of the league, and don't let anyone kid you: it was as tough then as it is now to motivate players and push them to play their best. Yes, it certainly helped to have George Mikan as your center, but there were a lot of other good teams around in the late 1940s and early 1950s. Only one, Minneapolis, was consistently successful.

Naismith in Springfield and began teaching it when he got to Buffalo. His players were all excellent athletes, and as the years wore on, they became familiar with each other's playing styles. The Germans won the Pan American Exposition Championship in 1901 and the Olympic Championship in 1905. As pros, from 1908 to 1911 they won 111 straight contests.

Burkhardt wasn't big on strategy, and in fact most coaches of the era weren't. They functioned more as organizers and managers. Any strategy was left up to the team captain or one of the other players. The original Celtics had two of the great basketball minds of the 20th century on their roster in the 1920s—center Joe Lapchick and guard Nat Holman—so they didn't really need a coach. Celtics manager John Whitty mostly made sure they got paid.

Left: New York Knicks coach Vince Boryla being herded off court after being thrown out of the game for protesting a technical foul called on him.

Above: Auerbach in 1986 with the NBA Championship trophy.
Right: Lenny Wilkens

The Coming of the Rens

On the other hand, Bobby Douglas, the long-time coach of the New York Renaissance team, was both a shrewd manager and coach. Douglas was born in the West Indies in 1882 and came to New York City in 1886. By 1900, Douglas was playing for amateur basketball teams in the Harlem area.

In 1922, Douglas at 40 was pretty much done playing in the amateur and semi-pro leagues in New York City, but he loved the game and wanted to continue in it, so he organized an all-black team. Douglas needed a home court. He had originally planned to name the team the Spartans, but when he approached the owner of the Harlem Renaissance Casino in New York City, he offered to name his team after the business if the casino would allow his team to play in the ballroom on the second floor. The deal was struck, and thus was born the New York Renaissance, or Rens for short.

The Rens were not just one of the first great black teams in pro history. They were one of the first great teams, period. Led by 6' 4" center Charles "Tarzan" Cooper (1924–44) and 6' 3" guard-forward William "Pop" Gates (1938–55), the Rens took on all comers, barnstorming from New York City to the Midwest. Both men played for the Rens during their glory years of the mid- to late 1930s, Cooper from 1929 to 1941 and Gates from 1938 to 1948. Both, along with Douglas, are in the Hall of Fame individually. The Rens were also enshrined as a team in 1963.

The Rens, like the Original Celtics and other great barnstorming teams, generally worked out offensive and defensive schemes on the road, as there were few days off to have practices. Douglas stressed tough man-to-man defense, crisp passing and looking for the open man.

The Rens lasted from 1922 to 1949 before disbanding. They compiled a 2,588–539 record in that span and, in the 1932–33 season, won 88 games in 86 days. In 1939, with Cooper, Gates and speedy playmaker Clarence "Fats" Jenkins, the Rens won the World Championship Tournament held in Chicago by defeating the Oshkosh All-Stars, 34–25.

Left: Pat Riley

The Coming of Red

Even before he became a coach for the Boston Celtics, Red Auerbach was known as a coach who stressed conditioning and running. This seems like a pretty basic concept, but it is surprising how few pro coaches in particular were very big on making sure their athletes were in shape. Even into the 1980s, many pro coaches believed that the best way to get in shape for an NBA season was to simply play oneself into shape.

Coaching conditioning was Auerbach's key to success. Jeez, the guy won everywhere he coached. And yet, for the most part, no one seemed too interested in how he did what he did.

As a 28-year-old coach with the Washington Capitols in the 1946–47 BAA/NBA season, Auerbach ran his guys into the ground in preseason. The result? A 17–1 record to begin the season, which essentially ended the Eastern division race after two months. The Caps didn't win the title that year, or the subsequent two years Auerbach coached them, because they weren't talented enough, but Red always got the most out of them.

To prove it wasn't a fluke, Auerbach took over the Celtics in 1950 and within six years began the most amazing dynasty in pro sports: 11 championships in 13 years (1956–69). The secret? There is no secret. Conditioning and good players are basically the two things that are key. Also, as Red says in his autobiography, "Somebody has to be in charge. And I'm it."

As the coach of the Minneapolis Lakers in their heyday, Johnny Kundla ran into the same problem Auerbach faced when the Celtics had Bill Russell: the "anybody-can-win-with-that-team" beef. Hey, the thinking went, Kundla had Hall of Famers George Mikan, Jim Pollard and Slater Martin through most of his "five-titles-in-six-years" run through the NBA Finals. So how could Kundla, a Hall of Fame coach himself, lose?

Well, it's never that easy. In fact, Kundla admitted recently that when the Lakers first signed Mikan in 1947, he overcoached a little bit. "We really went to George too much in the first part of that season," he recalled. "And teams were ready for us, and we lost four of the first five games he started for us."

Kundla decided to spread the offense around a little bit (which was greatly facilitated by Mikan's passing ability) and the Lakers went 39–11 the rest of the way en route to the NBL title in the 1947–48 season. That was the first of six championships in seven years, including the aforementioned five-for-six in the NBA, for Kundla.

One of Kundla's principal contributions to the game was creating the concept of the "power forward." The Lakers had drafted the 6' 8" Mikkelsen out of Hamline College to be a backup to Mikan, and for the first third of his rookie season Mikkelsen was on the bench, but Kundla realized that big Vern was just too darn good to be sitting. Mikkelsen started, with specific instructions: set screens, bang the boards and grab as many offensive rebounds as you can. Mikkelsen did a heck of a job; so good, in fact, that he parlayed it into a place in the Hall of Fame.

The Curse of the Modern Player

"It was," said Boston Celtic forward Kevin McHale several years ago, "a dark day in the NBA when Bill Sharman came up with that idea."

"That idea" was the "shootaround," a morning practice scheduled for the day of the game to get his players loosened up and ready to play that evening. Sharman, who was an advocate of stretching and conditioning when he was a player for the Boston Celtics,

BEST FIRST-YEAR COACHING STARTS EVER
1971–72: Bill Sharman, Los Angeles Lakers
69–13 (NBA champions)
1967–68: Alex Hannum, Philadelphia 76ers
68–13 (NBA champions)
1983–84: K. C. Jones, Boston Celtics
62–20 (NBA champions)
1973–74: Kevin Loughery, New York Nets
55–29 (ABA champions)
1976–77: Jack Ramsey, Portland Trail Blazers
49–33 (NBA champions)
1955–56: George Senesky, Philadelphia Warriors:
45–26 (NBA champions)
What Happened Next Year
1972–73 Lakers
Lost in NBA Finals to New York
1968–69 76ers
Lost in NBA East Finals to Boston
1984–85 Celtics
Lost in NBA Finals to Lakers
1974–75 Nets
Lost in ABA first round to St. Louis
1977–78 Blazers
Lost in NBA West semis to SuperSonics
1956–57 Warriors
Lost in NBA East semis to Syracuse

became an advocate of it when he became a pro coach.

"Sharman used to be stretching before the game, and we'd all be laughing at him," recalled his former teammate Bob Cousy.

The popular theory is that Sharman came up with the "shootaround" when he was first hired as coach for the Los Angeles Lakers in the 1971–72 season. Not so. Sharman began using the shootaround as early as the 1966–67 season, when he was a coach for the San Francisco (now Golden State) Warriors. The players hated it then, and they hated it when

Above: Abe Saperstein

career, Auerbach often brought veteran guard Irv Torgoff off the bench to provide an offensive spark in the 1946–47 and 1947–48 seasons, then went with Sonny Hertzberg when Torgoff was traded. And when the Baltimore Bullets came into the league in 1947–48, coach Buddy Jeannette had his own sixth man for several years: player Buddy Jeannette.

When New York hired former St. John's coach Joe Lapchick in 1947–48, Lapchick had his own version of the sixth-man concept, and it wasn't just one man.

In 1948–49, Lapchick's use of reserve Carl Braun played a huge role in the Knicks' upset of the defending BAA champion Baltimore Bullets. Braun, coming off the bench in Game 2 of the best of three series, scored 20 points in an 84–74 Knickerbockers win.

"Lapchick's strategy played an important part in the victory," noted the *New York Times*' Lou Effrat. "[Braun] came off the bench and soon made his presence felt. He concluded the night with a 20-point output that made him the individual high scorer." Two nights later, Braun had 16 points off the bench as the Knicks eliminated Baltimore, 103–99.

But Braun wasn't a reserve all the time. Lapchick tended to think more like a baseball manager than a basketball coach. Like his contemporary on the New York Yankees, Casey Stengel, Lapchick liked to shake up his lineup from time to time. Lapchick liked to give his team a different look, particularly in the playoffs, because he believed that using different lineups would make his team more difficult to defend.

For example, in addition to moving Braun in and out of the lineup Lapchick would also move forward-center Harry "the Horse" Gallatin on and off the bench. In later years, it would be other players like Nat Clifton or Ernie Vandeweghe coming off the bench for the Knicks.

In Rochester, Royals coach Lester Harrison had a philosophy similar to Lapchick's: he had a set starting lineup but would often shuffle his starters against a particular team. Guard Bob Davies was always in the starting lineup, but Harrison used Red Holzman and Bobby Wanzer almost interchangeably.

On the other hand, Lakers coach Johnny Kundla inevitably went with a set lineup and almost always brought the same players off the bench.

The fact is, the first great sixth man was Ramsey. Folks look at Frank Ramsey now and can't figure out how he's in the Hall of Fame, but Ramsey was the most versatile player of the late 1950s and early 1960s. He could guard players as tall as 6' 11" Nate Thurmond or players as quick as 6' 2" Carl Braun. He wasn't a great shooter, but he was a great scorer, and he loved to play in big games. The sixth-man concept certainly didn't start with "Rams,' but he was one of the best ever at it.

Above: Phil Jackskon

he began using it in Los Angeles. In fact, at a preseason team meeting with some of the Lakers veterans in 1971, Sharman broached the subject of having a midmorning practice the day of a game.

"What," asked one player, "do we do after the practice?"

"Easy," said Lakers guard Gail Goodrich. "Then we go wake up Wilt."

Ironically, Lakers center Wilt Chamberlain, a man who surely often marched to the beat of his own drummer, was one of the big supporters of the shootarounds and rarely missed one that season. Within a few years, every team was scheduling some kind of shootaround.

More modern coaches like Lenny Wilkins, Pat Riley and Phil Jackson aren't the innovators that some of their predecessors were. All three men are strong teachers, but all three depend greatly on holding the attention of their players by eliciting respect for their methods and communication skills. Wilkins, elected to the Hall of Fame as a player in 1989, and as a coach in 1998, is perhaps the most respected coach in the game today. His laid-back style belies a very shrewd student of the game.

Both Riley and Jackson are recognized as men who have been best able to convince the modern NBA player to subjugate his game for the common good. That, in part, is due to the reputation both men have enjoyed as coaches who can help their teams win World Championships. Riley has four and Jackson nine.

Both men have had to concede players some individual freedom, because the modern NBA functions on a hierarchy that places the star player on a platform well above that of the team's coach. In his autobiography, Lakers center Shaquille O'Neal admitted he was extremely upset that Jackson was giving Kobe Bryant more offensive leeway than he or his teammates.

Jackson, according to O'Neal, also made it clear that such a strategy would eventually pay off for the Lakers, and, essentially, it did. Los Angeles has now won three consecutive World Championships and is heavily favored to win a fourth in the 2002–03 season. Jackson and O'Neal had lunch before the 1999–2000 season, and Jackson outlined what he was going to do and how. He got O'Neal on board early, and the rest was relatively easy.

33 The Stylin' Moves
It's All About Looking Good

ORIGIN: Almost everybody had style in the 19th century. It was a stylish era

THE FIRST: Dr. James Naismith

THE ALL-TIMERS: Red Holzman, K.C. Jones, Chuck Daly, Pat Riley. All but Riley are in the Hall of Fame.

Right: Father Basketball, Dr. James Naismith. Left: Latrell Sprewell sporting pinstripes.

As long ago as 1891, when the game was invented, coaches or managers wore suits on the bench, unless they were playing coaches. Throughout sporting history, the style of most professional teams was to require a coach to wear a dress suit on the bench, except for baseball teams, whose managers have almost always worn their team's uniforms.

That suit-and-tie look held up in pro basketball until the 1960s, when style went out the window. The coaches for the American Basketball Association were particularly egregious. Larry Brown, who coached the Denver Nuggets from 1974 to 1979, was a major-league fashion victim. He often wore turtlenecks and Oshkosh B'Gosh overalls on

Red Holtzman always favored the conservative suit.

the bench, not to mention (this is true!) platform shoes.

The NBA was little better. In the 1970s, wide, airplane-wing lapels were the big thing. Everyone wore them, except the Knicks' Red Holtzman, who preferred conservative suits. The younger coaches often wore bellbottoms.

Jack Ramsey, as coach of the Buffalo Braves from 1972 to 1976 and later, when he took the helm of the Portland Trail Blazers from 1976 to 1986, insisted on wearing a particularly hideous checked sport coat that looked like it had been snagged from Goodwill.

The Celtics' Tommy Heinsohn, who coached in Boston from 1969 to 1978, often sported pastel turtlenecks and his own little checked suitcoat number, tastefully set off by his Prince Valiant haircut. The sidelines of Celtics-Braves contests of the early 1970s looked like a fashion show for the local School for the Blind.

The league was saved by K. C. Jones and Pat Riley, who coached for the Celtics and Lakers, respectively, through most of the 1980s. Jones preferred dark, tasteful, double-breasted suits, while Riley went with expensive silk jobs. Since the Celtics and Lakers were the two premier franchises in the league, other coaches were, thankfully, moved to follow those two. Detroit coach Chuck Daly also set the tone for the league with his exceptional fashion sense, which included sharp designer suits and ties.

These days, no self-respecting coach worth his salt will take the floor in anything less than a custom suit that runs into the hundreds or thousands of dollars. It's like Billy Crystal says: "If you look mahvelous, you'll feel mahvelous."

And they all look *mahvelous* these days.

FALL, 1961, BOSTON VS. SYRACUSE (BOXERS OR BRIEFS, RED?)

On March 25, 1961, the Celtics defeated the Syracuse Nats 120–107 in Game 4 of the best-of-seven Eastern Conference Finals. Boston would go on to win the series in five games. During the very rough contest, three Syracuse fans came out of the stands and attacked Celtics coach Red Auerbach.

This was probably beyond stupid, since Auerbach merely summoned his enforcers—6' 5" "Jungle Jim" Loscutoff, 6' 8" Gene Conley and 6' 7" Tommy Heinsohn—who promptly tossed the three nutballs back into the stands.

That, alas, wasn't the end of this little caper by any means. The next season, on the morning after the Celtics' first game in Syracuse since the brawl, Auerbach was awakened by a knock at his door. In his undershirt and underpants, he answered the knock. In the hallway of the hotel were a process server and a photographer from the Associated Press. The process server handed a startled Auerbach a document detailing a $750,000 damage suit leveled against him by the fans! And, of course, the photographer was on hand to capture the moment for posterity.

It was the first time an NBA coach had ever been photographed in his underwear. And it also answered a question nobody wanted to pose: boxers or briefs, Red? Well, for Red, it was white boxers with little designs on them. Very cute. The lawsuit, by the way, was settled out of court.

The Uniforms

Since those early days, uniforms and equipment have evolved considerably. The typical uniform of the basketballer of the 19th century included knee, elbow and thigh pads. It was a rough game.

Most teams wore sleeveless tops and have continued to do so. Some college teams have worn short-sleeved shirts and the Knickerbockers' Patrick Ewing (1985–2002) pioneered wearing a T-shirt under his jersey while an undergrad at Georgetown, but the NBA is pretty strict about not allowing that, so uniform design has been pretty, well, uniform from Day One in the league.

Footwear also evolved. Much is made of the jet-age, super-expensive sneakers of the

Wilt Chamberlain was the first to sport a wristband on court.

Dennis Rodman changed his hair color faster than he changed teams.

The time-honored Chuck Taylor. A classic.

modern NBA. NBA players put tremendous wear-and-tear on their feet, ankles and legs. They should have great shoes.

In the beginning, the best basketball shoes were high-topped leather models with a soft leather sole that offered little flexibility or support for the feet or ankles. That is not what they were constructed for in the early days of basketball, however. More than anything else, the early shoes had to be durable because players wanted them to last. In the latter days of the 19th century and the early years of the 20th, basketball players began using tennis shoes, which were low-topped, but more flexible.

The first basketball shoe was designed by A. J. Spalding and Bros, Inc. of Chicago in the early 1900s. Spalding sold a canvas shoe with a thick rubber sole. The undersole was pocked with holes for better traction.

In the summer of 1921, a professional player named Chuck Taylor walked into the Converse Co. of Chicago and complained that his feet hurt. He asked the executives for Converse to design a durable, flexible shoe specifically for basketball players. Converse agreed, and by the next year, Taylor was promoting the shoe himself.

In 1931, Converse added Taylor's signature to the shoes, and "Chucks" were born. Originally the high- or low-topped canvas shoes with rubber soles were only available in black or white. In the years to come, Converse would offer them in a variety of colors.

But the white high tops were the most popular. As of 2001, more than 500 million pairs have been sold. And Taylor is in the Hall of Fame as a contributor.

In the 1970s, Adidas, a company based in Germany, got into the basketball shoe business and began cutting into Converse's sales. Soon, Nike, Reebock, Pony and Puma all had basketball shoes on the market, but Taylor's "Chucks" were the originals.

Accessorize, Accessorize

The first wristband was worn in 1959 by Philadelphia Warrior Wilt Chamberlain. Actually, Wilt's wristband was just a rubber band that Chamberlain wore to remind him of his days when he was so poor he had to use rubber bands to keep his socks up and the rubber band on his wrist was a spare in case one of the ones on either sock broke.

During the 1968–69 season, Chamberlain again took the lead in this particular category, using wristbands tennis players wore to keep his hands dryer. By the 1969–70 season, Wilt became the first pro player to wear a headband. Again, it served a functional purpose: Chamberlain sweated so much he needed to keep the moisture out of his eyes. He was emulated by many pros, including Seattle Supersonic guard Donald "Slick" Watts (1973–79) who wore a headband on his shaved head.

The Hairstyles

Watts was the first NBA player to shave his head, but there were a lot of pro players who were just plain bald. Forward George "The Bird" Yardley (1953–60), 6'7" forward Toby Kimball (1966–75) and 6'2" guard Bob Weiss (1965–77) were all afflicted at a young age.

Hair got out of control as the 1960s unfolded into the 1970s. Many players, black and white, were letting their hair grow out. Kimball and Weiss were two unfortunate exceptions. Players like Julius Erving, of the New York Nets, Darnell "Dr. Dunk" Hillman, of the Indiana Pacers, and Artis Gilmore, of the Kentucky Colonels, sported luxurious afros throughout the 1970s. Bill Walton, of the NBA's Portland Trail Blazers, had long hair and a full beard in the early to mid-1970s.

Hair Today, Gone Tomorrow

Early in the 1981–82 season, after a series of lackluster games, the Lakers fired coach Paul Westhead and elevated assistant coach Pat Riley to the Lakers' head job.

The press conference announcing Riley's hiring was a confused affair, as Lakers owner Jerry Buss clearly wanted former Lakers star Jerry West to take over. West didn't want it, and handed Riley the job. The press conference also marked the beginning of Riley's "Elvis Look," in which he slicked back his hair. One Los Angeles sportswriter noticed.

"Pat," he asked. "Are you going to continue to wear your hair in that funny way?"

Riley laughed, but he kept the slicked-back look.

Dr. J and others sported luxurious afros in the 1970s.

By the 1987–88 season, Kareem Abdul-Jabbar's rapidly expanding bald spot moved him to shave off the rest of his hair. It looked funny at first, but a lot of players clearly liked the look. By the next season, those with and without hair-loss problems were doing it. When the Bulls' Michael Jordan began doing it in the early 1990s, baldness was a fashion statement in full swing. A large number of black players and some white players in the league began shaving their heads routinely.

The 1994–95 Houston Rockets won the NBA title with a championship record four baldies: Clyde Drexler, Kenny Smith, Sam Cassell and Mario Elie, not to mention assistant coach Bill Berry.

In the last five or 10 years, the hairstyle pendulum has come back almost full swing. Players are wearing their hair longer again, and many ballplayers style or color their locks. Dennis Rodman (1986–2000) was totally out of control the last five years or so of his career, changing hair color faster than he changed teams.

The Last-Second Moves

Larry Bird's Five Greatest Shots

Larry Bird, aka "Larry Legend," made a ton of wild shots in his NBA career. Here are the top five:

1. The Amazing Putback Late in the fourth quarter of Game 1 of the 1981 NBA Finals, Bird curled around a Robert Parish pick and spotted up for a jumper from about 18 feet out. The shot was short, though, and Bird raced to the basket to rebound the ball. He got to the baseline and corralled the rebound. Realizing he was falling out of bounds, he transferred the ball to his left hand and lofted a shot back into the basket. The ball went through the hoop and the Garden crowd went nuts. Boston won, 98–95.

"That," said Boston general manager Red Auerbach, "was the greatest shot I've ever seen."

2. Sixty Points in Your Face On March 12, 1985, Bird set a new all-time individual scoring record of 60 points against the Atlanta Hawks. He hit 22 of 36 shots, but in the fourth quarter, he was unconscious. At one point, with Antoine Carr all over him, he hit a fall-away 38-footer right in front of the Hawks bench with 18 seconds left. Several Hawks players literally fell off their seats in disbelief. The crowd, and remember this was a home game for Atlanta, began chanting "Lar-ry! Lar-ry! Lar-ry!"

3. I Told You So On February 26, 1983, the Celtics trailed the Phoenix Suns, 101–100, with two seconds left. Just before the ball was thrown in, Bird told Suns forward David Thirdkill he would win the game with a three-point shot. Sure enough, with Thirdkill hanging on him, Bird took the inbounds pass and hit a running 29-footer at the buzzer. Celts win, 103–101.

4. Magic Can't Believe It On May 30, 1987, the Pistons and Celtics were locked in a do-or-die Game 7 in the Garden. With about four minutes left, Bird launched a left-handed hook shot from about 18 feet out that banked in off the glass. The Celtics won the game 117–114. Out in Los Angeles, several Lakers were watching the game to see who they would face in the Finals. Magic Johnson later admitted he almost fell off his seat when the shot went in.

5. One That Didn't Count In the Celtics' first exhibition game in the Hartford Civic Center in September of 1987 against the Rockets, Bird and Celtics guard Sam Vincent were racing down the court on a fast break in the third quarter. Sam's pass was too far ahead of Bird, and Larry had to jump over the baseline to grab it. But there's no one to pass to, so he turns in midair and, falling out of bounds, throws a shot over the backboard that swishes. The basket was disallowed because the ball went over the glass, but the fans in Hartford went wild.

Five Players from the "Early Days" Who Could Play Now

1. Johnny Wooden, 5'10", Indianapolis Kautskys (1932–38) The crafty Wooden was an excellent playmaker, tremendous driver and relentless defender. Think John Stockton with a set shot.

2. "Jumpin' Jim" Pollard, 6'5", Minneapolis Lakers (1947–55) "Jumpin Jim" would fit right in with the NBA of the 21st century. The guy could jump out of the gym, run like a cheetah and could palm the ball

Bob Petit

with either hand. Put him down for 20 or so a game these days.

3. Robert "Bob" Pettit, 6'9", St. Louis Hawks (1954–65) Yeah, we know. Big and slow, but also a player able to shoot hook shots with either hand, set solid picks, rebound all day and night, pass, and go to the offensive boards as well as anyone except probably Moses Malone. This guy would do fine.

4. William "Pop" Gates, 6'3", various teams (1938–55) Possibly the best athlete playing basketball in the 1930s and 1940s. Fast, strong and possessing a set shot that put him out beyond three-point range, Pop would get the job done.

5. Harry "the Horse" Gallatin, 6'6", New York, Detroit (1948–58) Think Charles Oakley, only meaner.

The Real First Names of 10 Players

1. Walter "Ray" Allen

2. Demetrius "Tony" Battie

3. Daron "Mookie" Blaylock

4. Ulrich "Rick" Fox

5. Ronald "Popeye" Jones

6. Charles "Bo" Outlaw

7. Herman "J. R." Reid

8. LuBara "Dickey" Simpkins

9. Mayce "Chris" Webber

10. Gawen "Bonzi" Wells

LIST

The 10 Greatest Playoff Games

1. June 4, 1976: Boston 128, Phoenix 126 (3 OTs). NBA Finals, Game 5. The famed three-overtime contest. Little-used Celtics forward Glenn MacDonald is the hero with six points in the final overtime. The next year, he was cut in pre-season. The Celtics, after squeaking this one out, go on to win the NBA title the next game.

2. April 13, 1957: Boston 125, St. Louis 123 (2 OTs). NBA Finals, Game 7. Veteran stars Bill Sharman (9 points) and Bob Cousy (12 points) can't hit the broad side of a barn. Rookies Bill Russell (19 points, 26 rebounds) and Tommy Heinsohn (37 points) lead the way. Old pro Arnie Risen comes off the bench for Boston and hits for 16.

3. May 8, 1970: New York 113, Los Angeles 99, NBA Finals, Game 7. The most dramatic game in New York basketball his-

tory in a city that has a tremendous history. New York captain Willis Reed, battling a knee injury, is questionable for the contest. Just before the game is to begin, Reed comes trotting out onto the court. In the game, he hits his first two baskets and totally demoralizes the Lakers.

4. May 22, 1988: Boston 118, Atlanta 116, NBA Eastern Semifinals, Game 7. The Bird-Wilkins shootout. Dominique Wilkins (47 points) has his greatest game as a pro. The play of the game, though, was Larry Bird's length-of-the-court pass to Danny Ainge for a layup that essentially clinched the game. Classic Bird.

5. April 12, 1958: St. Louis 110, Boston 109, NBA Finals, Game 7. The Hawks' Bob Pettit scores 50, including 19 of the Hawks' last 21 points. The only time a Russell Celtics team loses in the NBA Finals.

Mookie Blaylock

6. May 7, 1994: Denver 98, Seattle 94 (OT), NBA West First Round, Game 5. The greatest upset in NBA history. The 42–40 Nuggets were led by center Dikembe Mutombo. The 63–19 SuperSonics won the first two games in Seattle by wide margins (24 and 10 points). The Nuggets won the next two in Denver, setting up the winner-take-all Game 5. The Sonics played just well enough to lose.

7. May 3, 1981: Boston 91, Philadelphia 90, NBA Eastern Final, Game 7. Bird's jumper with 18 seconds left wins it. The Celtics trailed by three games to one in this series and came back by winning the next three games, in which they trailed by double-digit deficits each game.

8. April 15, 1962: Boston 110, Los Angeles 107 (OT), NBA Finals, Game 7. The game is tied at 100 when the Lakers' Frank Selvy takes a jumper from the side with only seconds left. He misses. Bill Russell grabs the rebound and Boston wins in OT.

9. May 16, 1980: Los Angeles 123, Philadelphia 107, NBA Finals, Game 6. The Lakers go into Philadelphia without Kareem Abdul-Jabbar, who injured his ankle in the closing moments of Game 5. Kareem stays in

Boston v. Phoenix in 1976. Gerald Heard gets clear of Celtics John Havlecek (17) and Paul Silas.

Los Angeles, resting his ankle, on the theory that if the Lakers lose, he will be ready. But the Lakers don't lose. Earvin "Magic" Johnson, in his greatest playoff performance ever, has 42 points, 15 rebounds and seven assists. Jamaal Wilkes adds 37 as the Lakers win their first title in the Johnson era.

10. April 20, 1986: Boston 135, Chicago 131 (2 OTs), Eastern Conference First Round, Game 2. Michael Jordan's 63-point game. "That wasn't Michael Jordan out there," said Larry Bird after the Celtics squeaked out a win. "That was God disguised as Michael Jordan."

LIST
The Five Greatest Playoff Upsets in NBA History

1. Denver (3) over Seattle (2), 1994 Western Conference First Round.

This was the first time a Number 8 seed toppled a Number 1 seed in NBA playoff history. The SuperSonics won the first two games rather easily, and thought the series was in the bag. It wasn't.

Fun Fact: The SuperSonics were the best team (63–19) never to win a playoff series.

2. Golden State (4) over Washington (0), 1975 NBA Finals. The Washington Bullets, with future Hall of Famers Wes Unseld and Elvin Hayes, were heavily favored over the Warriors, led by their own future Hall of Famer, Rick Barry. In fact, most experts predicted a Bullet sweep. The Warriors, however, showed more poise down the stretch in all four games and stunned the experts, not to mention the Bullets.

"This was the greatest upset in NBA history," said Barry years later. Given that it was

the Finals and the Bullets were so heavily favored, he has a point.

Fun Fact: Prior to the season, the Warriors traded All-Star center Nate Thurmond to the Chicago Bulls for Clifford Ray, a move opposed by Warriors coach Al Attles. But Ray, an exceptional rebounder and passer from the pivot, was a better "fit" for the Warriors and helped them win the title.

3. Los Angeles (4), Baltimore (2), 1965 NBA Western Conference Finals. Record-wise, this wasn't a big upset, as Los Angeles won 49 games, the Bullets 37, but when you consider that the Lakers played almost the entire series without All-Star forward Elgin Baylor, it's a huge upset. Baylor was injured early in Game 1. Lakers guard Jerry West stepped up and averaged 46.3 points per game, still an NBA record for an individual in a playoff series.

Fun Fact: West (31.0 points per game) and Baylor (27.1) averaged 58.1 points per game for Los Angeles that year. The rest of the team averaged 53.8.

4. New York (3), Miami (2), 1999 NBA Eastern Conference First Round. This was the second time a Number 8 seed toppled a Number 1 in NBA playoff history. This was the strike-shortened season, so the Knicks, at 27–23, finished only six games behind the 33–17 Heat. Still, when Knicks guard Allen Houston's jumper finally dropped through the net in that improbable 78–77 win, it sucked to be a Heat fan.

Fun Fact: This was the second year in a row that the Knicks had won a winner-take-all contest on the road. The previous year they had done it in, you guessed it, Miami.

5. Houston (2), Los Angeles (1), 1981 NBA Western Conference First Round. The 40–42 Rockets against the 54-28 Lakers, who were also the defending World Champs, seemed a big mismatch in the first round, but after Houston won Game 1, 111–107, Los Angeles had to take notice. The Lakers evened the best-of-three series 111–106 in Houston, but the Rockets took the deciding contest, 89–86 in the Forum.

Fun Fact: The 40–42 Rockets remain the only sub-.500 team to make the NBA Finals. Houston lost to the Celtics in six games that year.

Three Players with Handicaps Who Played Professionally

George Glamack (1941–49) George Glamack, a 6'9" center, was a hook-shot artist who was so nearsighted he was called the "Blind Bomber." Glamack may have been blind, but he averaged double figures in points during his career in the NBA and the NBL, and was also the second leading scorer on the NBL champion Rochester Royals in 1946–47 with a 12.4 average.

"Fat Freddie" Scolari (1946–55) Fred was blind in one eye (we think it was his left eye, but nobody knew for sure), but the 5'11" Scolari was still one of the best point guards of his era and played in the second NBA All-Star Game, scoring 10 points for the winning Eastern squad.

"Pistol" Pete Maravich (1970–80) "Pistol" Pete Maravich had a congenital heart condition that was revealed after his death in 1988: he had only one coronary artery complex. People with normal hearts have two. In essence, Maravich played 10 years in the NBA with half a functioning heart. Children born with this anomaly usually don't live past 20. Doctors were astounded that

Willis Reed celebrates after the knicks beat the Lakers 113–99 in game 7 of the NBA Finals

Maravich not only lived twice as long, but was an All-Star pro athlete.

The Four Quadruple-Doubles

Much has been made about triple-doubles, but there have been four official so-called quadruple-doubles in NBA history. Here they are:

Nate Thurmond, Chicago Bulls (10-18-74): 22 points, 14 rebounds, 13 assists, 12 blocks

Alvin Robertson, San Antonio Spurs (2-18-86): 20 points, 11 rebounds, 10 assists, 10 steals

Hakeem Olajuwon, Houston Rockets (3-29-90): 18 points, 16 rebounds, 10 assists, 11 blocks

David Robinson, San Antonio Spurs (2-17-94): 34 points, 10 rebounds, 10 assists, 10 blocks (Note: In 1967, Wilt Chamberlain averaged a triple-double in points, rebounds and assists for the 15 playoff games played by the Philadelphia 76ers that year. Although blocked shots were not kept in those days, Chamberlain almost certainly, according to published reports,

recorded a quadruple-double, 24 points, 32 rebounds, 13 assists and, unofficially, 12 blocks, in the Sixers' first game against the Boston Celtics in the Eastern Conference Finals. He probably had another one in Game 5 of the same series, as he had, officially, 29 points, 36 rebounds, 13 assists and another 10 or so blocks, according to wire reports.)

Five Books about the NBA You Should Try to Find

These are books that are, alas, out of print, but that are worth looking up:

1. *Foul! The Connie Hawkins Story*, by David Wolf, 1972. An excellently researched book about the life and times of playground legend Connie Hawkins. Best part: Connie's ABA experiences.

2. *Maverick, More Than a Game*, by Phil Jackson, with Charles Rosen, 1975. Phil Jackson on the NBA in the 1970s, including groupies and stupid refs.

3. *Echoes from the Schoolyard*, by Anne Byrne Hoffman, 1977. Portraits of some of the all-time greats in their own words. Best part: the chapter about Joe Fulks.

4. *Loose Balls: The Short, Wild Life of the ABA*, by Terry Pluto, 1990. This is still available in a lot of stores, so run, don't walk, to get it. It's that good. Exactly what the title says. Stories from the days of the ABA. Best part: its all pretty good, but I loved the chapter on Wendell Ladner.

5. *Scientific Basketball*, by Nat Holman, 1922. More of a how-to book, but also includes wonderful tidbits about playing basketball in those early days. Best part: Holman on Joe Lapchick and why he's great.

Ten Things We Couldn't Leave Out

(but that you should know).

1
The Games of the Century

In 1948, Harlem Globetrotter owner-manager Abe Saperstein had an idea: he would challenge the Lakers in a one-shot "Game of the Century" and split the gate with Minneapolis. Saperstein reasoned, correctly, that Minneapolis and his Globetrotters were the most recognized teams on the planet. He figured fans would flock to see the two squads play.

Early in the 1947–48 season, Saperstein called Lakers general manager Max Winter and set it up. By the time the game had been scheduled, in the spring of 1948, the Globies had won 101 games in a row and the newspapers were speculating about the matchup between Mikan and the Globetrotters' Reese "Goose" Tatum.

The game drew a sellout crowd in Chicago, and the Globetrotters won, 61–59. Mikan outscored Tatum 24–9, but later admitted, "I was concentrating too much on showing up Tatum, completely forgetting I was just one cog in the team."

The two teams immediately agreed to several more "Games of the Century." The Globetrotters won the second game, 49-45, before 20,000 fans in Chicago in the spring of 1949. Max Winter demanded another rematch, and Saperstein was glad to oblige.

A few weeks later, Mikan scored 33 points, and the Lakers front line controlled the boards as the Lakers crushed the Globies, 68–53.

The Lakers won both contests in 1950, 76–60 and 69–54, and one of the big reasons was Minneapolis backcourtman Slater Martin. In Martin, the Lakers finally had a ballhandler at least as good as anyone the Globies had. Two more games were scheduled in 1951, but after the Lakers won again, 72-68, Saperstein called Winter and canceled the series. The games had drawn a combined 96,000 people, as Saperstein had expected, but there was one problem: his team didn't always win.

2
The Worst Game Ever

On November 22, 1950, the Fort Wayne Pistons hit on a way of trying to derail the powerful Minneapolis Lakers. They stalled the entire game, beating the Lakers, 19–18, in the lowest-scoring game in league history, but you know what? It almost didn't work.

The Pistons would get the ball and hold it at midcourt for sometimes a few minutes before taking a shot. The Lakers ran their offense every time they got the ball. Minneapolis led 13-11 at halftime, and 17-16 after three periods. Late in the game, the Lakers were ahead, 18-17. With time winding down, Fort Wayne center Larry Foust

Parish, Bird, and McHale. The greatest frontcourt in NBA history.

wound up with the ball and heaved in a hook shot with three seconds left for the game-winner. It was his only basket of the game.

"We snuck out of Minneapolis that night," admitted Fort Wayne owner Fred Zollner many years later.

3 The Best Drafts Ever

A lot of NBA observers believe that the Celtics' 1956 draft, which got them future Hall of Famers Tommy Heinsohn, K. C. Jones and Bill Russell, was the greatest draft in the history of the league. And it probably was, but not too far behind was the Minneapolis Lakers' draft prior to the 1949–50 season. In addition to picking up Bobby Harrison, a nine-year veteran who would be named to the 1956 All-Star Game (with another team, admittedly), the Lakers also drafted future Hall of Famer Vern Mikkelsen, a 6'8" banger who would give Mikan the relief he needed under the boards. Finally, Minneapolis also signed future Hall of Famer Slater Martin, a 5'10" guard who would quarterback the Lakers to four titles and the St. Louis Hawks to a championship.

4 The Best Trade Ever

The Celtics had originally owned the number one and number 13 picks in the NBA draft prior to the 1980–81 season. There was much speculation about who Boston would make the number one pick in the draft, with Louisville guard Darryl Griffith the principal choice.

Celtics general manager Red Auerbach knew the Celtics needed to get big guys for his front line, so he sent those picks to Golden State for center Robert Parish and the number three pick, which turned out to be Kevin McHale.

That move brought the Celtics the World Championship that year. Parish and McHale, with Larry Bird, evolved into the greatest frontcourt in NBA history. Carroll played 10 years in the NBA and made the All-Star team in 1987. Golden State's 13th pick was Ricky Brown, who played for five years in the league, averaging seven points per game.

5 The Only Way to Stop Mikan

The road was a tough place to play. Mikan, in his 1952 autobiography, recalled one incident in a game in Fort Wayne, Indiana, in the late 1940s. Late in the game, Mikan went to the free-throw line. Just as he was about to shoot, he felt a stinging sensation on his left leg. Then another sting on the seat of his pants. He mentioned it to referee Stan Stutz, believing it was a bee sting. Stutz pointed out that it was February, and that no one had seen the bee. Mikan shrugged and hit the free throw.

Later, with the Lakers up by only one point, Mikan was back at the free-throw line. He felt another sting in his lower back. Whirling around, he saw a BB pellet on the floor.

"Stan," he said to Stutz, pointing at the BB, "look. They're shooting at me."

Mikan made the free throw and the Lakers won, but they never caught the BB gun guy.

6 The Most Amazing Shot Ever

During the Harlem Globetrotters' tour of the world in 1952, "Goose" Tatum drop-kicked a basketball into the goal from beyond half-court, a feat that, up to that point, had been accomplished successfully only four times before in the Globetrotters' 25-year history. While the Globetrotters went wild, the Japanese crowd clapped politely.

Told that Tatum's feat was truly rare and amazing, the Japanese promoter reportedly shrugged.

"The fans in Japan believe the Globetrotters can do anything," he said. "So they weren't surprised."

7 The Closest Scoring Race Ever

The 1978–79 season was the year of the closest scoring race in the history of the league. Going into the final day of the season, April 9, Denver Nuggets guard David Thompson, in 79 games, had scored 2,099 points for an average of 26.57 points per game. San Antonio Spurs swingman George "Iceman" Gervin in 81 games had scored 2,169 points for a scoring average of 26.78 points per game.

Thompson had an afternoon game in Detroit. He went nuts, scoring 73 points in a 139–137 loss to the Pistons. He scored 32 points in the first period, on 13 baskets and six free throws, which broke a record jointly held by former Philadelphia Warrior Wilt Chamberlain and former St. Louis Hawks forward Cliff Hagan. Chamberlain's 31-point quarter came the night he scored 100 points against the Knickerbockers.

By halftime, Thompson had hit an amazing 20 of 23 field goals.

"They got me the ball and I was hitting," said Thompson after the game. "Everything I shot was going in during the first half, but I couldn't keep up the pace in the second half. I got a little tired."

Thompson finished with 73 points on 28 of 38 field goals, and 17 of 20 free throws. He also had seven rebounds and two assists. After the game, Thompson thanked his teammates for helping him to take the scoring title lead, and then apologized because the Nuggets had lost the game.

The Spurs had a night game against the New Orleans Jazz in the New Orleans Superdome. On the flight back from Detroit to Denver, Thompson found the Jazz-Spurs radio broadcast and began to listen to it. His record of 32 points in one quarter lasted about three hours. Gervin, after scoring 20 points in the first quarter against the Jazz, scored 33 in the second quarter on 12 baskets and nine free throws.

Gervin had 53 points at halftime. He had been appraised of Thompson's amazing performance, and figured out that he needed 59 points to break the record. After scoring the requisite six points in the third quarter, Moe took him out to a thunderous standing ovation from the Jazz fans, but as he later admitted during his induction ceremony to the Basketball Hall of Fame, he was a little nervous that his math hadn't been right. Gervin asked Moe to put him back in, and he hit a dunk and a jump shot to finish with 63 points. The Jazz players, said Gervin after

the game, did not want him to break the record.

"All the Jazz defenders were tough, and they kept a hand in my face all night," said the player called Iceman. "I was pressing early, and didn't have my rhythm, but I got it after seven or eight minutes."

Thompson admitted that he was a little peeved after Gervin slid by him to take the scoring record.

"But then again," he said, "there's no disgrace in coming in second to George Gervin."

8
The Origin of "Three-Peat"

The origin of the term "Three-Peat" came before the 1988–89 season, according to former Lakers guard Byron Scott. Scott recalled talking with former Lakers coach Pat Riley about the possibility of the Lakers winning three consecutive NBA titles just before the

season began. As Scott recalls it (and Riley, to our knowledge, has never denied it), he came up with the term.

It was Riley, however, who copyrighted the term, which apparently has earned Riley some endorsement dollars, although it is difficult to ascertain how much.

Scott thinks he knows.

"Yeah, tell Pat he owes me two or three million," laughed Scott just before the 2002 Finals.

9
The Punch That Nearly Killed

On December 12, 1977, the nastiest single punch in NBA history was unleashed by one of the most decent players in the league. That night, in Los Angeles, Houston center Kevin Kunnert and Lakers forward Kermit Washington were tussling for a rebound, which Kunnert eventually grabbed. After Kunnert fired an outlet pass, he and Washington got tangled up. Kunnert struck Washington with an elbow, and a frustrated Washington struck Kunnert several times in the face and shoulder with his fist.

Several players tried to break the fight up, including Lakers Center Kareem Abdul-Jabbar, who grabbed Kunnert. At this point, Rockets forward Rudy Tomjanovich was coming up behind Washington, in an attempt to keep the peace.

Washington later admitted he saw Tomjanovich coming at him out of the corner of his eye. Washington spun and unleashed a straight right hand that seemed to go right through Tomjanovich's head. Rudy T. cupped his face in his hands and

David Thompson in 1978.

Rudy Tomjanovich coaching the Houston Rockets in 1999

crashed to the floor. Bleeding from the nose and lip, he was helped off the court and taken to the hospital. An examination revealed Tomjanovich had sustained a double fracture of the jaw, a broken nose and a concussion. He required extensive surgery and was lost for the season.

"I saw him coming and just swung," said Washington after the game. "Now that I've talked to people, I understand Rudy wasn't going to fight. He's never even been in a fight. It was an honest, unfortunate mistake."

"It sounded," said Abdul-Jabbar succinctly, "like a melon hitting a cement sidewalk."

That punch earned Washington a 60-game suspension, a hefty (for the time) $10,000 fine and lost income to the tune of

$50,000 (players cannot collect their salary while on suspension).

The fallout from the Tomjanovich incident was more severe than just fines. Tomjanovich recovered, but played only three more years, retiring at age 32.

Washington, although he apologized for the incident, was vilified by many fans who saw the incident as being at least partly racial in nature. He and his family were subjected to outrageous vituperation. The animosity toward Washington was so intense that the Lakers traded him across the continent to Boston. To the credit of the fans in that city, Washington was warmly received and applauded for his hustling play, but the incident haunted Washington for the rest of his career and beyond.

10
The NBA-ABA All-Star Game

In 1971, the players for the National Basketball Association and the rival American Basketball Association agreed to play an All-Star game between the two leagues as a way to make a little money. The NBA didn't sanction the game, but that didn't matter, because the ABA did, and they arranged for the game to be broadcast.

The game was played in Houston on May 28, 1971. Elgin Baylor coached the NBA All-Stars, and Al Bianchi coached the ABA stars. The NBA starters were a Who's Who of pro basketball in the 1970s: guards Oscar Robertson and Dave Bing, center Nate Thurmond, and forwards John Havlicek and Dave DeBusschere started. Earl Monroe, Elvin Hayes, Walt Frazier and Billy Cunningham came off the bench. All nine of

these players are now in the Basketball Hall of Fame. The only player that didn't make it to the Hall from that squad was Lou Hudson, a late replacement for injured Lakers star Jerry West, another future Hall of Famer.

The ABA team started forwards Rick Barry and Willie Wise, center Zelmo Beaty and guards Charlie Scott and Larry Jones. Of that unit, only Barry is in the Hall of Fame. The substitutes were Mel Daniels, John Brisker, Steve Jones, Don Freeman and Roger Brown.

The NBA fell behind early, but rallied behind Frazier, who wound up with 26 points and was the game MVP. The final score was 125–120. A total of 16,364 watched the game.

The next year, the NBA hierarchy, by now battling the ABA in court, moved to block the game. The league warned its players that anyone caught participating in the contest would be fined and subject to suspension. That reduced the NBA roster talent-wise, although such stars as Wilt Chamberlain, Bob Lanier, Nate Archibald, Connie Hawkins, DeBusschere and Havlicek still showed up. The ABA had a little better squad than the previous year, with Dan Issel, Artis Gilmore and Julius Erving joining Wise, Brown and Daniels on the roster.

The game was great. The NBA squeaked out a 106–104 win, and Barry missed a very makeable three-pointer at the buzzer that would have given the ABA the victory. Lanier, with 15 points and seven rebounds, was MVP. But the uncertainty sowed by the NBA bigwigs kept attendance down, and NBA officials triumphantly announced that no one really wanted to watch these games. Right. Which didn't explain why the NBA scheduled 155 exhibitions with the ABA from 1971 through 1975.

Index

Abdul-Jabbar, Kareem, 19, 20, 61, 139, 146, 180. See also Alcindor, Lew
  career high, 25
  career record, 67
  drive shot and, 44
  fast break and, 187
  foul shot and, 49
  as high-scoring player, 172
  hook shots of, 23^24, 23^25
  pivot and, 112, 116, 118
  rejecting the ball, 99
  scoring championships, 22
  style and, 207
Abdul-Rauf, Mahmoud, 49
Abdur-Rahim, Shareef, 118, 131
Adams, Michael, 62
Africa, basketball in, 171
Ainge, Danny, 181
Alcindor, Lew, 20, 22, 23, 25, 118, 173, 174. See also Abdul-Jabbar, Kareem
All-America team, 145
All-Star games, 161, 174, 196, 215^16
Allen, Forrest "Phog," 199
Allen, Ray, 17, 148, 209
alley-oop shot, 34^39
Alonzo, Amos, 52
Amateur Athletic Union (AAU), 35, 47, 68, 83, 157, 183
American Basketball Association (ABA), 27, 29, 30, 37, 186–87
  Finals (1968), 127
  merged with NBA, 175
  rivalry with NBA, 215^16
  style and, 205
  three-point shot and, 59
American Basketball League (ABL), 151, 159, 173
Anderson, Nick, 106
Anthony, Greg, 17
Archibald, Lyman W., 57, 133
Archibald, Nate "Tiny," 40, 44, 44, 158, 159^60, 216
  passing moves of, 69, 70
  "playground" basketball and, 169, 175
  short stature of, 156, 157
Arizin, Paul, 10, 17, 162, 163, 163–64
Artest, Ron, 102
artful passing, 66–71

assists, 68, 80
Atlanta Hawks, 30, 81, 101, 118
  defensive standout, 108
  in NBA Finals (Eastern Conference), 177
  scoring records, 185
  stealing records, 94
  violations, 109
Atlantic Coast Conference, 84
Attles, Al, 10, 123
Auerbach, Arnold "Red," 48, 62, 77, 80, 108, 191, 198, 198
  conditioning of players and, 201
  fast break and, 185
  instructional book by, 79
  integration of NBA and, 196
  with NBA Championship trophy, 200
  player trades and, 213
  "playground" basketball and, 171^72
  tall players and, 114^15
  tough players and, 129
  trash-talking and, 190, 191, 193
  violent behavior of, 191^92

"baby hook," 21, 25
backboards, 53, 57, 157
  bank shot and, 60, 60, 61, 63, 63
  destroyed, 33
Bailey, Thurl, 101
Baker, Vin, 103
Baltimore Bullets, 33, 48, 49, 137, 159
bank shot, 60^63
Banks, Gene, 180
Barker, Cliff, 197, 197
Barkley, Charles, 45, 108, 162, 164, 166
  career triple-doubles, 137
  rebound games, 131
  trash-talking and, 190, 193
Barnes, Marvin, 75
Barnett, Dick, 192
Barnett, Rich, 146
Barnstable, Cliff, 141
Barros, Dana, 19
Barry, Brent, 17, 79
Barry, John, 89
Barry, Rick, 46, 87, 89

foul shot and, 49, 51
  as high-scoring player, 121, 122, 123^24, 172
  stealing the ball, 92, 95
basketball, 119, 183
  creation of, 8^10
  evolution of the ball, 44, 48
  "playground," 168–75
  racial integration of, 194–96
Basketball Association of America (BAA), 16, 21, 47, 48, 57, 134, 159
Basketball for the Player, the Fan and the C o a c h (Auerbach), 79, 193
Battie, Tony, 89, 209
Baylor, Elgin, 16, 75, 83, 95, 128
  as coach, 88, 215
  fake bank shot and, 61
  as high-scoring player, 120, 121, 121, 122–23, 172
  injuries, 185
  as rebounder, 135
Beacco, John, 11
Beard, Ralph, 10, 16, 69, 105, 141, 197
Beaty, Zelmo, 215
Beckman, Johnny, 88, 168, 171, 173
Bee, Clair, 17
behind-the-back dribble, 78^81
Bellamy, Walt, 134
Beloit College, 61
Belov, Alexander, 53, 53
Benjamin, Benoit, 152
Berry, Bill, 207
Best, Travis, 160, 161
Bianchi, Al, 146
Biasone, Dany, 196, 196
Bibby, Mike, 71, 80, 182, 186, 187
big guards, 144^49
Bing, David, 158, 165, 215
Bird, Larry, 24, 25, 29, 67, 172
  assist records, 74
  ball stolen from, 94
  career triple-doubles, 137
  drive shot and, 43
  fake bank shot and, 61
  foul shot and, 46, 46, 51
  greatest shots, 208

  as high-scoring player, 120, 122, 124–25
  no-look pass and, 73, 77
  passing moves of, 66, 70^71
  pick-and-roll play and, 86, 89
  set shot and, 59, 59
  stealing the ball, 95
  trash-talking and, 190, 190, 192, 193
Blake, Steve, 81
Blaylock, Daron "Mookie," 81, 209
Bob Cousy and the Celtic Mystique (Cousy), 69
Bogues, Tyrone "Muggsy," 81, 85, 100, 156, 156, 158, 160–61
Boilermakers (Purdue team), 42
Bol, Manute, 25, 102
  blocked shots and, 117
  giant size of, 150, 152, 155, 155
  rejecting the ball, 98
  three-point shooting statistics, 155
Borgmann, Bernhard "Benny," 41
Boryla, Vince, 199
Boston Celtics, 17^18, 21, 59, 80
  backboard smasher of, 33
  best draft ever, 213
  blowout stats, 62
  championships, 23, 61
  coaches, 202
  defensive standouts, 108
  Eastern Conference Semifinals (1953), 47
  fast break and, 182, 183, 185, 187
  foul shot and, 49
  integration of NBA and, 195, 196
  layup shot and, 55
  medium-size players in, 165
  in NBA Finals, 93, 95, 133, 139, 209, 210
  pick-and-roll play and, 86, 89
  scoring averages, 187
  stealing records, 94
  three-point conversions, 44
  trash-talking and, 190
  violations, 109
"Boston Massacre," 16
Boudreau, Lou, 159
bounce pass, 68, 183
Bowen, Bruce, 166
Boykin, Earl, 160

Boykoff, Harry, 139
Bradley, Bill, 27, 55, 162, 162, 164, 165–66
Bradley, Shawn, 117, 154
Brand, Elton, 33, 63
Brandon, Terrell, 161
Brandt, Charley, 140
Brannum, Bob, 129, 191
Bratton, Al, 55, 66^67
Braun, Carl, 17, 49, 56, 69, 203
Bridges, Bill, 135
Brisker, John, 215
Bristow, Allan, 107
Brookfield, Price, 16
Brown, Freddie "Downtown," 178
Brown, Hubie, 101
Brown, Kiesha, 80
Brown, Kwame, 143
Brown, Larry, 17, 38, 205
Brown, Roger, 177, 215
Brown, Walter, 185, 194, 196
Bruins (UCLA team), 38, 114
Bryant, Kobe, 30, 59, 167, 175
    alley-oop and, 38
    as "big guard," 144, 148, 148
    coaches and, 203
    crossover dribble and, 82, 85
    fast break and, 186, 187
    as one-on-one player, 176, 176, 180
    rejecting the ball, 102
    three-point conversions, 44
Buckner, Cleveland, 124
"buddy system," 87, 157
Buffalo Braves, 205
Buffalo Germans, 169, 198, 199
Burkhardt, Fred, 198, 199
Burleson, Tom, 150, 153
Buss, Jerry, 207

Camby, Marcus, 131
Campbell, Eldon, 63
Campus Confessions (1938 movie), 79
career field goal percentages, 19, 22, 59
Carter, Fred, 177
Carter, Vince, 128, 167, 175
    alley-oop and, 38
    as one-on-one player, 180
    "playground" basketball and, 169, 175
    slam dunk and, 26, 26, 30, 31, 32
Cassell, Buck, 54
Cassell, Sam, 207
Catholic Youth Organization leagues, 173
Cervi, Al "Digger," 10, 57, 69, 95

as coach, 163
    crossover dribble and, 83
    as defender, 105
    short stature of, 159
Chamberlain, Wilt, 59, 94, 135, 135–36
    in All-Star games, 216
    assists responsible for, 158
    career record, 67
    finger roll and, 54
    foul shot and, 49
    as high-scoring player, 123, 124, 125, 172
    hook shot and, 23, 25
    injuries, 185
    integration of NBA and, 195
    jump shot and, 19
    leg injury suffered, 178
    no-look pass and, 76^77
    pick-and-roll play and, 87
    pivot and, 112, 112, 113, 117^18
    "playground" basketball and, 169
    as rebounder, 132, 134, 147
    rejecting the ball, 98, 101
    "shootaround" and, 203
    slam dunk and, 26, 28^29, 31
    style and, 206^7
    trash-talking and, 192
Chambliss, Sharif, 75
Chaney, Don, 194
Chapin, Dwight, 79
Charlotte (N.C.) Hornets, 102, 160, 161, 185
Chase, William R., 67
Chattanooga Railites, 68, 113
Chenier, Phil, 106
chest pass, 68
Chicago Bulls, 15, 17, 30, 146
    in NBA Finals, 41, 95
    scoring averages, 187
    scoring records, 185
    violations, 109
Chicago Gears, 21, 62
Chicago Stags, 57, 58
Christie, Doug, 102, 108
Cincinnati, University of, 81, 145
Cincinnati Royals, 17, 86, 105, 140, 145
City College of New York, 171
Clark, Keon, 101
Cleveland Cavaliers, 30, 44, 71, 80, 84, 193
Cleveland Rosenblums, 105
Clifton, Nat "Sweetwater," 54, 138, 139–40, 194, 196, 203
coaches, 10, 25, 101, 133, 185, 198–203, 205. See also specific coaches
Collins, Doug, 53
Confessions of a Basketball Gypsy (Barry), 87, 123

Conley, Gene, 205
Connecticut League, 173
Cooke, Jack Kent, 185
Cooper, Chuck "Tarzan," 194, 196, 200
Cooper, Fred, 55, 66^67
Cooper, Michael, 18, 19
    alley-oop and, 34, 38
    layup shot and, 54
    set shot and, 56, 59, 59
Costello, Larry, 56, 59, 84
Cousy, Bob "Houdini of the Hardwood," 28, 81, 95, 158, 185
    alley-oop and, 34, 36, 36^37
    assist records, 74, 76
    behind-the-back dribble and, 78
    as coach, 44, 160
    crossover dribble and, 83
    fast break and, 183, 186
    foul shot and, 47
    hook shot and, 23
    jump shot and, 18
    no-look pass and, 72
    passing moves of, 66, 66, 69, 69
    pick-and-roll play and, 86, 88
    "playground" basketball and, 168, 173
    retirement of, 62–63, 105
Cousy on the Celtic Mystique (Cousy), 36
Cowens, Dave "Big Red," 93, 112, 118, 138, 139, 141, 187
Cronin, John, 11
crossover dribbling, 82^85
Cunningham, Bill, 180, 215

Dallas Mavericks, 17, 54, 59, 77, 81
    assist records, 84
    fast break and, 186
    scoring records, 185
Dallmar, Howie, 57, 79
Daly, Chuck, 181, 204, 205
Danbury (Conn.) Hatters, 173
Dandridge, Bob, 178
Daniels, Mel, 116, 215
Dantley, Adrian "A.D.," 42, 45, 162, 164, 166
Davies, Bob, 42, 48, 99, 105
    in All-Star Game, 163
    behind-the-back dribble and, 78
    crossover dribble and, 83
    passing moves of, 68, 69
    as "sixth man," 203
Davis, Antonio, 88
Davis, Baron, 96
Davis, William H., 56, 57
Dawkins, Darryl, 30, 33, 94, 152

DeBusschere, Dave, 27, 104, 106, 106–7, 108, 129, 215
defenders' moves, 104^9
Dehnert, Henry "Dutch," 41, 68, 112, 113
Denver Nuggets, 10, 30, 33, 38, 49
    assists, 68, 80
    coach of, 205
    goaltending leader of, 101
    team dunks, 36
DePaul University, 21, 139
Detroit Pistons, 25, 27, 42, 73, 80
    half-court defense of, 187
    one-on-one players in, 181
    opening tap stats, 88
    scoring averages, 187
Detroit Shock, 80
Deutsch, Robin, 10
Dickau, Dan, 38
Dickey, Derrick, 55
"digging in," 105
DiGregorio, Ernie, 75
Divac, Vlade, 88, 187
double dribble, 83, 84
Douglas, Bobby, 198, 200
drafts, best ever, 213
Drexler, Clyde, 137, 207
dribbling, 41, 78^85, 179
Driscoll, Jack, 157
drive shot, 40^45
Dudley, Charles, 178
Duncan, Tim, 24, 25, 98
    bank shot and, 60, 60, 63, 63, 63
    pivot and, 117, 118, 119
    rebound games, 131
    rejecting the ball, 103, 103
dunking, 26^33

"ear shot," 15
Eastern League, 173
Eaton, Mark, 23, 25, 101, 102, 117, 155
Echoes from the Schoolyard (Hoffman), 211
Edeshko, Ivan, 53
Edney, Tyus, 160
Edwards, LeRoy "Cowboy," 21, 25, 60, 61–62, 177
Effrat, Lou, 69
El-Amin, Khalid, 160
Elie, Mario, 56, 56, 58, 59, 207
Ellis, Dale, 63
Ellis, Leroy, 185
Embry, Wayne, 44, 86, 88, 89
Erving, Julius "Doctor J," 93, 107, 172
    in All-Star games, 216
    alley-oop and, 37

bank shot and, 61

finger roll and, 54

as one-on-one player, 176, 179, 180

passing moves of, 70

"playground" basketball and, 168, 169, 175

slam dunk and, 26, 26, 27, 28, 29

stealing the ball, 95

style and, 207

Eskridge, Jack, 16

Evansville University, 146

Ewing, Patrick, 88, 102, 115, 205

"eye fake," 73

Farnham, Dick, 11

fast break, 75^76, 182^87

"Fat Lady" phrase, 193

Faust, Henry, 199

Feerick, Bob, 19, 48, 59, 115

Ferry, Danny, 58, 58, 154

FIBA (International Basketball Federation), 53

finger roll, 54, 54

Finkle, Henry, 23

Finley, Michael, 59, 166, 186

Fisher, Robert, 161

Fitch, Bill, 153

"flopping," 41

"flushing" the ball, 35

footwear, 205^6, 206

Fort Wayne (Ind.) Pistons, 17, 27, 53, 95, 159, 212^13

forward pass, 89

Foster, Kit, 11

foul shot, 46^51, 133

Foul! The Connie Hawkins Story (Wolf), 211

fouls, 41

four-point play, 62, 63, 63

Foust, Larry, 135

Fox, Rick, 16

Francis, Steve "Franchise/Jumpin' Jack," 37, 38, 44, 70, 80, 85

Frazier, Walt "Clyde," 27, 87, 215
    alley-oop and, 37
    assist records, 74
    crossover dribble and, 82, 82, 83, 84
    "playground" basketball and, 169
    as rebounder, 135
    stealing the ball, 92, 95^96

Free, World B., 121

Freeman, Don, 215

Friddle, Burl, 16

Friedman, Marty, 57

Friedman, Max, 86, 87^88, 157

Fulks, Joe ("Jumpin' Joe"), 14, 15, 57
    behind-the-back dribble and, 79
    career field goal percentages, 19
    jump shot and, 15^17
    performance statistics, 16
    scoring record, 121
    set shot and, 58

Furey, Jim, 41

Gale, Lauren "Laddie," 15

Gale, Mike, 107

Gallatin, Harry "the Horse," 20, 48, 163, 209
    best rebounding games, 142
    as "little big man," 138, 139, 140
    as rebounder, 132, 134, 135
    as "sixth man," 203

"garbage men," 126^31

Garnett, Kevin, 24, 25, 101, 119, 166, 167

Gates, William "Pop," 200, 209

George, Devon, 103

Gervin, George "Iceman," 14, 54, 73, 147
    as "big guard," 144, 146
    fast break and, 182, 187
    as high-scoring player, 120, 120, 121, 123, 124, 124
    scoring average, 214

giant players, 150^55

Gilmore, Artis, 29, 132, 136, 207, 216

Glamack, George, 211

goaltending leaders, 101

Gola, Tom, 75, 144, 145, 145, 192

Golden State Warriors, 10, 49, 62, 155
    assists, 84
    layup shot and, 55
    scoring records, 185
    stealing records, 94

Goldpaper, Sam, 27

Gonzaga University, 38

Goodrich, Gail, 76^77, 103, 185, 203

Govan, Gerald, 130

Granick, Russ, 53

Grant, Brian, 88, 102

Green, Ricky, 178

Greer, Hal, 14, 19

Grevey, Kevin, 178

Griffith, Darrell ("Dr. Dunkenstein"), 30, 31, 38

Gross, Bob, 55, 77

Groza, Alex "the Nose," 115, 116, 141, 141, 142, 197

Guerin, Richie, 81

"gunners," 21

Hagan, Cliff, 25, 163, 164^65

Haggerty, George "Horse," 41

Hairston, Harold "Happy," 113, 185

hairstyles of players, 207, 207

Hakes, Stevie and Billy, 11

Halas, George, 151

Halbrook, Wade "Swede," 150, 153

half-court defense, 187

"half hook," 21

Hall of Fame, 10, 41, 88, 115, 127, 175
    ball stealers in, 92
    bank shooters in, 60
    behind-the-back dribblers in, 78
    "big guards" in, 144
    coaches in, 198, 199, 202, 203
    college players in, 15
    defensive standouts in, 104, 105
    fast break players in, 185
    foul-shot players in, 46
    "little big men" in, 138
    medium-size players in, 162, 163
    no-look passers in, 72
    pick-and-roll players in, 86
    player-coaches in, 42
    "playground" basketball and, 172
    rebounders in, 132, 135
    rejectors in, 98
    set shot players in, 58
    short players in, 156, 158, 160
    teams in, 200
    trash-talkers in, 190

Hamilton, Rip, 51

Hammond (Illinois) All-Americans, 159

Hannum, Alex, 61, 153, 164, 202

Hardaway, Tim, 82, 85, 85

Harlem Globetrotters, 26, 27, 54, 80, 139, 173
    dribbling and, 85
    drop-kick shot and, 213^14
    "Game of the Century" and, 212
    integration of NBA and, 195^96
    no-look pass and, 72, 73

Hassett, Joey, 121

Havlicek, John "Hondo," 31, 55, 129, 162, 165, 178
    in All-Star games, 216
    assist records, 74
    fast break and, 186, 187
    as high-scoring player, 121
    stealing the ball, 93

Hawkins, Connie, 26, 29, 132, 177
    in All-Star games, 216
    "playground" basketball and, 168, 169, 173–74

Hayes, Elvin, 166, 178, 215

Haynes, Marques, 85, 85

"Heavenly Twins," 86, 87, 88

Heerdt, Al, 199

Heinsohn, Tommy, 88, 183, 185, 186

Henderson, Gerald, 95

Hertzberg, Sonny, 170, 203

high post players, 115^18

Hill, Grant, 55, 137

Hillman, Darnell ("Doctor of the Dunk"), 29, 37, 207

Hoffman, Anne Byrne, 211

Hollyfield, Larry, 38

Holman, Nat, 40, 41, 68, 88, 157, 211
    as high-scoring player, 120, 121
    team strategy and, 199

Holy Cross, 80

Holzman, William "Red," 140, 141, 164, 166, 204, 205
    "playground" basketball and, 172
    as "sixth man," 203

"hook-dunk," 173

hook pass, 68

hook shot, 20^25, 121, 121

Hopkins, Bob, 201

Hornacek, Jeff, 19

Houbregs, Bob, 20, 23

Houston, Allan, 14, 17, 19

Houston Comets, 63

Houston Rockets, 37, 44, 49, 80
    assist records, 84
    in NBA Finals, 99, 102
    scoring averages, 187
    style and, 207
    tall players in, 151, 153^54
    violations, 109

Howell, Bailey, 126, 126, 127, 128, 129

Hudson, Lou, 215

Hudson River League, 157

Hughes, Kim, 10, 29

Hughes, Larry, 160

Hundley, Rod, 133

Hutchins, Mel, 17

Iba, Hank, 53

inbounds pass, 77

Indiana Pacers, 16, 17, 29, 33, 37, 116, 177
    as ABA champions, 33
    assist leaders, 80
    violations, 109

Indianapolis Jets, 16

Indianapolis Kautskys, 42, 50, 81

Indianapolis Olympians, 16, 69, 116, 197

integration, 194^96

Interstate League, 171, 173

Irish, Ned, 139

isolation plays, 180^81

Issel, Dan, 130, 138, 216
Iverson, Allan, 55, 82, 82, 148
  crossover dribble and, 84, 85
  fast break and, 184
  as high-scoring player, 120, 120, 124, 172
  no-look pass and, 76
  "playground" basketball and, 168, 169
  short stature of, 160
  stealing the ball, 96

Jackson, Inman, 72, 73, 80
Jackson, Mark, 17, 80, 137
Jackson, Phil, 27, 107, 198, 203, 203
  autobiography, 140, 166, 211
  in Hall of Fame, 198
Jacksonville Dolphins, 114
Jeannette, Harry "Buddy," 48, 59, 156, 158–59, 203
Jefferson, Richard, 143
Jenkins, Clarence "Fats," 200
Jersey City Skeeters, 173
Johnson, Charles, 178
Johnson, Dennis, 74, 95, 100, 102, 177
Johnson, Earvin "Magic," 59, 81, 101, 179
  alley-oop and, 34, 38
  assist records, 74
  assist-to-turnover ratio, 161
  as "big guard," 144, 144, 147, 147
  career triple-doubles, 137
  drive shot and, 40, 44^45
  fast break and, 186, 187
  hook shot and, 21, 21, 23, 25
  no-look pass and, 72, 75, 75
  passing moves of, 66, 67, 69
  pivot and, 113
  "playground" basketball and, 175
  as rebounder, 134
  season highs in NBA, 148
  stealing the ball, 95
Johnson, George, 25
Johnson, Gus, 33
Johnson, Kevin "KJ," 85
Johnson, Larry, 50, 162, 165, 166^67
Johnson, Lucas, 133
Johnson, Neil, 197
Johnson, Vincent "the Microwave," 84, 176, 181
Johnston, George T., 117
Johnston, Neil, 20, 22, 25
Jones, Bobby, 104, 107
Jones, Eddie, 102
Jones, K. C., 36, 37, 100, 185
  as coach, 124

crossover dribble and, 84
  as defender, 104, 105, 106
  fast break and, 186
  first-year coaching start, 202
  in Hall of Fame, 185
  integration of NBA and, 195
  no-look pass and, 75
  style and, 205
  as stylish player, 204
Jones, Larry, 215
Jones, Popeye, 143, 209
Jones, Sam, 93, 129, 185
  bank shot and, 60, 62, 62^63
  career field goal percentages, 19
  integration of NBA and, 195
  trash-talking and, 190, 192
Jones, Steve, 215
Jones, Wallace "Wah Wah," 197
Jordan, Michael, 97, 100, 109
  alley-oop and, 34, 38
  assist records, 74
  as "big guard," 144, 147, 149
  fast break and, 187
  foul shot and, 50
  as high-scoring player, 120, 121, 123, 172
  jump shot and, 15, 16, 19, 19
  layup shot and, 54
  as one-on-one player, 176, 180, 181, 181
  slam dunk and, 26, 30, 30^31
  stealing the ball, 92, 95, 97
  style and, 207
  trash-talking and, 190, 193
Joyce, Kevin, 53
Judkins, Jeff, 179
Julian, Alvin "Doggie," 80
jump shot, 14–19, 103

Kansas, University of, 63, 63, 199
Kansas City Blue Diamonds, 183
Kansas City^Omaha Kings, 33, 157, 158
Kareem (Abdul-Jabbar), 62
Kautsky, Ed, 50
Kautsky, Frank, 42
Keller, Bill, 44
Kenon, Larry "Dr. K," 27, 29^30
Kentucky, University of, 21, 25, 61, 141, 197
Kentucky Colonels, 29, 130, 207
Kerner, Ben, 192
Kerr, Johnny "Red," 53, 76
Kidd, Jason, 39, 80, 84, 85, 137
  behind-the-back dribble and, 78, 81
  drive shot and, 40, 45

layup shot and, 52, 54
  passing moves of, 71, 71, 72
  stealing the ball, 92, 96, 96^97
Kimball, Toby, 207
Kimbrough, J. R., 197
King, Bernard, 172, 190
King, George, 95
Kinne, Mike/Tom/Dave, 11
Kinsbrunner, Max "Mac," 82, 83
Knowings, Herman "Helicopter," 175
Kondel, Tom, 11
Kruminsh, Jan, 153
Kuberski, Steve, 129
Kundla, John, 10, 62, 114, 127, 198
  on overcoaching, 201^2
  "playground" basketball and, 170
  "sixth man" and, 203
  "three-peat" of, 199
Kunnert, Kevin, 215
Kupchak, Mitch, 178
Kurland, Bob "Foothills," 10, 116, 152
  alley-oop and, 34, 35, 35, 36, 37
  as "little big man," 139
  rejecting the ball, 98, 98, 99^100
Kurpaska, Jeff, 11

Ladner, Wendell, 126, 127, 130
LaFrentz, Raef, 103
Laimbeer, Bill, 95, 165
Landsberger, Mark, 61
Langston University (Oklahoma), 85
Lanier, Bob, 25, 181, 216
Lapchick, Joe, 116, 133^34, 151, 169
  "playground" basketball and, 170
  as rebounder, 132
  "sixth man" and, 203
  team strategy and, 199
LaRusso, Rudy ("Roughhouse Rudy"), 126, 127–29
LaSalle University, 145
Lavelli, Tony, 22
Layden, Frank, 102
layup shot, 27, 41, 52^55, 57
Leary, Dick, 57
Lee, Clyde, 129^30
Lee, Greg, 38
Leonard, Bob "Slick," 177
Leonard, Chris, 57
Lever, Fat, 137
Levingston, Cliff, 177
Lewis, Raymond, 168, 175
Lexington Avenue Armory (NYC), 48
"little big men," 138–43
Lloyd, Earl, 194, 194, 196, 197
"lob shot," 35

Lobo, Rebecca, 137
Logan, Johnny, 69
Long Island University, 17
Longley, Luc, 107
Loose Balls: The Short, Wild Life of the ABA (Pluto), 211
Los Angeles Clippers, 33, 36, 63, 81, 88, 109, 185
Los Angeles Lakers, 15, 18, 21, 23, 28, 59, 67
  artful passers of, 69
  blowout stats, 62
  coach of, 202
  dribbling and, 85
  fast break and, 182, 185, 187
  "Game of the Century" and, 212
  layup shot and, 55
  in NBA Finals, 41, 61, 95, 133, 145, 209, 210
  opening tap stats, 88
  players' height, 114
  scoring averages, 187
  scoring records, 185
  team dunks, 36
  three-point conversions, 44
Los Angeles Sparks, 137
Los Angeles Stars, 177
Loscutoff, Jim ("Jungle Jim"), 129, 186, 191, 205
Loughery, Kevin, 180, 202
Louisiana State University (LSU), 74, 80, 81
Louisville, University of, 31
Love, Bob "Butterbean," 146
Lovelette, Clyde, 114
Loyola of Chicago, 98, 99
Lucas, Greg, 113
Lucas, Jerry, 27, 105, 118, 138, 138, 140, 140–41
Lucas, Maurice, 129
Luisetti, Angelo "Hank," 10, 17–18, 57, 78, 78, 79^80
Lump, Ray, 17, 48

Macauley, Ed ("Easy Ed"), 115, 135, 163, 185, 196
MacCulloch, Todd, 119
Mader, Dave, 75
Madison Square Garden, 121
Mahnken, John, 115
Mahorn, Rick, 131
Maier, John, 199
Malone, Karl "the Mailman," 45, 51, 89, 95, 118
  as "garbage man," 129

layup shot and, 55
pick-and-roll play and, 86, 86, 89
pivot and, 113, 115
Malone, Moses, 137, 165, 166, 180–81, 193
Mandic, John, 16
Manigault, Earl "the Goat," 26, 168, 173–75
Maravich, Pete "Pistol," 72, 72, 74, 74, 81
behind-the-back dribble and, 80^81
crossover dribble and, 83, 84
handicap of, 211
pick-and-roll play and, 88–89
Marbury, Stephon, 44, 45, 45, 55, 73, 169
Marks, Sean, 131
Martin, Kenyon, 101
Martin, Slater "Dugie," 17, 114, 212, 213
as defender, 104, 105
no-look pass and, 75
short stature of, 156, 159
stealing the ball, 92, 93
Mashburn, Jamal, 24, 44
Mason, Anthony, 17, 182
Maverick, More Than a Game (P. Jackson), 106^7, 140, 166, 211
Maxwell, Cedric, 131, 190, 192^93
McAdoo, Bob, 17, 83
McBride, T. K., 11
McCarty, Walter, 58
McCracken, Jack, 66, 68
McCray, Rodney, 151
McDermott, Bobby, 56, 57^58, 59, 120, 121–22, 159
McDyess, Antonio, 33, 131
McGill University, 8
McGinnis, George, 29
McGrady, Tracy, 34, 37
McGuire, Al, 172^73
McGuire, Dick ("Tricky Dick"), 66, 69, 81
no-look pass and, 72, 73, 75
"playground" basketball and, 168, 172–73
McHale, Kevin, 21, 31, 95, 147, 177
as defender, 108
rejecting the ball, 100
on the "shootaround," 202
McIntyre, Rod, 114
McLemore, McCoy, 121
McMahon, Jack, 105
McMillian, Jim, 103, 185
medium-size players, 162^67
Meier, Al and Dave, 11
Melchionni, Bill, 27
Meminger, Dean, 27
Memoirs of an Opinionated Man (Russell), 192
Memphis Grizzlies, 60, 77

Memphis Pros, 116
Memphis State University, 38, 75
Meschery, Tom, 100
Miami Heat, 84, 102, 109, 143, 185
Miasek, Stan, 59
Michigan State University, 147
Mikan, George, 28, 35, 58, 212
agility of, 36
bank shot and, 60, 60, 62
career high, 25
coaches and, 199, 202
foul shot and, 49
height of, 152
hook shot and, 20, 21–23, 22
jump shot and, 16
as "little big man," 139
pivot and, 112, 114, 114
as rebounder, 135
rejecting the ball, 99, 99^100
shot with BB pellets, 213
slam dunk and, 27
trash-talking and, 191
Mikkelsen, Vern, 114, 126, 127, 163, 202, 213
Miles, Darius, 33, 101
Miller, Andre, 44, 71, 80, 81, 84, 190
Miller, Ed, 199
Miller, Reggie, 14, 16, 16^17, 33, 192
as "big guard," 144, 147, 148
career field goal percentages, 19
foul shot and, 51
four-point play and, 62
trash-talking and, 192
Milwaukee Bucks, 23, 25, 44, 77, 118
blowout stats, 62
in NBA Finals, 139
"point-forward" concept and, 145
scoring records, 185
Milwaukee Hawks, 125
Minneapolis Lakers, 17, 21, 22, 62, 183
best draft ever, 213
trash-talking and, 191
"worst game ever," 212^13
Minneapolis Timberwolves, 49, 50, 68, 77, 108, 109, 119
missed shots, scoring off, 126^31
Mitchell, Tom, 11
Mogus, Leo, 16
Mokray, Billy, 185
Moncrief, Sidney, 108
Monroe, Earl "The Pearl," 27, 81, 215
as one-on-one player, 176, 176, 179, 179^80
"playground" moves and, 175
Montreal Shamrocks, 8
Moore, Johnny, 157
Morey, Pete, 11

Morey, Tim, 11
Most, Johnny, 95
Most Valuable Player award, 137, 142, 143, 159, 196
Motta, Dick, 178, 193
Mourning, Alonzo, 138, 138, 142, 143, 143
"Move, the," 61
Mullaney, Joe, 178^79, 185
Mullin, Chris, 102
Murphy, Calvin, 46, 49, 129, 156, 156, 157, 159
Mutumbo, Dikembe, 131

Naismith, James J., 8^10, 17, 55, 61
coaches and, 199
dribbling and, 84
"first team" of, 121
foul shot and, 47
as man of style, 204, 204
"playground" basketball and, 175
rules of basketball and, 66
YMCA and, 170
Nance, Larry, 30, 54, 94, 100
Nash, Steve, 46, 51, 54, 81, 89, 186
Nater, Swen, 165
National Basketball Association (NBA), 15, 16, 22, 80, 205. See also NBA Finals
absorption of ABA, 27, 30, 175
All-Star Games, 30, 73, 118, 163
best set shooters, 59
goal percentage crown, 17
integration of, 195^96
official rule book, 67
playoffs, 24, 47, 124, 209–10, 210–11
Retired Players Association, 10
rivalry with ABA, 215^16
scoring records, 121
steals officially recorded by, 94
top rebounding games, 136
24-second clock invented, 183, 196
National Basketball League (NBL), 15, 21, 33, 42, 68, 158
National High School Championship Tournament, 68
Naulls, Willie, 195
NBA Finals, 41, 45, 178, 193. See also National Basketball Association (NBA)
assist records, 74
bank shot in, 61
"big guards" in, 145
defensive moves in, 104
Eastern Conference, 93, 177, 205

first (1947), 57
hook shots in, 21, 23, 25
Kundla's "three-peat" (1950), 199
"little big men" in, 139, 140, 142
pick-and-roll in, 87
rebound shots in, 133
rejecting the ball in, 99, 102
steals in, 95
Western Conference, 151
NCAA (National Collegiate Athletic Association), 35, 36, 38, 42
finals, 114
leading scorers in, 125
rebounders in, 145
semifinals, 75
tournament, 101
Nelson, Don, 118, 139, 145, 155
Nevitt, Chuck, 155
New Jersey Nets, 44, 45, 55, 76, 101, 185
New Orleans Hornets, 44, 63, 96
New Orleans Jazz, 83, 88^89, 214
New York Jewels, 83
New York Knickerbockers ("Knicks"), 14, 17, 19, 73, 84
alley-oop and, 37
artful passers of, 69
foul shot and, 48
integration of NBA and, 196
"little big men" in, 140
merger of ABA and NBA and, 27
in NBA Finals, 99, 102, 209
"playground" basketball and, 172, 175
scoring records, 185
stealing the ball, 96
violations, 109
New York League, 173
New York Liberty, 63, 137
New York Nets, 27, 30, 116, 130, 202
New York Public School Athletic League Hall of Fame, 172
New York Renaissance ("Rens"), 93, 119, 195, 200
New York State League, 47, 157, 158
New York Treat 'Em Roughs, 171, 173
New York University, 171
New York Whirlwinds, 41, 57, 88
New York^Penn League, 57
Newburgh (N.Y.) Tenths, 157
nicknames, of players, 81
Nixon, Norm, 44, 147
no-look pass, 72^77
North Carolina, University of, 30, 83^84
North Carolina State University, 37, 153
Novak, Mike, 98, 99, 114, 157
Nowitzki, Dirk, 17, 77, 89, 186

Oakley, Charles, 126, 127, 128, 131
O'Brien, Jim, 149
Ohio State University, 23
Olajuwon, Hakeem "the Dream," 45, 92, 97, 117
    pivot and, 112, 118
    quadruple-double of, 211
    rejecting the ball, 98, 99, 102
Olowakandi, Michael, 88
Olympics, 31, 35, 53, 53, 101, 153, 169
O'Neal, Jermaine, 88, 101, 103
O'Neal, Shaquille ("Shaq"), 20, 24, 25, 33, 107
    alley-oop and, 38
    autobiography, 154
    bank shot and, 63
    behind-the-back dribble and, 81
    coaches and, 203
    fast break and, 186, 187
    foul shot and, 49
    no-look pass and, 77
    opening tap stats, 88
    pivot and, 112, 112, 115, 118, 119
    rebound games, 131
    as rebounder, 136, 137
    slam dunk and, 30, 32
O'Neill, Jonathan, 168
opening tap, 88
Oregon, University of, 15
Original Celtics, 112, 113, 119, 134, 151, 200
    evolution of basketball and, 68
    formation of, 41
    playing venues, 169
Orlando Magic, 37, 49, 76, 94, 109
Orr, Louis, 94
Ortiz, Gonzalo and Joe, 169
Oshkosh All-Stars, 21, 200
Ostertag, Greg, 118, 136
Otten, Don, 117, 139, 150, 150, 152^53
Outlaw, Charles, 167, 209

Page, Harlan "Pat," 104, 105
Pan American Exposition Championship, 199
Parish, Robert, 21, 25, 49, 86, 89
passing moves, 66^77
Patterson, Steve, 114
Paultz, Bill, 27
Payton, Gary "the Glove," 33, 59, 79
    alley-oop and, 37
    assists, 80, 84
    behind-the-back dribble and, 81
    crossover dribble and, 85
    as defender, 104, 105,·108, 109

layup shot and, 55
passing moves of, 71
Perkins, Sam, 41
Pettit, Bob, 61, 125, 164, 166, 172, 209
Philadelphia 76ers, 10, 28, 77, 123, 175
    assist records, 84
    coach of, 202
    goaltending leader of, 101
    layup shot and, 55
    in NBA Finals, 93, 145
    stealing records, 94
    three-point conversions, 44
Philadelphia Warriors, 15, 17, 22, 25, 28, 79
    fast break and, 185, 186
    in NBA Finals, 57, 87
Phillips 66ers, 34, 35, 68, 116
Phoenix Suns, 29, 30, 33, 45, 209
    assists, 80, 84
    dribbling and, 85
    stealing records, 94
pick-and-roll, 86–89
Pierce, Paul "The Truth," 17, 167, 175
    alley-oop and, 38
    as "big guard," 148, 149
    drive shot and, 45
    as high-scoring player, 124, 125
    as one-on-one player, 180, 181
    pick-and-roll play and, 89
    three-point conversions, 44
Pierce, Ricky, 108
Pippin, Scottie, 74, 95, 109, 137
pivot (offensive move), 112–19
"playground" basketball, 168^75
Pluto, Terry, 211
Podoloff, Maurice, 183, 196
"point-forward" concept, 145
points, stats on, 88
Pollard, Jim ("Jumpin' Jim"), 26, 127, 159, 174, 208–9
    in All-Star Game, 163
    pivot and, 114
    "playground" basketball and, 170
    slam dunk and, 27
    stealing the ball, 92, 93
Pollock, Harvey, 10
Porter, Kevin, 76
Portland Trail Blazers, 31, 77, 155
    assist totals, 68
    blowout stats, 62
    coach of, 202, 205
    goaltending leader of, 101
    layup shot and, 55
    in NBA Finals, 102
    opening tap stats, 88
    team dunks, 36
Potapenko, Vitaly, 19, 143

Powell, Elaine, 80
Price, Mark, 46, 49
Purdue, University of, 42
"push shot," 57

quadruple-doubles, 211

Radinovic, Velimir, 133
Radojuevic, Alek, 158
Rambis, Kurt, 69, 131
Ramsey, Frank "Rams," 10, 185, 205
    as defender, 108
    fast break and, 186
    as "sixth man," 202, 203
Ratliff, Theo, 101
Ray, Clifford, 22, 89
Reading (Penn.) Coal Barons, 173
Reason, Anthony, 38
rebounders, 132–37, 165
Redlein, George, 199
Reed, J. R., 43
Reed, Willis, 27, 37, 49, 141, 169
Reid, Herman "J.R.," 209
Reinhart, Bill, 185
reject (defensive move), 98–103
Renick, Jesse, 34, 35, 37
Rice, Glen, 62
Richardson, Michael Ray, 96–97, 137
Richardson, Quentin, 39
Richmond, Mitch, 62, 63
Riley, Pat, 143, 185, 198, 201, 203
    style and, 204, 205, 207
    "three-peat" and, 214
Risen, Arnie, 10, 16–17, 22, 68, 141
    on behind-the-back dribble, 80
    as center player, 116
    pivot and, 115
    as rebounder, 135
Robertson, Alvin, 92, 96–97, 211
Robertson, Oscar, 18, 27, 42, 81
    as "big guard," 144, 145–46, 146, 179
    crossover dribble and, 84
    drive shot and, 43, 43^44
    passing moves of, 66, 70, 71
    pick-and-roll play and, 86, 88, 89
    as rebounder, 134, 136, 149
    trash-talking and, 192
Robinson, Clifford, 16, 130
Robinson, David, 33, 52, 88, 115, 119, 211
Robinson, Flynn, 185
Robinson, Leonard "Truck," 88
Roche, John, 121

Rochester Royals, 16, 22, 48, 68, 140
    drive shot and, 42
    fast break and, 185
    pivot players, 115
Rodgers, Guy, 113
Rodman, Dennis "the Worm," 104, 107, 127
    as defender, 107, 108, 109
    as rebounder, 131, 132, 132, 137
    style and, 207
Rohde, William, 199
roll pass, 68
Rollins, Wayne "Tree," 98, 101, 117
Rookie of the Year award, 137, 142, 159
Rose, Jalen, 17, 102
Rose, Malik, 131
Rosen, Charles, 211
Rowe, Curtis, 114
Rucker, Holcombe, 169, 173
Rucker Tournament, 169, 173
Ruggles, Edwin P., 120, 121
Ruland, Jeff, 129
Russell, Bill "Eagle with a Beard," 69, 117, 118, 122, 191
    alley-oop and, 34, 36
    assist records, 74
    as defender, 106
    fast break and, 186
    in Hall of Fame, 185
    height of, 153
    integration of NBA and, 195, 195
    layup shot and, 55
    no-look pass and, 77
    pick-and-roll play and, 86, 86, 88
    as rebounder, 132, 133, 135, 135^36
    rejecting the ball, 98, 100, 100^101
    retirement of, 186
    slam dunk and, 28, 28
    stealing the ball, 93
Russell, Byron, 15, 181
Russell, Cazzie, 62, 140
Russell, John "Honey," 58, 104, 105
Russian players, 116, 153

Sabonis, Arvidas, 24, 150, 155
Sacramento Kings, 17, 25, 33, 45, 59, 71, 118
    assist records, 84
    fast break and, 182, 186, 187
    opening tap stats, 88
    scoring records, 185
    stealing records, 94
    violations, 109
Sadowski, Edward "Big Ed," 177
Sailors, Kenny, 14, 14, 15, 17

career field goal percentages, 19
crossover dribble and, 83
drive shot and, 42
set shot and, 58
St. John's University, 82, 83, 139, 171, 172
St. Louis Bombers, 69
St. Louis Hawks, 25, 115, 164, 209, 213
Sampson, Chris, 11, 151, 152
Sampson, Ralph, 150, 153
San Antonio Spurs, 24, 25, 30, 33, 146
blowout stats, 62
fast break and, 182, 186^87, 187
opening tap stats, 88
scoring averages, 187
team dunks, 36
San Antonio Warriors, 108
San Francisco, University of, 36, 100
San Francisco Warriors, 87, 140
Sanders, Thomas "Satch," 104, 106, 118,
186, 195
Saperstein, Abe, 73, 85, 196, 202, 202, 212
Schayes, Dolph, 41, 123, 163
layup shot and, 52
pivot and, 115
as rebounder, 132, 132, 134^35
Schenectady (N.Y.) National Guard,
Company E, 182, 183
Schwartz, Greg, 11
Scientific Basketball (Holman), 211
Scolari, Fred J. ("Fat Freddie"), 42, 81,
197, 211
crossover dribble and, 83
as defender, 105
foul shot and, 47, 48
set shot and, 59
scorers (high-scoring players), 120–25
Scott, Byron, 214
Scott, Charlie, 82, 83, 83^84, 99, 215
Seattle Super Sonics, 17, 19, 33, 59
alley-oop passers, 37
assists, 80, 84
defensive standout, 108
dribbling and, 85
layup shot and, 55
in NBA Finals, 102, 178
opening tap stats, 88
tall players in, 153
World Championship and, 201
secondary break, 183
Sedran, Barney "Mighty Mite," 57, 86,
87–88, 156, 157^58
Selvy, Frank, 74, 125, 133
Semjonova, Uljana, 116
Senesky, George, 202
set shot, 56^59
Seton Hall University, 42, 79
Seymour, Paul, 27–28, 191

Sharman, Bill, 10, 14, 18, 88
career field goal percentages, 19
as coach, 76, 185, 198
first-year coaching start, 202
foul shot and, 46, 48, 51
retirement of, 62
"shootaround" and, 202^3
Shaw, Brian, 77
Sheboygan (Wisc.) Redskins, 129
Shelton, Lonnie, 83
"shootaround," 202
Short, Robert, 121
short players, 156^61
Shoun, Clyde, 150, 151
"Showtime," 76, 187
Sikma, Jack, 51, 108
Silas, James "Captain Late," 146^47, 187
Silas, Paul, 135, 139
Simonson (first foul-shot player), 46
Simpkins, LuBara "Dickey," 209
Sixers, 19, 33
"sixth man," 202^3
Skiles, Scott, 76
Skoog, Meyer "Whitey," 17
"skyhook," 23, 25, 118
slam dunk, 26^33
"slap pass," 70
Sloan, Jerry, 135, 144, 146, 146, 147
Smith, Elmore, 103
Smith, George, 145
Smith, Kenny, 207
Smith, Phil, 178
Smith, Steve, 166
Sparta Club, 61
spin dribble, 179
Sprewell, Latrell, 63, 106
Springfield College, 52, 56, 67, 92, 120, 121
Stackhouse, Jerry, 40, 44, 85, 102, 162, 167
Stagg, Amos Alonzo, 54^55
Stanford University, 79
Starks, John, 17, 62, 89, 99
stealing the ball, 92^97
Steinmetz, Christian, 60, 61
Stockton, John, 80, 161, 181
behind-the-back dribble and, 81
passing moves of, 66, 66, 70, 70, 71
pick-and-roll play and, 86, 89, 89
Stojakovic, Peja, 17
Stojakovic, Predrag, 187
Stokes, Maurice, 166
Stoudamire, Damon, 45, 78, 81, 85, 160,
161
style, 204^7
Sullivan, Brian, 10
Swift, Stomile, 60
Syracuse Nationals, 17, 27, 28, 47, 153
drive shot and, 41

fast break and, 187
layup shot and, 52, 53
in NBA Finals, 95
trash-talking and, 191

Tatum, Reese "Goose," 212, 213
Taylor, Brian, 27
Taylor, Chuck, 206
Taylor, Rolard, 124
Teague, Robert L., 121
techniques
alley-oop, 34
bank shot, 60
behind-the-back dribble, 78^81
"big guard," 144
coaching, 198
crossover dribble, 82
defenders' moves, 104
drive shot, 40
fast break, 182
foul shot, 46
"garbage man" moves, 126
hook shot, 20
jump shot, 14
layup shot, 52
"little big man" moves, 138
for medium-size players, 162
one-on-one moves, 176
passing moves, 66, 72
pick-and-roll, 86
pivot, 112
"playground" basketball, 168
recovering rebound shots, 132
reject play, 98
scoring, 120
set shot, 56
for short players, 156
slam dunk, 26
stealing the ball, 92
trash-talking, 190
for very tall players, 150
Thomas, Isiah, 54, 78, 81, 82, 95
Thomas, Kurt, 143
Thompson, David, 19, 37, 37–38, 169, 214
Thompson, Tina, 63
Thompsonville Big Harts, 173
"three-peat," 199, 214
three-point line, 57, 59
Thurmond, Nate, 87, 108, 135, 211, 215
Tidrick, Hal, 134
Tiger Pause, 11
Tomjanovich, Rudy, 215
Toney, Andrew, 19, 180^81
Torgoff, Irv, 203
Toronto Raptors, 30, 33, 68, 88, 175

Towe, Monte, 38
Towery, Carlisle, 16
trades, of players, 213
"trailer," 185
Trapp, John Q., 185
trash-talking, 190^93
Trentons (New Jersey team), 47, 55, 67
Trinity Midgets, 132, 133
triple-double, 134, 137
Troy (N.Y.) Trojans, 47, 68, 99
Trujillo, Michael, 168
Tucker, Trent, 121
turnovers, 85
Twyman, Jack, 17, 19
Tyler, Terry, 100

UCLA (University of California, Los
Angeles), 24, 34, 35, 38, 100, 102
UMass (University of Massachusetts), 29
underhand passes, 68
uniforms, 205^6
Unruh, Paul, 145
Unseld, Wes, 132, 137, 138, 140, 142–43,
143, 178
Urquhart, Mike, 11
Utah Jazz, 15, 19, 30, 38, 67, 102
assists, 68, 80, 84
layup shot and, 55
in NBA Finals, 95
pick-and-roll play and, 86
stealing records, 94
Utah Stars, 27, 174
Utica (N.Y.) Utes, 157

Van Excel, Nick, 45, 80, 84
Van Horn, Keith, 49, 130
Van Lier, Norman, 131, 146
Vance, Dave, 130
Vancouver Grizzlies, 80, 94, 185
Vanderweghe, Ernie, 203
Viani, Bruce, 11
View from Above, A (Chamberlain), 54
violations, 24-second, 109
violence, 191^92, 215
Virginia Squires, 29, 146

Wachter, Ed, 20, 21, 99
fast break and, 183
foul shot and, 47
passing moves of, 68
pivot and, 114

Wachter, Lew, 21, 68, 183
Walker, Antoine, 55, 59, 71, 80
Walker, Chet "the Jet," 93, 146
Wallace, Ben, 88, 103, 108
    as "garbage man," 126, 126, 130, 131
    as rebounder, 131, 137
Wallace, Rasheed, 131
Walton, Bill, 24, 25, 31, 152
    alley-oop and, 34, 35, 38
    no-look pass and, 77
    rejecting the ball, 102
    style and, 207
Wanzer, Bobby, 48, 163, 172, 203
Warner, Ed, 173
Washington, Kermit, 215
Washington, Tom "Trooper," 126, 127, 130
Washington, University of, 23
Washington Bullets, 102, 152, 175, 178
Washington Capitols, 42, 47, 114, 185,
    194, 196
Washington Mystics, 80
Washington Wizards, 44, 51, 88, 143
Watts, Earvin, 81

Weatherspoon, Teresa, 63, 63
Webber, Chris, 33, 59, 118, 187, 209
Webster, Marvin, 143
Wedman, Scott, 16, 19
Weiss, Bob, 207
Wells, Gawen "Bonzi," 209
West, Jerry, 14, 15, 16, 18, 129
    assist records, 74
    career field goal percentages, 19
    drive shot and, 42, 44
    foul shot and, 47
    injuries, 185
    as one-on-one player, 176, 177, 178,
        178–79
    pick-and-roll play and, 87
    rejecting the ball, 100
    stealing the ball, 92, 92, 93^95, 95
Westhead, Paul, 207
White, Jahidi, 88
White, Jo Jo, 60, 63, 63, 181, 187
Whitehead, Jerome, 151
Whitty, John, 199
Wicks, Sidney, 114

Wilkins, Dominique ("Human Highlight
    Film"), 26, 30, 31, 172, 177
Wilkins, Lenny, 75, 173, 198, 200, 201,
    203
Williams, Jason, 72, 77, 81, 175
Williams, Michael, 49
Williams, Nate, 178
Williams, Ron, 178
Williamson, Corliss, 89, 125
Williamson, John ("Super John"), 180
Winning the Hard Way (Auerbach), 196
Winter, Max, 212
Wisconsin, University of, 17, 61
Wise, Willie, 108
Wolf, David, 211
Women's National Basketball Association
    (WNBA), 63, 126
Wooden, John "India Rubber Man," 10,
    81, 208
    as coach, 100
    drive shot and, 40, 42
    foul shot and, 50
Woolpert, Phil, 100

World Championship, 21, 41, 88, 158,
    163, 175
World Professional Basketball Tourna-
    ment, 195, 200
Worthy, James, 55, 187
Wyoming, University of, 14, 15

Yale University, 22, 54^55
Yao Ming, 150, 154, 154
Yardley, George "the Bird," 10, 17, 27–28,
    95, 101, 207
"yo-yoing," 179
Young Men's Christian Association
    (YMCA) clubs, 8, 46, 55, 67, 168,
    170–71, 199

Zaslofsky, Max, 48, 56, 56, 58, 58, 59
Zinkoff, David, 28, 80